POWER TOOL MAINTENANCE

McGraw-Hill Book Company | New York
St. Louis
San Francisco
Düsseldorf
Johannesburg
Kuala Lumpur
London
Mexico
Montreal
New Delhi
Panama
Rio de Janeiro
Singapore
Sydney
Toronto

POWER TOOL MAINTENANCE

Daniel W. Irvin

Educational Director
Power Tool Division
Rockwell Manufacturing Company

Power Tool Maintenance

Library of Congress Catalog Card Number
76-126174
32050

1 2 3 4 5 6 7 8 9 0 VHVH 7 9 8 7 6 5 4 3 2 1 0

This book was set in Melior by Progressive Typographers, and printed on permanent paper and bound by Von Hoffmann Press, Inc. The designer was Merrill Haber; the drawings were done by John Cordes, J. & R. Technical Services, Inc. The editors were Cary F. Baker, Jr., and Cynthia Newby. Sally Ellyson supervised production.

Preface

The most common and continuous problem of the shop instructor and the cabinet shop or job shop owner is preventive maintenance and alignment of their shop equipment, primarily power tools. Downtime in industry means a loss of money, but this can often be recovered by various means. Downtime in a school always means a loss of educational time to a student, which may well be lost forever.

Industry has its share of maintenance problems, but educators have even more because the equipment must withstand severe and often abusive use by inexperienced students. Most instructors would agree that students have an innate curiosity about thumbscrews, star wheels, knurled knobs, and other adjustment features, even though they do not understand their functions. Moreover, power tools and machinery are generally used for a longer period of time in a school shop than in an industrial environment.

The basic format for *Power Tool Maintenance* has been refined for ten years, through college credit workshops and clinics held in all sections of the United States. The following is a partial list of clinic locations where forty hour sessions have been held, usually as a part of a summer school program:

Appalachian State Teachers College
  Boone, North Carolina
Broward County School System
  Fort Lauderdale, Florida

Arizona State University
  Tempe, Arizona
Colorado State College
  Greeley, Colorado

v

Dade County School System
  Miami, Florida
Fairmont State College
  Fairmont, West Virginia
Georgia Southern College
  Statesboro, Georgia
Kent State University
  Kent, Ohio
Millersville State College
  Millersville, Pennsylvania
Moorhead State College
  Moorhead, Minnesota
Nebraska State College
  Kearney, Nebraska
Stout State University
  Menomonie, Wisconsin
University of Idaho
  Moscow, Idaho
University of North Dakota
  Grand Forks, North Dakota
Western Washington State College
  Bellingham, Washington

Eastern Michigan University
  Ypsilanti, Michigan
Fresno State College
  Fresno, California
Gorham State College
  Gorham, Maine
Mankato State College
  Mankato, Minnesota
Montana State University
  Bozeman, Montana
Murray State College
  Murray, Kentucky
Northern Illinois University
  De Kalb, Illinois
University of Hawaii
  Honolulu, Hawaii
University of New Mexico
  Albuquerque, New Mexico
Western Michigan University
  Kalamazoo, Michigan

The many requests that manufacturers get from both colleges and school systems concerning service, parts information, and clinic possibilities verify the definite and urgent need for instructional information in logical sequence presented in text form.

Part 1 covers terminology. Speaking the language of the trade is necessary in communicating with service people, distributors, and manufacturers. A planned system of troubleshooting is presented, primarily to build confidence in a method of checking a machine in enough detail to diagnose a problem. Knowledge of belts, bearings, pulleys, and lubrication is necessary for even the most elementary diagnostic effort, disassembly, assembly, or alignment check.

Part 2 covers specific information on power tools most commonly found in the school shop or laboratory, or a typical job or cabinet shop. Each stationary power tool is covered logically from introductory, preventive maintenance, and alignment viewpoints. Portable electric and portable air tools are discussed in Chaps. 19 and 20.

Part 3 includes a chapter on the types of motors and controls most often used on stationary power tools and a chapter on much-needed information concerning maintenance files, parts manuals, where and how to order parts or parts manuals, guarantees, and the general service relationships between the manufacturer and the user.

Recognition and thanks are most certainly due to a great many persons and companies who assisted directly or indirectly in producing this book. For permission and encouragement: F. P. Maxwell, Executive Vice-president, Rockwell Manufacturing Company. For photos, permissions, and sample manuals: Ames Publishing Company, Paul Eisenberg, Managing Editor; Amsted Industries, Allan D. Pedrick, Marketing Manager; DoAll Company, John W. Smith, Production Promotion Manager; Fairfield Engineering and Manufacturing Company, Allan D. Pedrick, Marketing Manager; Furnas Electric Company, Carl F. Witschonke, Manager; Gates Rubber Company, Robert B. Lainhart, Senior Advertising Specialist; Hitchcock Publishing Company, Roland Laboissonniere, Vice-president, and Darrell Ward, Executive Editor; K. O. Lee Company, Phil J. Braunstein, Advertising Manager; KTS Industries, Inc., H. Dykema, Sales Manager; Marathon Electric Manufacturing Corporation, Alfred P. Sirois, Manager Advertising and Sales Promotion; New Department-Hyatt Bearings, Division of General Motors Corporation, W. S. Matthews, Technical Literature Supervision; Newman Machine Company, Inc., J. Gillespie, Vice-president; Oliver Machinery Company, J. Dykstra, Sales; R. A. Ness and Company, Ray Ness, owner; Wilton Tool, a Division of Wilton Corporation, Charles Roudane, General Sales Manager. For picture help: George Winklmann. For art help: Jack Nofsinger. For special photos and photography: Jack Moore. For technical help and editorial checking: Harold Jonas, E. B. Meynard, W. S. Matthews. For typing, composing, and blind faith: Sandy Collaizzi, Jean Walkiewicz, Elinor Irvin.

Daniel W. Irvin

Contents

POWER TOOL MAINTENANCE

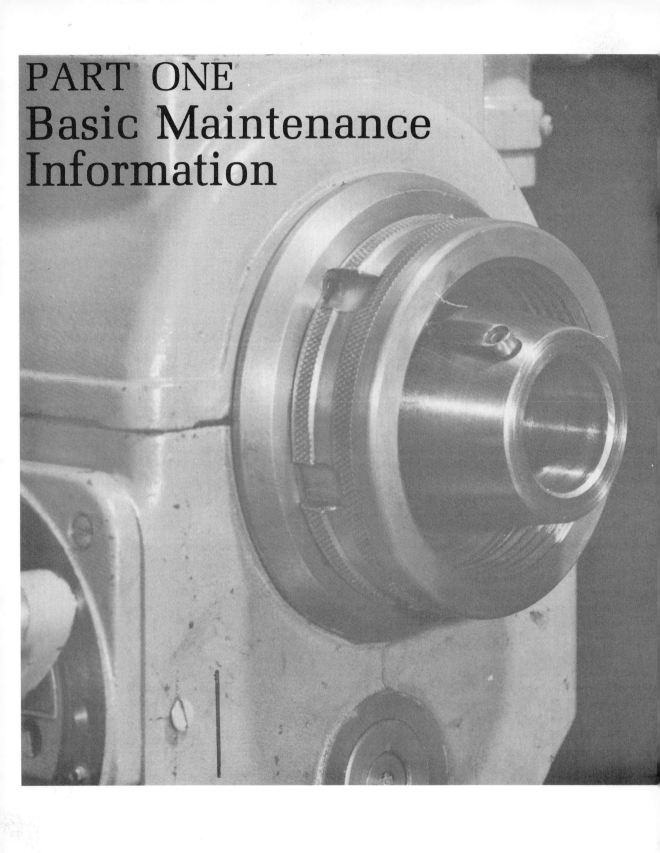

PART ONE
Basic Maintenance Information

CHAPTER ONE

Definition of Terms

Every science, occupation, trade, or job has its own specialized jargon which is often understood only by those engaged in it. This is also true of general areas, such as occupations in which machinery or machines are somehow important, regardless of the specific industry. The same terminology is used and understood by the designer, the engineer, the operator, the maintenance man, the teacher, and the salesman. To avoid inaccuracy, delay, misunderstanding, and even excessive costs at every level, a specialized vocabulary must be used. It is particularly important in communication regarding maintenance.

When two words are used together to describe a part or operation, the meaning of the compound is usually greater than the simple addition of separate definitions. The correct academic meaning for various terms is easily found in *Webster's Seventh New Collegiate Dictionary* which is readily available to the mechanic, industrial education teacher, or homeowner. A more detailed and specific definition can be found in technical or engineering references, but they are often too technical for common use. The explanations, which follow the academic definitions or paraphrased definitions taken from *Webster's Seventh New Collegiate Dictionary*, indicate the mechanics concept of meaning and fall somewhere between the accurate but academic vocabulary and the strict technical terminology.

In the following pages are terms frequently used in describing machine tools, power tools, machine parts, accessories, and methods of construction or operation of equipment in the medium size and price category. It is well to remember that any given word may have a completely different meaning in another industry or in everyday life.

FIG. 1-1*a*

ARBOR

A shaft on which a revolving cutting tool is mounted; on a cutting machine, a spindle that holds the work to be cut.

One of the most confusing words to define accurately is "arbor" because of its similarity to other terms, such as spindle, shaft, and mandrel. The actual meaning in reference to a specific part can vary in different parts of the country, in different industries, and even among people engaged in the same occupation, depending on their background. It is generally accepted that the shaft or spindle in a circular saw, radial saw, or cutoff machine may be called an arbor. By rule of thumb, it is horizontal. (*See Shaft; Spindle.*) (Fig. 1-1*a*)

BEARING

A machine part in which a journal, pin, or other part turns.

The purpose of any type of bearing is to reduce friction. In most cases, this is effected by moving parts such as balls or rollers in an assembled package (Fig. 1-1*b*). If no moving parts are used, friction is usually reduced by using a lubricant on particular metals or oil-impregnated metal parts.

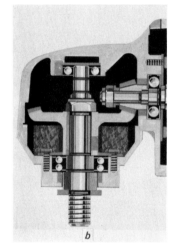

FIG. 1-1*b*

BED

A flat or level surface; a supporting surface or structure.

The precision frame of a metal lathe or wood lathe. The headstock, tailstock, and other assemblies either are fastened to the bed or are adjustable only in relation to it. In machine tools such as a metal planer, the bed can also hold the workpiece.

BELT

A continuous band of tough, flexible material for transmitting motion and power.

Most medium-priced stationary tools and machine tools are belt driven. There are many kinds of drive belts designed to do specific jobs, such as work with a variable-speed mechanism. Compared with a gear drive, chain drive, or direct-drive unit, a belt-drive machine is, with few exceptions, less expensive and easier to maintain, and more speeds are quickly obtainable.

Stock removal also is accomplished by abrasive belts variously designed for specific materials (Fig. 1-2). Each minute and separate piece of abrasive material bonded to the belt might be considered a bit because of its cutting action. (See *Bit*.)

BIT

The replaceable part of a compound tool that performs such a function as drilling or boring.

The cutting tool used with a drill press, metal lathe, or router is called a bit, e.g., drill bit, tool bit, router bit. In most cases, it is a single-point cutting tool (Fig. 1-3). (See *Belt; Blade; Disk; Knife; Wheel.*)

BLADE

The cutting part of an implement.

The cutting tool used with a great variety of saws, e.g., circular saw blade, band saw blade, scroll saw blade, bayonet saw blade. Each tooth of a blade acts as an individual bit. (See *Bit*.)

BOLT

A metal rod or pin for fastening objects together, usually with a head at one end and a screw thread for a nut at the other.

The nut and bolt is the most common fastener. A great variety can be found in most pieces of equipment. To perform specific functions, unusual head shapes, lengths, or shoulder sizes are often used. Although in most cases these are not "specials," they are not generally stocked by most distributors. Care should be taken not to mix them with common or regular bolts.

BOSS

A protuberant part or body.

This usually small raised area of a casting is often machined and used as a locating point, a positive stop, a fastening position, or a bearing surface. It is used also to control distance accurately. Often this saves machining the entire surface of the casting (Fig. 1-4).

BRACKET

A fixture projecting from a wall or column.

A bracket is often used to mount a switch or starter in a convenient posi-

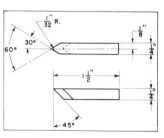

FIG. 1-2

FIG. 1-3

FIG. 1-4

tion. A stronger bracket, even cast iron, might be used to support a complete assembly inside the machine.

BUSHING

A usually removable cylinder lining for an opening (as of a mechanical part) used to limit the size of the opening, resist abrasion, or serve as a guide.

A bushing is often used to support a control shaft where it enters a cabinet; for instance, a circular saw cabinet (Fig. 1-5). It often takes the place of a bearing where speed and heat are not factors. Hardened bushings are used also to guide a drill bit quickly and accurately, particularly when starting a hole. They often eliminate the need for a boring or drilling machine of greater precision. They are easily replaced.

FIG. 1-5

CABINET

An upright case; a chamber.

A supporting stand, usually made of sheet steel, which is an integral part of the machine. Often major assemblies are bolted or welded to the cabinet. A floor-model circular saw is a good example. This definition does not apply to a steel stand (enclosed or open) which merely holds the machine at a working height, serving the function of a bench.

CAM

A rotating or sliding part that imparts or receives motion.

Many lathe tailstocks and woodworking lathe tool rest supports are clamped to the bed by cam action. Usually this is accomplished by the cam's being made of a round shaft. The cam-type action is achieved by having the center of rotation off center, producing an eccentric movement and resulting in the squeeze or clamping action desired. Often machine tools have cam actions in their control mechanisms.

CENTER

One or two tapered rods which support work in a lathe or grinding machine and about or with which the work revolves.

In metalworking and woodworking lathes, the work is normally held between the headstock and tailstock. The centers actually support the work. The shank is usually a No. 2 or No. 3 Morse taper fitting into a corresponding internal taper in the head- and tailstock. The point of the center is usually 60 deg, but many kinds are available for both wood and metal turning. A hardened center is used in the tailstock, usually identified by a groove or a ground ring, because this center does not turn with the work. Ball bearing tailstock centers are available also (Fig. 1-6).

FIG. 1-6

CHAMFER

A beveled edge.

The edge of a cast-iron table, saw table, drill press table, etc., is almost razor-sharp when the machining, grinding, or milling is completed. This sharp right-angle corner or edge is usually touched off or broken with a file. The chamfer or bevel produced is not noticeable but very necessary for safe assembly and operation.

CHUCK

An attachment for holding the workpiece or the tooling in a machine such as a drill press or lathe.

In a portable drill or drill press, the chuck generally holds the cutting tool, a drill bit, reamer, plug cutter, etc. These rather small three-jaw drill chucks are often referred to as Jacobs chucks, although this is a brand name rather than a type designation (Fig. 1-7a).

FIG. 1-7a

Chucks used on a metal lathe are usually three-jaw, four-jaw, or six-jaw units. The four-jaw chucks usually have independent control for each jaw so that odd-shaped material can be clamped or work can be turned on an eccentric. Lathe chucks have also reversible step jaws for both internal and external holding.

Collect chucks hold the work by being drawn or forced into a self-releasing taper. This causes the sections of the chuck, really jaws, to be reduced in diameter, clamping either the work or the tool (a rod or a router bit). In some applications, these chucks are called spring chucks.

CLIP

Any of various devices that grip, clasp, or hook.

This is similar to a bracket, but by rule of thumb much smaller and lighter. Clips are often used to control or restrict any movement of electric wiring internally in a machine. This might be true inside a drill press head if a remote push-button station is built into the front of the head and the magnetic starter is mounted outside and in the rear. A table extension might be supported by clips. Many kinds of clips are used for various purposes (Fig. 1-7b).

FIG. 1-7b

COLLAR

A ring or round flange to restrain motion or hold something in place.

A collar might well be considered an extremely thick washer. In some

cases, provision is made to fasten the collar to a shaft with a taper pin, roll pin, or setscrew when it is used to control movement (Fig. 1-8). To control space, for example, as with a shaper collar, the thickness and diameters are extremely accurate.

COLLET

A metal band, collar, ferrule, or flange. (*See Chuck.*)

COLUMN

A supporting pillar, usually round.

A typical and instantly visual example is the main frame of a drill press. The round shaft or column is the supporting member for the base, table, and head.

Columns are used also for support, rigidity, and accuracy and to allow for adjustment in many radial saws, woodworking shapers, grinders, and other equipment. They are sometimes used as stiffeners in extended fabricated cabinets (Fig. 1-9).

COTTER PIN

A metal pin split so that the ends can be bent after insertion through a slot or hole.

These pins are used to secure a castle or castellated nut in an exact position in relation to the shaft and assembly. They are used also merely as a stop to keep more or less loose items, such as a washer, from falling off the end of the shaft into expensive gearing.

cpm (also written CPM)

This is a standard abbreviation of "cuts per minute," or the number of knife cuts measured in minutes. Some machine specifications indicate only cpm which is related to the number of knives, the diameter of the cutter, and the rpm, without regard to the rate of feed. Some indication as to the cuts per inches of feed is often a better guide to the potential lack of chatter or smoothness of cut. Oftentimes this can be expressed by other specifications, such as the linear feet per minute of feed or the inches of stock cut per minute.

CUTTING TOOL

A sharp tool for such operations as stock removal, abrading, drilling, boring, and grinding. (*See Belt; Bit; Blade; Disk; Knife; Wheel.*)

DISK (also spelled DISC)

A thin, circular object.

Usually a disk is a heavy paper circle with an abrasive coating. Different sizes or diameters are available, with a variety of grits and cutting abrasives. Such disks are fastened to the metal disk of an abrasive finishing machine with an adhesive. They are easily replaced when loaded or worn. Tungsten carbide disks are available also and can be mounted on a circular saw arbor or grinder shaft.

Regardless of the size or type of grit, each small piece of abrasive material acts as a cutter bit and turns off a chip in the same way as a lathe bit. The chips are so small and there are so many that normally they are considered dust.

DOG

A usually simple, mechanical device consisting of a spike, rod, or bar with an end adapted to holding, gripping, or fastening.

A dog has a clamping device which surrounds the work at one end and a bent tail at the other end. When it is properly clamped to the work in a metal lathe with the tail extended through a slot in the drive plate, the work is driven or revolves with the lathe spindle. A great many sizes, styles, and kinds are available.

DOVETAIL WAY

A flaring tenon or mortise.

A dovetail way is used to assure accuracy and rigidity for parts or assemblies which must be adjusted or moved slowly. The method used in many jointers to mount the tables to the base casting is an excellent example (Fig. 1-10). A dovetail uses a gib and gib screws for one adjustment system providing rigidity in two directions, vertical and horizontal.

FIG. 1-10

There are several other advantages, including lower manufacturing cost and therefore lower selling price, because accuracy is controlled by field adjustment rather than original precision machining. (See *Gib*.)

DOWEL PIN

A pin fitted into the matching holes of two abutting pieces to prevent motion or slippage.

An extract location can be duplicated by using dowel pins when dismounting and mounting an assembly. Actual holding is done with cap screws, bolts and nuts, etc. Two pins are usually sufficient; for instance, in the upper left and lower right corners. A typical application is holding a gearbox in position to assure proper meshing of a mating external gear.

DRIFT

A tool for ramming down or forcing something.

A wedge used to break the holding power of a taper. Usually a sharp easy tap is enough, with the drift inserted into the slots at the end of the female taper. The drift for a Morse taper is itself tapered 1¾ in. in 12 in., although it is usually not longer than 6 in. (See *Key, center key.*)

FEED ROD

The device that carries forward the material to be operated upon.

A feed rod, usually square or hexagonal in shape, is used to move an assembly; for instance, the carriage of a metal lathe. The assembly can usually be stopped or started by clutch action while the feed rod remains in motion.

This movement might be done also with a lead screw or a round threaded rod, primarily needed for thread-cutting operations.

A positive stop rod in a screw machine, which controls or moves the work or the cutter, is often called a feed rod. The control rods in a bed turret are a good example.

FENCE

A barrier to mark a boundary.

A fence is a control assembly, usually adjustable. In a jointer, the fence normally controls squareness. In a circular saw, the fence controls the width of the cut and its straightness, when ripping (Fig. 1-11).

FIG. 1-11

FIXTURE

A permanent appendage or structural part.

Fixtures, by rule of thumb, are fastened to the machine and guide, hold, or position either the cutting tool or the work (Fig. 1-12). Often they are designed for continuous production runs and are complicated enough to be considered a machine redesign. The original purpose of a machine can be completely changed by a fixture. (See *Jig.*)

FIG. 1-12

FLANGE

A rib or rim for strength, for guiding, or for attachment to another object.

A flange might be considered a precision washer, shaped or precision-machined to be thicker at the rim. In many cases, the inside flange is actually a part of the spindle or arbor, or is electrostatically welded in place. This is done prior to final machining so that the arbor and inside flange will have a precision-square and concentric relationship. The outside flange is drilled or machined to fit snugly on the arbor. A good example is a typical circular saw arbor assembly.

A flange on a shaft is a vertical extension of a shoulder. A specific piece of webbing cast into the underside or rear of most iron castings to prevent warpage is also called a flange. This term can be applied to various stiffeners inside a sheet-steel cabinet.

fpm (also written FPM)

This is a standard abbreviation of "feet per minute," relating to either the speed or the rate of feed of a machine. For instance, the peripheral speed of a grind wheel might be 6000 fpm, or the rate of feed or wood through a planer might be 21 fpm. In other words, fpm designates the number of times, measured in feet, the same point on the wheel passes the tool rest; or the amount of wood, measured in feet, that passes under the cutterhead in one minute.

In the case of feeds, the manufacturer's specifications must be accepted, or an actual test must be made to verify accuracy. The following formula and example using a 7″ × 3450 rpm grinder are applicable where speeds rather than feeds are involved:

$$\frac{\text{Diameter in inches} \times \text{pi} \times \text{rpm}}{12} = \frac{7 \times 3.1416 \times 3450}{12}$$

$$= \frac{21.9912 \times 3450}{12}$$

$$= \frac{75869.6400}{12}$$

$$= 6322.47 \text{ fpm}$$

GASKET

Hemp or rope for making pipe or other joints fluid-tight; packing for the same purpose made of other material (such as rubber).

A thin seal, usually made of various paperlike materials, used to seal in oil or seal out dirt is called a gasket. Liquid or paste-type seals also are used, usually for special purposes involving gasoline or other solvents which might destroy a normal gasket. Both types are used for some applications. The cover plate on a gearbox is a typical area requiring a seal or gasket.

GEAR

A toothed wheel.

FIG. 1-13

Bevel Gear

A pair of these gears are made to transmit power with the shafts at an angle, and often at right angles. Many different varieties of teeth are used, and the sizes of the two gears can be different for a mechanical advantage (Fig. 1-13).

Bull Gear

A bull gear is usually the largest gear in the gear train or set of gears. It is common in metal working machines and machine tools, such as a lathe, shaper, or planer. It is sometimes large enough to have a flywheel effect and is often the main driving gear for the machine.

Pick-off Gear

These are the outboard gears in the gear train driving the lead screw or feed rod on a metal lathe not equipped with a quick-change gearbox. They must be picked off and changed or repositioned to obtain different desired feeds or threads per inch.

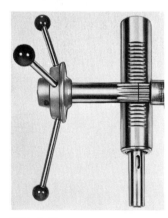

FIG. 1-14

Pinion Gear

This is the smallest gear of any type in any gear train or set of gears. It is usually referred to in conjunction with a gear rack, as in "rack and pinion." In a drill press, the pinion gear is almost a spline cut into the shaft controlling the depth, and the rack is cut into the rear of the quill (Fig. 1-14). This is fast-acting. In a circular saw, in which the pinion is a worm gear and the rack is cut into the trunnion, the action is much slower. (See *Rack.*)

Worm Gear

A shaft or gear with the teeth cut in a spiral, almost like threads, is a worm. It is mated with a rack or normal gear to provide reasonably slow movement. It is normal to drive the rack or gear with the worm. This process is usually not reversible.

GIB

A plate of metal or other material machined to hold other parts in place, to afford a bearing surface, or to provide means for taking up wear.

The metal bar or strip inserted between the internal and external parts of a dovetail way is the gib. It not only takes up most of the space but is usually indented to receive the points of the setscrews which apply the pressure needed for adjustment. It protects the machined cast-iron way from damage. (*See Dovetail Way.*)

GROMMET

An eyelet of firm material to strengthen or protect an opening or to insulate or protect something passed through it.

A grommet is similar to a bushing but is not normally a precision part; it is often made of plastic, fiber, or rubber as well as metal. A grommet is often inserted in a drilled hole of a metal part to help guide or protect either the part or a wire or rod which is loosely inserted. A rubber grommet might protect an electric cord from insulation damage.

GUIDE BLOCK

A contrivance for steadying or directing the motion of something (Fig. 1-15).

FIG. 1-15

Guide blocks either can restrict movement or may be a part of the system activating some movement. In some band saw guide assemblies, they prevent the blade from twisting or turning under cutting pressure. In a transmission or lathe headstock, they may be the sliding internal fingers that slide a gear in or out of mesh. They are usually found in pairs and are sometimes called shoes. (*See Shoe.*)

HEADSTOCK

A part of a lathe that holds the revolving spindle and its attachment.

This term, commonly used in reference to a lathe, may also apply to a screw machine, horizontal boring mill, or for that matter even a drill press. It performs the final step in the power source for the piece of equipment.

HOUSING

A casing (an enclosed bearing) in which a shaft revolves; a frame or other support for mechanical parts.

The outside case of a transmission or gearbox is called a housing. By rule of thumb, it is removable as an assembly rather than being a part of the basic frame or castings.

INSERT

Something placed between objects to make them secure.

A table insert is a removable table section to make the replacement or adjustment of a cutting tool easier or possible (Fig. 1-16). For instance, in a scroll saw, a table section is removable for blade changes and yet allows the work to be supported close to the blade. For a table saw and shaper, different sizes and shapes of inserts are available to accommodate the various cutting tools which might be used.

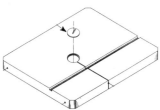

FIG. 1-16

JIG

A device used to maintain mechanically the correct positional relationship between a piece of work and the tool.

A jig, by rule of thumb, is not fastened to the machine but guides, holds, or controls the movement of the workpiece or cutting tool. A jig will usually increase the safety and accuracy of the operation and also speed production. A tenoner used on a circular saw is a good example.

JOURNAL

The part of a rotating shaft, axle, tool, or spindle that turns in a bearing.

The journal is the part of a spindle, usually hardened, where contact is made with the bearing. In this sense a sleeve or poured bearing, but not a ball bearing, is implied.

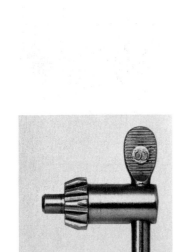

FIG. 1-17

KEY

A small piece fitting into a groove which controls motion between parts.

Center Key

Center keys are available in all Morse taper sizes from No. 1 to No. 6 and are used to drive, by wedging action, the taper shank tool out of the spindle socket or sleeve. Center keys with a taper of $1\frac{3}{4}$ in. per foot are often called a drift.

Chuck Key

Most small drill chucks are opened or closed by a chuck key, which has a bevel gear matching a bevel gear on the chuck body (Fig. 1-17). A pin inserted into a hole in the chuck forms the pivot point. This controls all three jaws equally. (On drill chucks that are hand-tightened, the key is eliminated.)

Cotter Key

(*See Cotter Pin.*)

Standard Key

Usually a square key providing a positive drive. Keyways one-half the depth of the key are milled in the shaft and in the cutter, pulley, or driven part.

Woodruff Key

This key provides a positive key drive for a shaft which must be threaded, is tapered to a small size, or for some other reason cannot have a keyway extending the complete length. The key itself is similar to a straight square key except for a half-moon extension, not quite as long as its whole length. The Woodruff key is held in position when this round section is placed into a corresponding slot milled in the shaft. A typical use is to drive the lower wheel on a band saw.

KNIFE

A sharp cutting blade or tool.

The tool bit or the cutter bit in a woodworking jointer or planer is commonly known as a knife. It is usually sold, installed, or sharpened only in sets because of the dynamic balance requirements of the cutterhead. The head itself is functionally the chuck or toolholder in these machines. (*See Bit.*)

KNURL

One of a series of small ridges or beads on a metal surface to aid in gripping (Fig. 1-18).

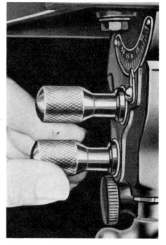

FIG. 1-18

Knurls on a knob or handle section of a workpiece are formed by the pressure of ridges on two hardened rollers. The ridges on the rollers are slanted in opposite or nearly opposite directions, making a diamondlike design in the workpiece.

LEAD SCREW

To direct on a course or in a direction. A continuous helical rib-spiral.

The most obvious example is the threaded shaft which drives the carriage, particularly in thread cutting on a metal lathe. In most small lathes the lead screw acts also as a feed rod for normal cutting operations. A worm gear is virtually a short lead screw although not usually manufactured with the same precision.

MITER GAGE

A square with an arm adjustable to any angle.

A miter gage is a sliding jig. The head, which holds or controls the workpiece, can be set at any angle from 45 deg right to 45 deg left. The most frequent setting is 90 deg, at a right angle to the blade or cutting tool. The miter gage slides in a milled slot in the table surface. (*See Jig.*)

NUT

A perforated block, usually of metal, that has an internal screw thread and is used on a bolt or screw for tightening or holding something.

Castellated Nut or Castle Nut

FIG. 1-19

These hexagon nuts usually have six projections, equally spaced at the top, forming slots which are usually not quite as thick or deep as the normal part of the nut itself. The projections have the same internal diameter as the nut body, are threaded, and form three slots across the top of the nut (Fig. 1-19). The slots are lined up with a hole in the bolt or stud, allowing insertion of a cotter pin. The outside diameter of the projections is usually smaller than that of the nut so that the head and bent legs of the cotter pin do not extend much farther than the nut itself. A typical use is to control exactly the pressure on the bearing assembly of a band saw lower wheel shaft. With a cotter pin inserted, the assembly can be neither tightened nor loosened by wheel movement or vibration.

Hexagon Nut

FIG. 1-20

As the name indicates, these nuts are six-sided; they are normally called hex nuts. Their shape makes possible the use of box end or open end wrenches and allows the nut to be tightened or loosened in small working space. Socket wrenches provide fast action. Sizes, finishes, threads, materials, and types are almost unlimited (Fig. 1-20).

Self-locking Nut

Many methods are used to provide self-locking. The most common is the use of radial slots, which result in sections of slightly decreased diameter. A similar locking system can be devised with a fiber or plastic insert fitted into a slot or hole in the threads. This type of nut is a stop nut as well as a locknut. It will hold its position firmly once the locking threads or the insert is fully engaged. Some nuts are available with a lock washer welded or attached to one flat surface.

Speed Nut

Speed nuts or Tinnerman nuts consist of a small piece of sheet metal or even spring material, slightly curved, with a hole drilled or punched in the center. Usually the metal has a slight cut, parallel to the outside edge and tangent to the hole diameter. This allows each side to follow the threads of the bolt. The curved side will flatten out when the bolt is tightened, securing the assembly. Since there is no wrench for a speed nut, it is usually held by hand while the bolt is turned into it. Speed nuts are used only when there is no stress or weight and the parts do not normally require removal, such as blank cover plates, nameplates, or scales.

Square Nut

These four-sided nuts are used where working or turning space is not a problem. They are less expensive than equivalent hex nuts. A typical use is fastening a motor to a motor mount. They are often used with carriage bolts for crating machinery.

Wing Nut

These nuts are used where adjustment is frequent and absolute tightness is not vital. Rather than being square or hexagonal, the body of the nut is usually round. The nut is loosened or tightened by two winglike projections which provide leverage for the thumb and forefinger.

Wire Nut

Wire nuts are usually made of insulating plastic with a metal insert. Their purpose is to join or splice mechanically two or more electric wires quickly, eliminating the need for solder or tape. The joint can easily be taken apart by merely unscrewing the nut, although the connection can be considered permanent.

OILER

A receptacle or device for applying oil.

These small cups for holding lubricating oil are normally found on metalworking machines, not on woodworking machines. They usually are pressed into a hole in a casting and have a spring top or cap.

PAWL

A pivoted tongue or sliding bolt on one part of a machine that is adapted to fall into notches so as to permit motion in only one direction.

A pawl is often used to control the amount of movement, usually in even steps. An example is its use in the feed mechanism on most metalworking shapers.

FIG. 1-21

PILLOW BLOCK

A block or support used especially to equalize or distribute pressure (Fig. 1-21).

A pillow block usually supports and surrounds a bearing, with the bearing seat ground into the block. This allows quick, easy replacement of an assembly while maintaining precision accuracy. This use is typical for jointer head assembly.

PINION

The smallest of a train or set of gear wheels, designed to mesh with a larger wheel or rack. (See *Gear, pinion gear*.)

PLATEN

A flat plate of metal, especially one that exerts or receives pressure.

A platen is usually associated with an abrasive belt machine and backs up the belt at the work area. This makes possible accurate or square removal of stock. The metal disk of a disk finishing unit is sometimes called a platen.

PULLEY

A wheel used to transmit power by means of a band, belt, cord, rope, or chain.

By rule of thumb, a pulley is a series of sheaves cut in one wheel or assembly (Fig. 1-22). These can have the same diameter for high torque transmission or different diameters for changing speeds. In the latter case it is called a step pulley and usually has a matching pulley with the step diameters reversed; only one belt is used. A pulley can be flat (slightly crowned) or made with a groove to match the belt shape. (See *Sheave*.)

FIG. 1-22

QUILL

A hollow shaft often surrounding another shaft.

This housing usually controls the accurate in-and-out movement of a spindle or arbor. The quill may house the bearings also and is usually removable as an assembly. A good example of this is a drill press quill, controlling movement up and down and containing the spindle bearings.

RACK

A bar with teeth on one face for gearing with a pinion or worm gear (Fig. 1-23).

The teeth cut in the curved lower part of a circular saw trunnion are a rack. The teeth milled in the rear of a drill press quill are a rack. Most gear racks are the part receiving the motion from a pinion gear, either a small regular gear or a worm. (*See Gear, pinion gear.*)

RAIL

A bar extending from one support to another; a track.

In most cases, the fence on a circular saw or band saw is supported by, and slides on, guide rails. These can have many shapes, such as round or square; they may also be hollow or solid and made of various materials. The front rail is often calibrated in "inches from the blade" for fast fence settings. Guide rails are frequently referred to as guide bars.

RAM

Any of various guided pieces for exerting pressure.

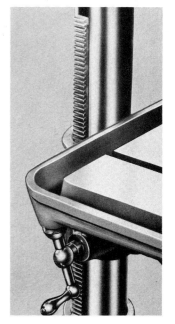

FIG. 1-23

This term is most often used to describe the quill in the tailstock of a lathe. Rams are often designed with a self-releasing or knockout feature when fully retracted. This ejects the tapered shank of the center or cutting tool. Other rams have a tang slot for insertion of a draft or center key. The sliding arm of a metal working shaper, some radial arm saws, and some radial drill presses also are called rams.

RING

A circular band of metal or other material; an enclosed circular or other area.

Hog Ring

A heavy retaining ring not usually a complete circle, used to hold a drill press return spring confined, under tension, and in a small package for easy handling, shipment, and installation.

O Ring

A rubber or plastic type of ring usually used as a seal to control liquid or air flow where movement of parts is necessary. It is used also to cushion or control shock between two parts.

Retaining Ring

These are often called snap rings or True-Arc rings, the latter a brand name. These rings are often used to position a bearing on a shaft or to hold an assembly from moving on a shaft. They are actually spring clips, suitable for both external and internal applications. Open-type rings can be pushed on a shaft and also forced off with a screwdriver even between assemblies. A more closed type of ring is usually used at the end of a shaft and must be opened with special pliers for installation or removal. The rings have holes in each end for this purpose. Unlimited varieties of rings are used, but they all usually seat in a slot cut in the shaft at a controlled depth. There are also completely closed rings which depend on internal or external fingers for holding power on a shaft without a slot (Fig. 1-24).

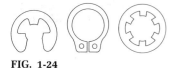

FIG. 1-24

ROD

A slender, usually round, square, or hexagonal bar (as of wood or metal). (*See Feed Rod.*)

ROLL PIN

A type of spring taking the form of an open cylinder (Fig. 1-25).

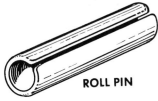

ROLL PIN

FIG. 1-25

Roll pins are used for numerous purposes, usually in place of a taper pin, a screw, or even a cotter pin. They are tapped into a hole or mating holes in two parts (a shaft and a collar) slightly smaller in diameter than the pin itself. The pin contracts, forming a secure bond because of its spring action. It must be tapped or driven out with a punch. Roll pins are often used for prepositioning assemblies before bolts are tightened and for positive stops. They are available in numerous sizes.

rpm (also written RPM)

This is a standard abbreviation of "revolutions per minute," or the number of times, measured in minutes, a shaft, pulley, or wheel will rotate 360 deg. In most cases, the motor is marked or labeled with the rpm. To ascertain the correct speed for the cutter, blade, or spindle, the following formula will work if any three elements are known:

$$\frac{\text{Motor pulley diameter}}{\text{Spindle pulley diameter}} = \frac{\text{spindle speed in rpm}}{\text{motor speed in rpm}}$$

If you are connecting a motor to a shaft in one step with a belt drive, the correct spindle speed is easily obtained by changing pulley sizes. If a jack shaft is used, the formula must be used twice.

SCREW

A continuous helical rib used to attach, fasten, or close.

Cap Screw

There is an almost unlimited variety of cap screws, differing primarily in the style of head. For example, flat head, fillister head, hexagonal socket head, fluted head, round head, and button head. The only things they have in common are a definite shoulder, a head, and a reasonably small size. Unlike a bolt and nut, which forms a clamp, a cap screw is usually threaded and tightened directly into a tapped hole in a casting (Fig. 1-26*a*).

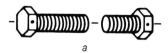

a

FIG. 1-26*a*

Drive Screw

Drive screws are often referred to by a brand name, Parker-Kalon screws. They are not turned but driven into the work. Any turning action is due to the large helix angle serrations on the screw body. Generally intended to be permanent, drive screws are used to hold nameplates, serial number plates, direction or instruction plates, and scales to a machine.

Self-tapping Screw

This screw can be driven or turned into a hole of the proper size without previous tapping of the hole. Depending on the type of threads on the screw, the material in the hole is displaced or cut to form a similar thread. Normally, a sheet-metal screw will distort the metal enough to make the holding action similar to that of a nut. In thicker material the threads are actually pushed into the sides of the hole or are cut by the tapered starting threads of the screw. These tapered entering threads have multiple cutting edges, similar to a tap.

Setscrew

Small screws with internal hex sockets, no external head, and continuous threads are commonly called Allen setscrews, the brand name. These sock setscrews can be tightened below the surface of the work and come with various types of ends or points, e.g., dog point. Other setscrews generally have a small external square head, not much larger than the screw body. Many kinds of heads and points are available to serve various purposes.

FIG. 1-26*b*

Thumbscrew

Small screws with a rather large single handle, formed to fit the thumb and the first finger, are called thumbscrews. A typical use is tightening the chuck jaws on a scroll saw. They are used where a wrench might be inconvenient for frequent loosening and tightening (Fig. 1-26*b*).

SERRATION

Having marginal teeth pointing forward toward the apex.

Most drive screws and even small studs are serrated; they are driven or tapped into the starting hold. The ridges, either straight or slightly helical, either force similar ridges into the hole or are spread out into the lands on the drive screw. This action gives extremely good holding power and often makes them very difficult to remove. Serrations are cut also into the end of a shaft to match duplicate serrations in a handwheel, ensuring both no-slip action and a great variety of positions.

SHAFT

A continuous helical rib; a commonly cylindrical bar used to support rotating pieces or to transmit power or motion by rotation.

Although any quill, spindle, rod, or similar part might be correctly called a shaft, it is better to use a more definite term or at least add some further explanation to this word. The extensions of a motor armature are called shafts. (*See Arbor; Spindle.*)

SHANK

The straight part of a nail or pin; a part of an object by which it can be attached.

This term usually refers to the part of a drill bit, reamer, or cutting tool which is held by a taper, chuck, or toolholder. Specific tools are often described by this term, such as "straight shank drill" or "taper shank drill."

SHEAR PIN

To become divided; to cut.

These pins are designed to shear off or break when the torque or load becomes excessive. Their purpose is to protect other expensive or difficult-to-replace mechanisms from damage. For instance, the quick-change gearbox on a metalworking lathe may be protected by a shear pin connecting the lead screw with the main shaft in the gearbox. In most cases, the material and thickness of the shear pin are accurately engineered to break or shear before expensive gearing is damaged.

SHEAVE

Any grooved wheel or pulley (Fig. 1-27).

This term is generally applied to a single V groove drive wheel or only one of the V grooves in a pulley containing more than one groove. A four-step pulley is also a four-sheave pulley.

FIG. 1-27

SHIM

A thin, often tapered slip which fills out or levels up.

A shim is usually a thin, accurately sized piece of metal used for minute and usually permanent adjustment. Shims are used both to take up wear in older machines and to bring assemblies into perfect alignment in new units. In either case, they become an actual part of the machine. Shims can be made of any material. For instance, wood can be used to level a machine or to prevent tipping due to an uneven floor. A wedge might be considered an adjustable shim.

SHOE

A device that retards, stops, or controls the motion of an object.

In most cases, the word "shoe" refers to brake shoe and specifically indicates the area that contacts the part in motion. Often the shoe is easily replaceable because of frequent use and hard wear. A shoe may be very small, contacting only a limited area, or it may completely wrap around a shaft or spindle. Many materials are used, depending on the speed, torque, and other factors. A shoe is used also as a follower and might be called a guide or even a guide block. (See Guide Block.)

SHOULDER

A lateral projection or extension.

A shoulder is formed by an instant change in the diameter of a shaft. Shoulders are used to position various parts, gears, or bearings or to limit the travel or movement of such items. The presence of a shoulder may indicate the direction of removal for a bearing or even the entire shaft.

SLEEVE

A tubular machine part designed to fit over another part (as a hollow axle or bushing).

A sleeve is often used to reduce the size of a hole or to restore a worn hole to its original size. It is often very thin, measured in thousandths of an inch. (See Bushing.)

FIG. 1-28

SLINGER

An instrument for throwing; a tubular ring for spreading a solution by centrifugal force.

A slinger is usually a special flange with slots or holes for slinging or throwing by centrifugal force (Fig. 1-28). Lubricating oil, cutting fluid, or coolant is often literally thrown at the correct area by a slinger. The fluid is often pumped directly through the hollow spindle to the slinger flange. An abrasive cut-off machine is an excellent application of this principle.

SOCKET

An opening or hollow that forms a holder.

The internal part of a tapered spindle which accepts a taper shank drill is a socket. The wrench or set of wrenches with one or more handles and many interchangeable adapters to fit various sizes of nuts is a socket set.

SPACER

A material used to produce or arrange space between objects.

Space between parts can be created in many ways, but the term "spacer" usually refers to a washer, sleeve, or other similar device. In most cases, spacers are precision-made in regard to length or width and are used to keep working parts in alignment with the mating parts of other assemblies. Spacers are used also to take up lash or slack in an assembly. (See Sleeve; Washer.)

SPANNER

A wrench, especially one having a pin in its jaw to fit a hole or slot in an object.

A spanner wrench is designed to tighten or loosen a part that is not accessible with a normal wrench, usually because of interference due to a spindle, arbor, shaft, or possibly a shoulder or deep inset. Tightening with a spanner wrench is sometimes necessary to prevent indiscriminate adjustment or removal of a part. There are many types of spanners using a variety of systems. One pin, no pins—one hook, two pins. The latter is usually a flat spanner.

SPINDLE

A horizontal or vertical axle revolving on a pin or pivot ends.

A spindle performs exactly the same function as an arbor but by rule of thumb it is mounted in a vertical position. Examples are a drill press and a woodworking shaper. The exception is a lathe spindle.

SPLINE

A key that is fixed to one of two connected mechanical parts and fits into a keyway in the other.

Two or more equally spaced keyways cut into a shaft are usually called a spline. The number of keyways is limited only by their size and the diameter of the shaft. In most cases, splines are cut into two mating parts such as a pulley and a spindle, allowing for both continued rotation and in-and-out movement (Fig. 1-29). A spline can also reduce the transmission of vibration or shock between moving parts, with no loss of torque.

SPOT FACE

A small extent of face, at the place of action, in a responsible or accountable position.

A spot face provides an accurate plane usually surrounding a hole and often eliminates the need to machine a full casting. The hole may be drilled, but the spot-facing operation is usually done with a single-point cutting tool even though it may be a part of, or fastened to, the drill bit. The spot-faced area is always lower than the surrounding casting.

SPRING

An elastic body or device that recovers its original shape when released after being distorted; a source of action or motion.

Many types of springs are used in the operation of machinery. A flat coil spring, like a clock spring, is usually used to return the drill press quill to its original position. Round coil springs can be used to eliminate lash or play in a shaft. Small pieces of flat spring stock are used to keep constant tension on an adjustment. Wave washers and even roll pins might be considered springs. (See *Roll Pin; Washer, wave.*)

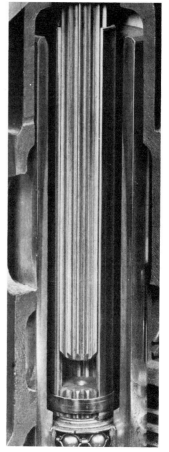

FIG. 1-29

STUD

Any of various infixed pieces (as a rod or pin) projecting from a machine and serving chiefly as a support or axis.

A stud is normally threaded at both ends and is first tightened into a major casting or assembly. A second part, cover, or assembly is then slipped on the stud and held in place with a nut. Studs are used where the casting depth or other restrictions prohibit the use of a bolt. Studs are used also for exact positioning of an assembly.

T SLOT

A T slot is the part of a clamping or holding device, cast or milled into a work surface or table (Fig. 1-30). A T bolt, with its head in the slot, can be

FIG. 1-30

used with a nut for clamping a tight or firm grip on the work or fixture. This is true for drill presses, milling machines, metalworking shapers, and similar machines. A sliding jig can be held to the table with a T slot without restriction of its movement parallel to the table. For instance, the miter gage used with the circular saw often slides into a T slot milled in the table. There are many methods and variations that accomplish the same general results without milling out a complete T slot.

TABLE

The upper, flat surface; a horizontal stratum.

The table is usually the flat, horizontal working surface of the machine. When the arbor or spindle tilts, the table is stationary, and vice versa. Most tables contain tapped holes, slots, or other means to facilitate attaching fixtures or using jigs. In machine tools, the table can often move or rotate during operation.

TAILSTOCK

The adjustable or sliding head of a lathe containing the dead center.

This unit, which houses the adjustable ram, slides on the lathe bed to compensate for a long or short workpiece. It can be adjusted from front to rear either for alignment with the head stock or to cut a long taper. The tailstock merely supports the work during normal turning, but cutting tools can be mounted in the ram. Although in a screw machine the tailstock is replaced by a turret, the latter can be used also as a tailstock when necessary.

TAPER

Something used to produce a gradual diminution of thickness, diameter, or width.

Brown and Sharp Taper

This is a standard self-holding taper widely used to hold tooling in milling machines and other machine tools, e.g., end mills. The Brown and Sharp taper runs $1\frac{3}{4}$ in. per foot.

L-00 Taper

This rather long, steep taper is used in conjunction with a key for accurate alignment and positive drive on many small and medium-sized metal lathe spindles. The chuck plate or faceplate is drawn up on the taper and held by a threaded flange nut or draw nut on the spindle. The snug fit must be broken by reversing the draw nut with a spanner wrench. This type of drive is often written as L-00 or L00 taper drive or tapered key drive (Fig. 1-31).

FIG. 1-31

Morse Taper

This is a standard self-holding taper used on the shanks of reamers, counterbores, toolholders, drills, and lathe centers. Morse tapers run about ⅝ in. per foot with a slight difference between sizes. The most common is a No. 1, 2, or 3, commonly used as a socket in drill press spindles, lathe spindles, and rams.

Pipe Taper

This taper is always internally or externally threaded and ensures a tight fit between the pipe and the fitting without using a shoulder, nut, or other method. The two parts literally run out of threads, owing to the taper, and automatically tighten.

R-8 Taper

This taper is normally used in milling machine sprindles and, of course, for the collets which are used. It is very short and self-releasing; it is used only to draw the collet tight on the work or tooling with accuracy.

Taper Pin

A taper pin is driven into a matching hole, drilled and taper-reamed, usually through two parts, such as a collar and a shaft, where adjustment is not considered necessary. It has been standardized at ¼-in. taper per foot and is usually about 1 in. long though available in any length to match a particular application.

No. 33 Chuck Taper

This is a very short self-holding taper used to hold small chucks and other adapters on a spindle, usually a drill press. The chuck, with its internal taper, is drawn on the external taper of the spindle with a threaded collar and spanner wrench. This taper is often called a Jacobs taper because of the popularity of this particular brand of chucks (Fig. 1-32).

FIG. 1-32

TEMPLATE

A gage, pattern, or mold.

A template can be a simple, full-sized paper pattern or a complicated guide system for reproducing duplicate parts. A template is used also to eliminate complicated measuring for work infrequently done. Simple portable router templates are usually homemade of ⅛-in. hardboard, but intricate mechanical hinge-butt templates or guides are commercially available. Oftentimes an original part is used as a template to make a duplicate item. For instance, a torn gasket can be used as a pattern or template to make an accurate replacement.

TIE ROD / TIE BAR

A structural element (as a beam, rod, or angle) holding two pieces together; something that serves as a connecting link.

The front and rear trunnion assembly of a circular saw is often held together and accurately spaced by a tie rod. Tie rods or bars may be used also to strengthen a steel cabinet.

TORQUE

A turning or twisting force.

The actual power or turning power of a motor. It is vital, regardless of the type or drive, that all possible torque developed by the motor be transmitted to the spindle, arbor, or working parts. Any slippage, binding, or similar problem will affect the machine operation and possibly the work.

TRUNNION

Pivot; either of two opposite gudgeons on which a cannon is swiveled.

In most cases, tilting arbors, spindles, or tables ride on a trunnion or pair of trunnions. These assure ease of movement and also maintain correct alignment of the parts involved. A trunnion is an extension of a pivot point (Fig. 1-33).

FIG. 1-33

WASHER

A flat, thin ring or a perforated plate used in joints or assemblies to ensure tightness, prevent leakage, or relieve friction.

Fiber Washer

These washers are most often used to reduce friction against a collar, shoulder, or boss. They have a tendency to retain any lubricant which might be used.

Lock Washer

Any one of several types of washers intended primarily to keep a nut from backing off because of vibration. Some of these washers are split and actually act as a spring. Others have projections or teeth which dig into the nut, the work face, or both (Fig. 1-34).

FIG. 1-34

Spacer Washer

A washer of a controlled thickness to separate two parts accurately. These are sometimes hardened and are often accurate to thousandths of an inch.

Wave Washer / Spring Washer

This washer, which looks as if it were waved, could easily be classified as a spring. In fact, thin washers of this kind are usually made of spring steel. Their most common use is to preload a bearing or to resiliently take up slack or lash in a shaft.

WHEEL

A circular frame, capable of turning on an axle.

Although a sleeve or even a gear might be considered a wheel, the most common usage implies a handwheel (Fig. 1-35). A handwheel is used for manual control of a mechanism, and a locking feature is often included to hold the setting in its proper position. A handwheel, a knurled knob, or a ball crank handle are often interchangeable, but the handwheel usually provides greater leverage.

The term "wheel" is also used to mean grinding wheel. Grinding wheels come in many sizes and shapes, with various grinding characteristics. They are actually cutting tools with abrasive or cutting material bonded into a solid circular unit. Each separate piece of abrasive material is a cutter bit.

FIG. 1-35

WHIP

The flexible, threshing motion of a vibrating object.

Whip action in a shaft is normally undesirable. If it occurs, the shaft is acting as a torsion bar or spring and is being twisted when started or stopping by excessive torque. Whip action may also indicate that the shaft should be of a larger diameter or should be made of a harder material. This action can be present also in a long thin workpiece that is held between centers.

WIPER

Something used for wiping (as a towel or sponge).

A wiper, usually of felt or similar material, is used to keep the ways or track free from grit, dust, coolant, and other harmful material. Wipers are found on moving assemblies, primarily in the machine tool class, such as a saddle and tailstock of a metal lathe, and also on the carriage assemblies of radial saws. Some band saws have brush wipers for blade cleaning during operation. Felt wipers are used also to distribute lubricant.

YOKE

An arched device; a clamp or similar piece that embraces two parts to hold them up or unite them in position.

Many assemblies or single parts used to hold a mechanism at both ends might be called yokes. The most obvious example is the casting holding the motor in a radial saw cutting head assembly. A yoke is usually open, similar in basic design to a C clamp, allowing for controlled movement of the suspended assembly.

You may wish to add to this list from your personal experience.

_____

_____

_____

CHAPTER TWO

General Troubleshooting

The normal distributor or manufacturer is often notified by letter or even by telephone that his customer's machine "isn't running," "doesn't work right," or "is broken." Even after extensive questioning, he can obtain no really usable information to analyze the problem. This situation naturally leads to an actual service call, often for a minor adjustment like tightening a setscrew, or for advising purchase of a new belt. Two main disadvantages result from inadequate information and a subsequent service call: first, there may well be a charge for the service and, secondly, valuable production or educational time is lost.

It is important that the customer check the machine and analyze the probable cause or at least report the effect on either the unit or the work. If this is done, the cause of the problem is usually found and corrected by the teacher or operator. Even if a distributor or manufacturer is contacted, many problems can be solved or successful suggestions made for correction if adequate information is given in a letter or by telephone.

There are two major reasons for the customer's lack of adequate information or analyzing ability. The first is purely psychological. "I never took one apart before," "I was afraid I couldn't get it back together," "I never thought of checking it out myself," and "I wouldn't go near it if it wasn't running right" are typical comments. The second reason is a real lack of knowledge about exactly what to look for or, possibly even more important, a method or system for analyzing the trouble. There are, of course, many other reasons; for instance, the fear of voiding a guarantee or

FIG. 2-1

FIG. 2-2

FIG. 2-3

warranty, a service agreement with a distributor or manufacturer, or ignorance of usable terminology concerning the problem or the machine.

The lack of confidence and method can be overcome by a simple process of elimination. Most machines, regardless of size, are an assembly of component parts or assemblies. The assemblies or areas should be inspected for proper working order individually and, if possible, even separated from the total machine. A vibration problem in any machine might warrant a close check of all assemblies involved, but a strange click in the headstock of a lathe would eliminate any inspection of the tailstock.

The following checklist, in sequential order, indicates the cause of most vibration or unusual noise problems that can be corrected before they become serious:

1. CHECK THE MOTOR
The motor should be disconnected from the machine by removing the belt (or the coupling on a direct-drive unit) (Fig. 2-1). Unusual noise or defective motor bearings can be detected. Loose end bells or other mechanical trouble spots can be checked. Line voltage and amp draw should be checked with meters. The motor should be turned over by hand and also run under power.

2. CHECK THE BELTS AND PULLEYS
Belts and pulleys should be inspected periodically. Broken sections in a pulley or even cracks will throw it out of balance and cause vibration, and they will cause excessive wear to the belt. Frayed belts also will cause vibration and should be replaced (Fig. 2-2). The V groove in the pulley should be checked for wear. The belt should not bottom but should ride on the sides of the sheave.

3. CHECK THE SETSCREWS
Even a slight movement between a shaft and pulley will produce a sound very similar to a worn or bad bearing. In addition to the noise caused by a loose setscrew, serious damage can be done to both pulleys and shafts. The loosening of the screw will allow the pulley to move slightly, forcing the screw to dig into and destroy the flat on the shaft, alternately left and right (Fig. 2-3). If loose enough, the pulley may rotate independently of the shaft, or vice versa, scoring the shaft completely. Movement or slippage also has a tendency to enlarge both the bore of the pulley and the threaded setscrew hole. If a key is used other than a flat on the shaft for positive drive, the keyway in both the pulley and the shaft can be widened or actually destroyed. If a tight setscrew has a tendency to loosen when the machine is in operation, there are several ways to correct the problem:

a. Replace the setscrew with a longer screw; more threads give more holding power.
b. Replace the normal setscrew with a cone point, cup point, or serrated setscrew—to bite in and hold.

c. Replace the single setscrew with two setscrews, one driven in on top of the other to act like a locknut (Fig. 2-4).

d. Use a commercial product such as Locktight.

e. Drill and tap the hole for a larger setscrew.

f. Drill and tap a new hole in the pulley hub.

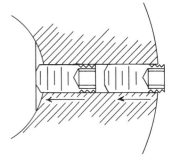

1566520

FIG. 2-4

In many cases, the pulley must be replaced, the flat on the shaft must be filed smooth, or the key must be replaced or turned over. In extreme cases, the shaft must be replaced or turned down to a smaller diameter.

Setscrews used for adjusting gibs, holding collars in place, or similar jobs normally do not cause noise or damage, but their proper adjustment is directly related to the accuracy of the machine.

4. CHECK THE PULLEY ALIGNMENT

Regardless of the purpose or location of a belt drive, the pulleys or sheaves must line up exactly (Fig. 2-5). Even a slight misalignment will cause vibration, produce less torque transmission, and naturally lead to excessive pulley and belt wear. A straightedge or plumb line can be used to assure that the pulleys are in the same plane. The position on both sides of the center line should be checked to make sure one of the pulleys is not tipped. It may be necessary to reposition a motor mount or move a pulley slightly on a shaft to accomplish this alignment. By rule of thumb, the pulley should be as close to the bearing as possible to avoid distortion of the shaft or damage to the bearing or bearing seat.

FIG. 2-5

5. CHECK THE ARBOR OR SPINDLE

The arbor or spindle, when disconnected from the drive mechanism, can usually be rotated by hand. By turning slowly back and forth, you can feel a worn or dirty bearing. The complete assembly should then be removed and the bearings checked individually (Fig. 2-6). This check is easily made by holding the outer race in one hand while turning the inner race with a finger of the other hand. A visual check should also be made of the bearing seals, the outside and inside of the bearing case, and the bearing seats in the machine. A rough sealed-for-life bearing cannot be washed out, repacked with grease, resealed, or otherwise repaired; it must be replaced. It might be noted that bearing seals are most often damaged by rough or careless installation.

FIG. 2-6

A damaged or bent spindle or arbor can cause many problems affecting both the machine itself and the accuracy of the work. In most cases, actual damage is obvious, but a slight deflection or runout is hard to check visually with the spindle in the machine. Probably the best way to check for runout is to use a dial indicator while turning the spindle slowly by hand. In a woodshop or cabinet shop an indicator may not be available, but a rough check can still be made. When the spindle is rolled on a flat surface, like a saw table, it will lope or roll at different speeds if not perfectly straight. Light can usually be seen between the spindle and the table, or a feeler gage leaf can be inserted in this space, indicating spindle deflection. Any runout in an arbor or spindle will decrease bearing life, cause vibration, and naturally affect accuracy. It is usually easier and less expensive to replace a defective or bent arbor than to attempt any straightening.

6. CHECK THE CUTTING TOOL

It should be obvious that all cutting tools must be both sharp and properly sharpened. A drill bit must be straight to drill an accurate hole. A saw blade must not wobble and must be balanced. Jointer blades must all be the same height. A band saw blade must be welded or brazed correctly, smoothly, and in line. A router bit or shaper cutter must have each lip ground in exactly the same manner (Fig. 2-7).

FIG. 2-7

This list could be expanded almost infinitely in view of the many types of machines, materials, and cutting tools. Many machine problems start with dull, out-of-balance, or otherwise defective cutters, leading directly to bent shafts, worn bearings, ruined guides, vibration, and inaccurate work.

If only because of the increasing physical effort needed—to say nothing about the lack of accuracy—a student, teacher, or carpenter will soon be forced to stop work long enough to sharpen a dull hand saw. A machine also works harder and less accurately with dull cutting tools. Although harder to measure instantly, the excessive strain on belts, pulleys, bearings, shafts, motors, and all working parts is both obvious and expensive within a short time.

There is an old trite saying about using "the right tool for the job." It is never more true than when applied to power equipment of any type. This is, of course, why there are rip blades, crosscut blades, skip tooth blades, spur bits, straight shank drills, side milling cutters, helical milling cutters, three-wing cutters, bonded wheels, aluminum oxide belts, and literally thousands of cutting tools available, each designed to run at a specific speed, to cut a specific material. Each has its individual characteristics in regard to rake angles, balance, method of sharpening, length of life, or hundreds of other similar or special considerations. One thing they all have in common is the ability to do a specific operation or cutting job easier, faster, or more accurately than other cutting tools.

If the six points listed above are checked, there is an excellent chance that the problem can be corrected on the spot without added expense or lost time. Even if instant correction is not possible, the problem may well be isolated by this process and easily explainable in terms of ordering parts or requesting specific service.

Incidentally, this is a good general plan to follow in regard to preventive maintenance, possibly every year in a normal shop situation. The only procedure which it might be wise to skip is the actual removal of bearings and shafts as long as no roughness or runout is obvious. Not removing them would lessen the possibility of accidental damage to bearing seals, bearing seats, and precision arbors or spindles.

There are many basic rules of thumb, usually learned the hard way or through experience, related to the disassembly of machines and equipment. A few are listed here, but any mechanic could add to them very quickly:

1. At least scan the parts manual to become generally familiar with the particular machine.

2. Clean with a solvent all areas to be checked or disassembled. Setscrews, snap rings, and other small features can be completely hidden by dirt and grease.

3. Identify the place and purpose of setscrews, roll pins, snap rings, taper pins, and other features.

4. Locate shoulders or other restrictions in order to determine the direction in which a shaft or bearing must be removed.

5. Use a wood block, mallet, or soft metal hammer when tapping free a shaft or assembly.

6. Any roughness on the end of the shaft should be filed smooth before removing a pulley or bearing.

7. Remove parts in order and lay them out in order for cleaning and inspection unless you are completely familiar with the machine or assembly.

8. Care should be taken not to damage bearing races by prying on a bearing during removal or tapping on the seal when reassembling.

9. If in doubt, replace any questionable part while the unit is disassembled to avoid future problems and disassembly a second time.

10. Lubricate where necessary with the proper lubricant while the assembly is apart.

11. A seemingly concentric part may have a front and rear, a left and right, or even be worn in a "seated" or more workable position. There is often a similar but not duplicate right and left part. They should be reassembled in their respective positions, even though the two parts may have been the same when both were brand new.

12. After cleaning and lubricating, carefully assemble all the parts in proper order. Use the parts manual as a guide.

The real key to success is confidence, which could be considered a combination of common sense and patience. When used with a parts manual for direction, these two attributes practically guarantee the expected results, even for an amateur.

The following is a list of "common" tools and equipment necessary for basic maintenance repair or alignment:

1. Screwdrivers: large, medium, small, stubby, offset, regular, Phillips blades

2. Pliers: regular combination, needle nose, side cutting, vise grip, internal and external retaining ring, large slip joint or water pump type

3. Hammers: large and small ball peen, plastic or other soft face, wood mallet

4. Wrenches: set of open and box end, set of Allen wrenches, pipe wrench; special wrenches supplied with machine

5. Files: large and small, flat mill, three-square, round

6. Hack saw: adjustable frame 10″, 12″

7. Drive or pin punches: 4″ long, $\frac{1}{16}$″, $\frac{1}{8}$″, $\frac{3}{16}$″, $\frac{1}{4}$″

8. Center punch: 4″ length

9. Combination square: 12″ blade

10. Rules or scales: 6′ folding, 6′ tape, 6″ steel scale

11. Knife: 3″ sloyd, trimming (razor), putty

12. Scratch awl: 6″ scriber with handle

13. Wheel puller: small adjustable bearing/wheel puller

14. C clamps: small, medium

15. Lubricants: machine oil, penetrating oil, hard wax or other dry lubricant

16. Abrasives: fine and medium, steel wool, emery paper

17. Pencils, chalk

18. Flashlight

19. Safety glasses

The following tools and equipment can often make the job go faster or are needed to solve a specific problem. In most cases, they are available in the shop area or can be obtained close by:

1. Volt-amp meter

2. Dial indicator

3. Magnetic holder

4. Thickness or feeler gage

5. Precision level

6. Socket wrench set

7. Torque wrench

8. Framing square

9. Aviation or tin snips

10. $\frac{1}{4}$″ or $\frac{3}{8}$″ electric drill

11. Wire wheel and adapter

12. Set of drills

13. Tap and die set
14. Set of nut runners
15. Screw extractor set
16. Bar clamps
17. Adjustable hand screws
18. Hand tapered reamer
19. Small wrecking bar or pinch bar
20. Wire strippers
21. Bench brush
22. Paintbrushes
23. Solvent
24. Masking tape
25. Friction tape
26. Gasket material
27. Gloves
28. Rags
29. Extra bolts, nuts, washers, cotter pins, and other standard parts

CHAPTER THREE
Belts and Pulleys

In many cases, unsatisfactory operation of power tools or machine tools is directly related to the belts and pulleys. Not only is this true in the case of minor noises or vibration, but over an extended period of time, it is often found to be the basic reason for major maintenance problems. In spite of this fact, most medium-sized machines in the modern cabinet shop, metal shop, or school shop are belt driven.

DIRECT DRIVE

FIG. 3-1

Until 35 years ago, most machines were driven directly off the motor shaft (Fig. 3-1)—therefore the term "direct drive." Others were driven by flat belts, possibly through line shafting of some type. The direct-drive system of transmitting power is subject to almost no torque loss, but it offers few other advantages. The design of the machine is restricted by the motor size and specifications. Normally, the speed is controlled by set standards for the motor itself without regard to the correct speed for the cutterhead, spindle, or type of operation. Other speeds may be available, but the special motor cost is usually restrictively high. In case of serious motor problems, necessitating removal, valuable time may be lost during the repair period. It is often difficult to obtain a substitute or replacement motor because at least the shaft size, mounting feet and holes, and shaft height must be exactly the same as for the original motor.

Direct drive is still common and is used on such equipment as grinders, radial saws, and planers. In these cases, either the advantage of full torque transmission far outweighs other considerations or the motor itself is a major assembly.

The cutting tool, such as a saw blade or grinding wheel, is often mounted directly on an extended motor shaft. Any connection to another shaft is always made with a flexible coupling (Fig. 3-2). Care should be taken to make sure the two shafts line up as accurately as possible to avoid wear, vibration, and even shaft or bearing damage. Usually the motor is the only adjustable assembly.

FIG. 3-2

FLAT BELT DRIVE

The flat leather belt drive, which was common for many years, is almost a thing of the past. There is probably only one major manufacturer still using flat belts in their equipment design. All flat belts run on a cone pulley, which is convex or has a slightly larger diameter in the center, gently rounding off to a small diameter at each edge. The belt tends to ride on and climb to the high area and is thus kept on the pulley. Examples of this principle are a band saw wheel or tire and the drum on a belt sander.

Although the flat leather belt can provide a very satisfactory drive and avoids many of the problems incident to the direct drive, it has definite disadvantages depending on the application. Unless the belt is purchased in a specific length and already spliced, splicing can be a real problem. It involves punching or drilling the belt ends in the proper pattern, possibly cutting grooves in the belt to bring the lacing flush with the surface, and lacing by hand. Flat leather belts also can be spliced by using wire belt hooks (Fig. 3-3); this is often done by machine. The hooks or loops in each end of the belt are meshed together and a pin is inserted, allowing for flexibility but holding the ends together. Possibly the best method of belt splicing is to splice the belt itself without lacing or metal hooks. At each end a long taper, 5 or 6 in., is cut with a knife or even a hand plane (Fig. 3-4). The tapers are then glued together with a good acetone cement and clamped tightly until dry. The major advantage of this method is the absence of noise, vibration, or cone pulley damage because there is no obvious break in the belt.

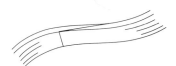

FIG. 3-3

FIG. 3-4

Other types of flat belt drives are often used on high-speed or very high-speed drill presses and grinders (Fig. 3-5). Such continuous belts, usually made of rubber or synthetic material, are used primarily to eliminate vibration. Flat belts, either spliced or continuous piece, are considered more vibration-free than V-belts under the same conditions.

Many modern drives in portable tools now use timing belts, or flat belts with gear rack formed on the inside. The belt teeth mesh with teeth on the driving and driven gears (Fig. 3-6) to provide a positive nonslip drive;

FIG. 3-5

41

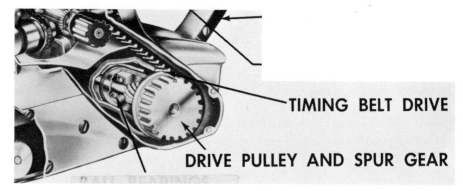

TIMING BELT DRIVE

DRIVE PULLEY AND SPUR GEAR

FIG. 3-6

in most cases they perform no actual timing function. This type of drive is usually less troublesome and more maintenance-free than a chain or gear train (enclosed in a case) that requires periodic check and lubrication.

V-BELT DRIVE

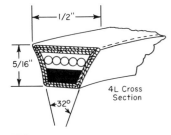

FIG. 3-7

FIG. 3-8

The V-belt drive is probably the most common drive method used on today's medium-sized power tools and machine tools. It offers the designer, the manufacturer, and the user many advantages over the direct drive and the flat leather belt systems.

The space saved by the use of a sheave or V-pulley rather than the crowned pulley is possibly as high as 75 percent. This factor gives the design engineer much greater freedom to produce a cleaner, smaller unit. Because it is seldom necessary to provide bearing support at both ends of a sheave, less space is required. With no reduction in space, more pulley steps can be used for changing speeds.

Since V-belts pull on both sides, they provide excellent pulling power and transmit almost all the usable torque developed by the motor or driving pulley. As increased torque or breaking effort is applied to the drive pulley, the V-belt actually digs in and grips both pulleys tighter and deeper. Because of this, V-belts have a very low rate of power loss.

Sometimes the power transmission problems are beyond the capacity, or torque transmitting capabilities, of a single or a normal V-belt. Belt manufacturers and machine designers have solved this problem, usually in either of two ways. First, V-belts are now available which contain wire cords rather than only fiber cords (Fig. 3-7). These increase belt life and pulling power primarily by limiting the amount the belt will stretch, thereby decreasing slipping. Alternatively multiple-belt drives are also used to decrease stretching and slipping (Fig. 3-8). The belts may be completely separate but matched; they may be separate but vulcanized together at the top (Fig. 3-9); or they may be totally molded together (Fig. 3-10). In any case, the purpose is the same. An additional benefit, particularly on a long run, is that the belts which are vulcanized, or actually one piece, have less tendency to turn, whip, or come off the pulley.

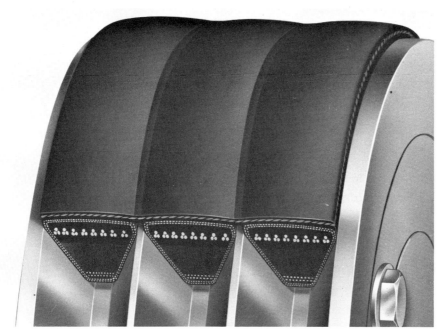

FIG. 3-9

FIG. 3-10

Other than misalignment or the use of lubricants and belt dressing, the greatest enemy of the V-belt is heat. This can sometimes be overcome in the field by adjustments in tension, realignment, or cleaning, but basically it is the belt manufacturer's problem.

Along with the various belt sizes and methods of construction, as related to both torque and heat buildup, the cog or compass belt was developed. V-belts of this kind usually have steel wire cords for greater strength, but their most obvious difference is the notched or cog construction on the inside of the belt (Fig. 3-11). The notches or cogs, although seeming to serve a timing or gear purpose, are really intended to perform two very different functions. First, because they expose more belt surface

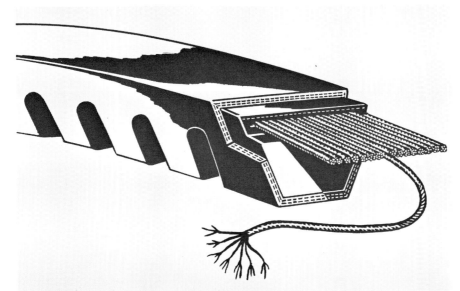

FIG. 3-11

to the air, they will dissipate heat faster and the belt will run cooler than a conventional belt. There is also less internal heat and friction, and the combination of wire construction and cog design allows greater torque transmission with a V-belt of smaller cross section. Secondly, the cog design allows the same size of V-belt to go around a smaller sheave than normally possible and still maintain full contact and full pulling power.

Naturally, all brands or all sizes of V-belts are not the same. Each designer, working with torque requirements as well as other factors, chooses a specific belt for a specific job. It is therefore wise to duplicate the V-belt exactly when replacement is necessary. Many types of rubber and synthetic materials are used as the core or inside, many fabrics are used to cover the belt, and many types and kinds of cords are used. Usually a substitute is not satisfactory.

Standard V-belts are available in five different cross-sectional sizes lettered from A to E (Fig. 3-12). Most equipment in the medium price and size class is designed to use an A or B section belt. The greater sheave size required for, and the greater torque transmission possible with, larger belts are not generally necessary to handle the workload.

The following is a list of suggestions covering V-belts, their use, and maintenance:

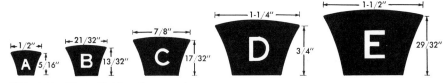

FIG. 3-12 (Gates Rubber Company)

1. Always turn off the power when checking any drive mechanism (Fig. 3-13). Watch it run *and* watch it come to a stop. Do not touch belts or sheaves until it has completely stopped. Unplug the machine from the power source or turn it off at the master control panel to make sure the power cannot be turned on accidentally.

FIG. 3-13 (Gates Rubber Company)

FIG. 3-14

2. All belt drives should be completely guarded (Fig. 3-14). Often a partial guard is worse than none at all because it gives the operator a false sense of security.

3. Do not use belt dressing on V-belts (Fig. 3-15). If apparently needed because of slippage, look for the real cause.

FIG. 3-15   (Gates Rubber Company)

FIG. 3-16

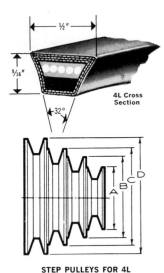

STEP PULLEYS FOR 4L
CROSS SECTION BELTS

FIG. 3-17

FIG. 3-18 (Gates Rubber Company)

4. On a multiple-belt drive, always replace the complete matched set at the same time. Never replace one belt, but purchase the complete set from one manufacturer (Fig. 3-16). Belts from different manufacturers can have different characteristics. Even two unmatched belts with the same catalog number from one manufacturer can be slightly different in length.

5. Make sure you use the correct size and type of V-belt to match the sheaves (Fig. 3-17) and the recommendation of the equipment manufacturer. Many problems can be solved by purchasing replacement belts from the equipment manufacturer, using his catalog number.

6. Proper tension is important for trouble-free service (Fig. 3-18). There are many methods for testing it, including mechanical gages or tension testers. Probably, the method is less important than the results. Regardless of how it is done or checked, the lowest tension at which the V-belt will not slip under full load is the correct tension. Too little tension causes belt slapping and slippage; too much causes vibration, sheave wear, and bearing wear.

7. Exact alignment of pulleys or sheaves is vital to belt life, pulley life, and bearing life (Fig. 3-19). Misalignment is the original cause of many seemingly unrelated machine problems.

FIG. 3-19 (Gates Rubber Company)

Gages are available for checking both the size and the amount of wear on V-belts and sheaves. When the sheave gage is inserted into the sheave (Fig. 3-20), you should be able to detect no more than $\frac{1}{32}$ in. of wear on either side. If the wear is excessive or the groove misshapen, the sheave should be replaced. The V-belt should fit into the belt gage (Fig. 3-21), and the crown should match the appropriate size line. Wear is indicated by the crown falling below the line.

The V-belt should never touch the land at the bottom of the V groove of the sheave. Such contact indicates an extremely worn sheave, a worn belt, or the wrong size of belt. The result is vibration and a definite loss of torque transmission through slippage.

The accompanying chart is a troubleshooter's guide concerning V-belt drive problems.

FIG. 3-20

FIG. 3-21

Trouble-Shooters' Guide for V-Belt

Trouble Area and Observation	Cause	Remedy

BELT STRETCH BEYOND TAKE-UP

Trouble Area and Observation	Cause	Remedy
Belts stretch unequally.	Mis-aligned drive, unequal work done by belts.	Realign and retension drive.
	Belt tensile member broken from improper installation.	Replace all belts with new matched set, **properly** installed.
All belts stretch about equally.	Insufficient take-up allowance.	Check take-up and follow allowance in Gates design manuals.
	Greatly overloaded or under-designed drive.	Redesign using Gates manuals.

SHORT BELT LIFE

Trouble Area and Observation	Cause	Remedy
Relatively rapid failure; no visible reason.	Tensile members damaged through improper installation.	Replace with all new matched set, properly installed.
	Worn sheave grooves (check with groove gauge).	Replace sheaves.
	Under-designed drive.	Redesign using Gates manuals.
Sidewalls soft and sticky. Low adhesion between cover plies. Cross-section swollen.	Oil or grease on belts or sheaves.	Remove source of oil or grease. Clean belts and grooves with cloth moistened with alcohol, benzene or gasoline.
Sidewalls dry and hard. Low adhesion between cover plies. Bottom of belt cracked.	High temperatures.	Remove source of heat. Ventilate drive better.
Deterioration of rubber compounds used in belt.	Belt dressing.	Never use dressing on V-belts. Clean with cloth moistened with alcohol, benzene or gasoline. Tension drive properly to prevent slip.
Extreme cover wear.	Belts rub against belt guard or other obstruction.	Remove obstruction or align drive to give needed clearance.
Spin burns on belt.	Belts slip under starting or stalling load.	Tighten drive until slipping stops.
Bottom of belt cracked.	Too small sheaves.	Redesign for larger sheaves using Gates manuals.
Broken belts.	Object falling into or hitting drive.	Replace with new matched set of belts. Provide shield for drive.

FIG. 3-22

The newest development in V-belts is the Polyflex belt (Fig. 3-22), designed by the Gates Rubber Company. Through licensing agreements the same type of belt will probably be made by other large belt manu-facturers.

These new belts are very different from normal V-belts in size, shape, and material. They are much smaller, yet their pulling power or torque transmission is equal to, or better than, that of the normal-size belt. The belt angle is 60 deg rather than the 36 or 42 deg on a regular V-belt. This

Drives

If your V-belt drive is properly designed and properly installed, it needs very little maintenance. Occasionally, however, a drive may be accidentally damaged or knocked out of adjustment. Changing operating requirements or environmental conditions may lead to problems. This guide is designed to help you discover these problems before they cause machine downtime — and to help you correct them quickly.

Trouble Area and Observation	Cause	Remedy

BELT TURNOVER

	Cause	Remedy
	Excess lateral belt whip.	Use Gates PowerBand Belt.
	Foreign material in grooves.	Remove material — shield drive.
	Mis-aligned sheaves.	Re-align the drive.
	Worn sheave grooves (check with groove gauge).	Replace sheave.
	Tensile member broken through improper installation.	Replace with new matched set **properly** installed.
	Incorrectly placed flat idler pulley.	Carefully align flat idler on slack side of drive as close as possible to driveR sheave.

BELT NOISE

	Cause	Remedy
	Belt slip.	Re-tension drive until it stops slipping.

IMPROPER DRIVEN SPEED

Observation	Cause	Remedy
Incorrect driveR - driveN ratio.	Design error.	Use correct sheave sizes.
Spin burns on belt.	Belt slip.	Re-tension drive until belt stops slipping.

HOT BEARINGS

Observation	Cause	Remedy
Drive over-tensioned.	Worn grooves — belts bottoming and will not transmit power until over-tensioned.	Replace sheaves. Tension drive properly.
	Improper tensioning.	Re-tension drive.
Sheaves too small.	Motor manufacturer's sheave diameters not followed.	Redesign drive using manuals.
Poor bearing condition.	Underdesigned bearings or poor bearing maintenance.	Observe recommended bearing design and maintenance.
Sheaves out too far on shaft.	Error or obstruction problem.	Place sheaves as close as possible to bearings. Remove any obstruction preventing this.
Drive under-tensioned.	Belts slipping and causing heat build-up.	Re-tension drive.

results in more belt surface being supported by the side wall of the sheave. Correct belt tension is maintained for a longer time without adjustment. The top of the Polyflex belt is ribbed for greater flexibility. The ribbing and the small size are visible evidence that this is a different kind of belt.

The material used and the method of manufacture are also very different. The actual material is a special polyurethane compound that results in greater flex resistance and superior abrasion resistance. It also has a higher coefficient of friction, permitting use of a 60-deg belt angle.

FIG. 3-23

In general the same rules apply in regard to maintenance or adjustment of these new belts except that more tension is necessary. The increased tension in no way causes vibration, as it might with the conventional V-belt, because of the one-piece cast body and balance of the Polyflex belt. Naturally the sheave must match the belt. Therefore it is impossible simply to interchange the two types of belts without changing the sheaves or pulleys.

With respect to design, it is obviously possible to provide more steps on a pulley of the same size and depth. It is possible also to provide the same original number of steps in a much smaller package (Fig. 3-23). Because of the many advantages to machine designers and to the final users, these belts will no doubt become more common in a very short time. They are presently used by at least two machinery manufacturers on new equipment, one horizontal milling machine and one drill press.

VARIABLE-SPEED BELTS

The variable-speed belt found on variable-speed drive systems is for all practical purposes an extremely wide V-belt. Often as wide as 1 ½ in., it gives the variable-speed pulley space enough at the bottom to close in, allowing the belt to ride at the top of the V groove (Fig. 3-24).

FIG. 3-24

When open, the belt rides near the bottom. The variable-speed belt pulls on both sides and is tapered to match the sides of the groove. All the normal suggestions regarding alignment, lubrication, and tension, already mentioned for the normal V-belt, apply to the variable-speed belt.

PULLEYS AND SHEAVES

Any pulley wobble or runout can be easily detected by sight check during turning by hand. This indicates that the sheave body is not perpendicular to the hub or the bore. Normally, it cannot be straightened and should be replaced. The setscrew hole also should be checked for an oversize or loose condition, and the V groove or grooves should be checked for wear. Even when these conditions prove satisfactory, the sheave or pulley can still cause vibration problems due to improper balance. There are two normal methods of checking or indicating proper balance, static and dynamic. Static balancing (Fig. 3-25) is done with the pulley or sheave in a stationary position or fixture. Dynamic balancing (Fig. 3-26) is done or checked with the pulley rotating at high speed. Since the centrifugal force action will indicate proper balance more accurately, it is the preferred method. With die-cast or cast-iron pulleys, this is done in a special balancing machine fixtured to drill out or remove material in the heavy area, producing the desired balance.

Pressed-steel pulleys or sheaves are generally considered adequately balanced; if necessary, material must be added to produce a better balance. They are also generally less expensive than a solid or cast pulley because no machinery is required, but balancing is not usually as accurate.

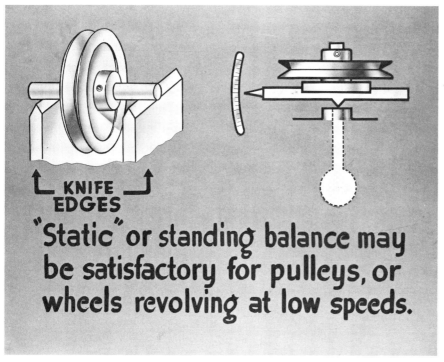

KNIFE EDGES

"Static" or standing balance may be satisfactory for pulleys, or wheels revolving at low speeds.

FIG. 3-25

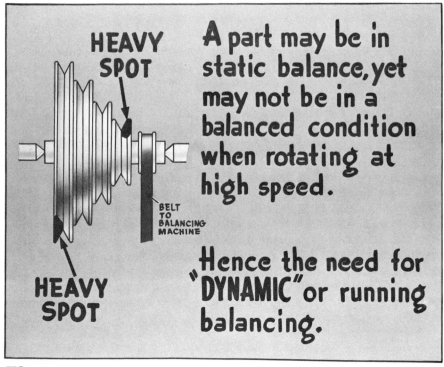

FIG. 3-26

COMBINATION DRIVES

Particularly on larger equipment, many manufacturers may use a combination of different types of drives. The basic drive for a machine might be belt driven, either flat belt or V-belt, although the final drive to the spindle or arbor could be actual gearing (Fig. 3-27). Such a combination

FIG. 3-27

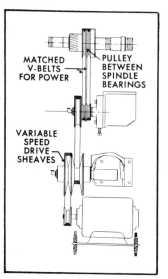

FIG. 3-28

may conserve space or accomplish a specific engineering or mechanical purpose. It could be related to a control or a torque factor. For instance, the design engineer might think it necessary, for customer convenience, to provide a variable-speed system although the workload required a high torque, close coupled drive. He might combine these into one system (Fig. 3-28) providing the benefits of both types of drives in one package. Step pulleys alone can provide quite a range of speeds (Fig. 3-29). With planetary gearing built into the drive pulley, even lower speeds are available (Fig. 3-30).

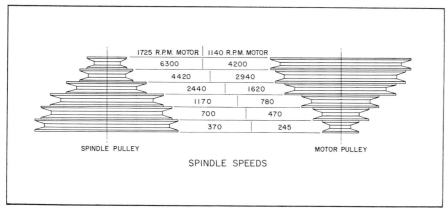

	1725 R.P.M. MOTOR	1140 R.P.M. MOTOR
	6300	4200
	4420	2940
	2440	1620
	1170	780
	700	470
	370	245
SPINDLE PULLEY		MOTOR PULLEY

SPINDLE SPEEDS

FIG. 3-29

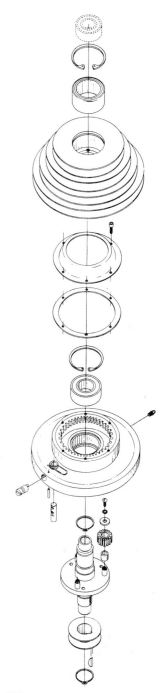

FIG. 3-30

CHAPTER FOUR
Bearings

Most of the bearings in the machine tools, stationary power tools, and portable tools used in commercial and school shops fall into one of the following categories:

1. Ball bearings
2. Tapered roller bearings
3. Cylindrical roller bearings
4. Needle roller bearings
5. Sleeve bearings

Product engineers do considerable research and conduct many tests before establishing either the kind or quality of bearings to be installed in a specific machine. The five kinds mentioned above are available in many different sizes, types, and tolerances. In general, the bearings utilized by the machine are the most practical for the application, considering the cost and the quality needed. Two major factors involved in bearing expense are size and tolerance. Although "tolerance" is often referred to as "class fit" to indicate the accuracy or lack of runout, these two terms are related, but not synonymous. As bearing precision increases, the tolerances on dimensions, out-of-roundness, taper, run out, etc., become smaller. Naturally, the tolerances on the shaft and housing mounting fits also are held to closer limits for higher-precision grade bearings.

The first four kinds of bearings listed contain moving parts and are all called antifriction bearings. They are all basically constructed of two hardened steel rings, tracks, or races, with hardened steel balls or rollers spaced between the rings.

Ball bearings usually have a separator which keeps the individual balls evenly spaced (Fig. 4-1). Tapered roller bearings are adjustable with movable inner or outer race (Fig. 4-2a). Cylindrical or straight roller bearings are similar in construction to ball bearings except that rollers are used instead of balls (Fig. 4-2b). Needle roller bearings usually have no separator and often have no inner race, fitting or rolling directly on a hardened shaft or spindle (Fig. 4-3a). The sleeve bearing, regardless of the material, depends entirely on the thin film of oil or lubrication maintained between the bearing surface and the shaft or spindle. In the latest theories of hydrodynamic lubrication, antifriction bearings too may depend on a thin film of oil in the load-carrying zones.

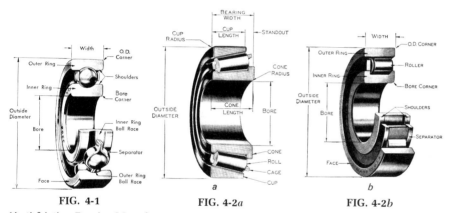

FIG. 4-1
(Anti-friction Bearing Manufacturers Assoc.)

FIG. 4-2a

FIG. 4-2b

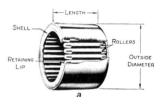

FIG. 4-3a (Anti-friction Bearing Manufacturers Assoc.)

BALL BEARINGS

The most common bearings in use today are, without a doubt, ball bearings. Most of these are now sealed and are referred to as sealed-for-life. The bearing manufacturer greases the open unit, seals the grease in and the dirt out, and supplies the bearing as a ready-to-run assembly. No maintenance or preventive maintenance is needed or even possible. The external parts can be wiped clean, but the bearings cannot be washed inside and repacked with grease. Once the seals are broken or damaged (Fig. 4-3b), the grease soons runs out, or is pumped out, dirt enters, and the bearing is destroyed. It is not repairable and should be replaced. Extreme care should be taken when replacing defective bearings, or removing and reinstalling the original bearings. Any pressure, tapping, pulling,

FIG. 4-3b (Anti-friction Bearing Manufacturers Assoc.)

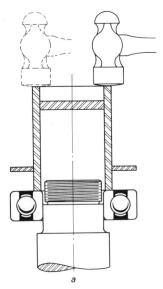

FIG. 4-4a (New Departure,
Hyatt Bearings, Division of
General Motors Corp.)

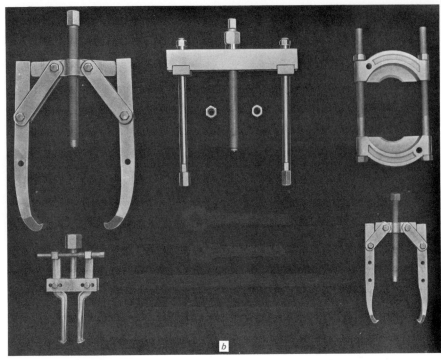

FIG. 4-4b (New Departure, Hyatt Bearings, Division of General Motors Corp.)

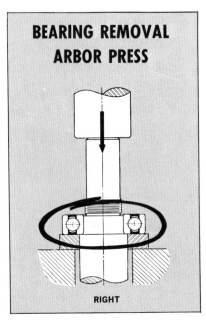

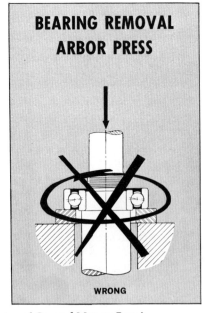

FIG. 4-5 (New Departure, Hyatt Bearings, Division of General Motors Corp.)

56

or driving must be done on either the inner or outer race or ring. The race tapped depends on whether the bearing is being mounted on a shaft (inner race) or into a bearing seat (outer race). Tapping should be done with a guide, even a piece of pipe of the right diameter, to distribute the blow evenly (Fig. 4-4a). Even the slightest tap on one of the seals may cause quick bearing failure. Incidentally, seal damage is probably a major cause of bearing failure. Bearing pullers are available, similar to wheel pullers, which maintain an even pressure on the race (Fig. 4-4b). Care should be taken that the fingers or arms of the puller actually pull on the inner race and do not touch the seals. If the shaft or assembly can be removed from the machine, an arbor press or even a drill press (not running) is useful. Steady even pressure is the safest and best method, but the same precautions concerning the inner and outer race hold true (Fig. 4-5) regardless of whether the bearing is being removed or installed. If the inner race is tight on the arbor or shaft, penetrating oil is often needed to help break it loose.

There are many kinds of seals used for specific purposes. Sometimes they even extend beyond the width of the races. A combination of materials is used when the application is particularly destructive, for instance, when the bearings are to be used for an abrasive finishing machine (Fig. 4-6). These are known as double-sealed bearings. They can be double-sealed on only one side or on both sides. Usually the two shields are visually different. The bearings must be replaced with the same side of the bearing in the same position as the original, or in the same position as when it was removed.

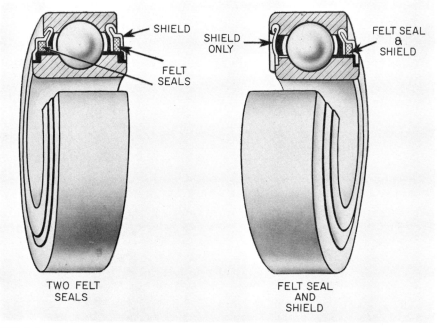

FIG. 4-6

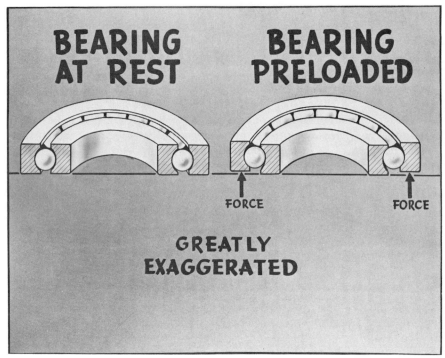

FIG. 4-7

The accuracy or tolerance of a ball bearing is directly related to the cost. This is the major reason why two bearings of exactly the same external dimensions and manufactured by the same company will vary so greatly in price. Bearings are precision-graded A, B, C, D, E; A has the closest tolerances and is also the most expensive. In order to maintain a reasonable cost and yet provide the accuracy needed, comparatively inexpensive bearings are sometimes preloaded. This is done by forcing the outer race in one direction and the inner race in the other direction, thus closing the space between races and bearings (Fig. 4-7). This usually decreases the overall life of the bearing somewhat but greatly increases the accuracy while holding costs and prices down. In many cases this preloading is done by the tool or equipment manufacturer rather than the bearing manufacturer. In general, among major bearing and tool manufacturers, preloaded bearings are scientifically preloaded. They are very precisely matched and ground, and they are relatively expensive. When this care is taken, the life of the preloaded bearing is not affected. Preloading can be done through the use of ground shoulders, sleeves, or wave washers. The amount of preloading must be controlled, for excess pressure can damage the bearing or open the seals. In some cases, a cartridge assembly, factory preloaded, is supplied as a component part of a machine and is replaceable as a unit (Fig. 4-8). Double-row, preloaded ball bearings, in the same case or race package, are also available from bearing manufacturers.

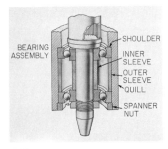

FIG. 4-8

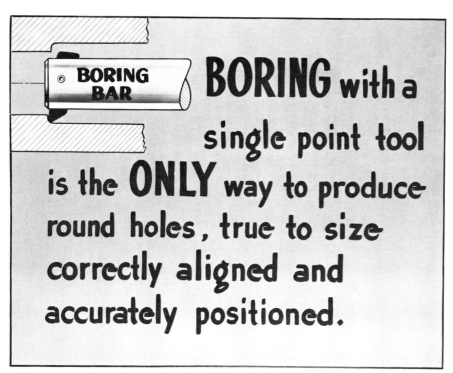

BORING with a single point tool is the ONLY way to produce round holes, true to size correctly aligned and accurately positioned.

FIG. 4-9

Since the outer race of the bearing usually fits tightly—a push fit into a bearing seat—and becomes a part of the casting as far as alignment is concerned, it is vital that the bearing seats be accurately machined (Fig. 4-9). If a cast or predrilled hole to be used eventually as a bearing seat is out of position, the single-point tool will cut deeper into one side and correct the location (Fig. 4-10). This is usually done on a jig borer or a metal lathe.

When replacing a bearing, it is important to wipe out or thoroughly clean the bearing seat. Dirt or even a small chip forced between the bearing and the side of the seat or under the bearing can cause many problems. The bearing may be squeezed or distorted, with consequent shortening of its life. Misalignment also may decrease its life and possibly bend an arbor or shaft. It can make the bearing almost impossible to remove. The casting itself may be cracked or damaged so that even a new bearing, properly installed, will be loose or misaligned.

The inner race must fit tightly on the shaft, spindle, or arbor, and usually this requires a precision-ground surface for proper fit and alignment (Fig. 4-11). Dirt, grit, or other foreign material should be wiped off the shaft and also from the inner race before the bearing is pressed on or installed.

When completely assembled, the two races should, for all practical purposes, become a part of their separate assemblies. The bearing races should not turn in the seat or on the shaft.

In modern machines and power tools, open and unshielded ball bear-

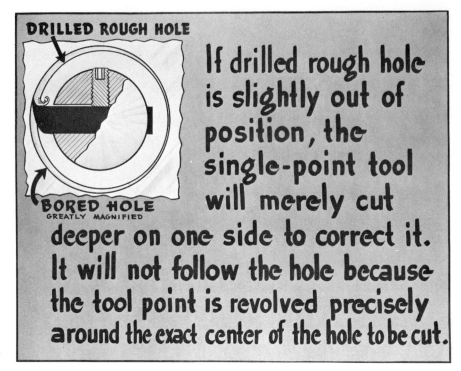

DRILLED ROUGH HOLE

BORED HOLE
GREATLY MAGNIFIED

If drilled rough hole is slightly out of position, the single-point tool will merely cut deeper on one side to correct it. It will not follow the hole because the tool point is revolved precisely around the exact center of the hole to be cut.

FIG. 4-10

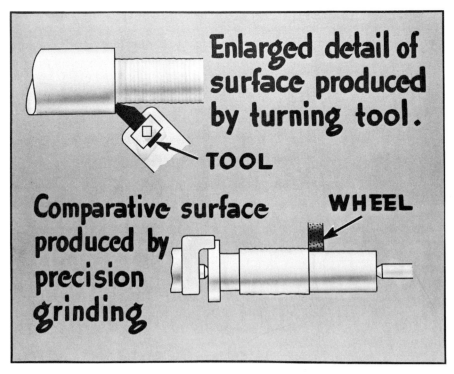

Enlarged detail of surface produced by turning tool.

TOOL

Comparative surface produced by precision grinding

WHEEL

FIG. 4-11

ings are just about history. If possible, they should be replaced with sealed-for-life bearings. If this is impossible, they should be washed out with a solvent and repacked with grease, according to the manufacturer's instructions.

TAPERED ROLLER BEARINGS

In most cases, these bearings are found in heavier equipment or where controlled accuracy or frequent adjustment is important. Such control may be needed because of heat expansion of a spindle, due to speed and workload, or simply because of weight and possible combinations of both radial and thrust load (Fig. 4-12). Explicit instructions for both adjustment and lubrication of tapered roller bearings are always spelled out by the machine manufacturer, and they should be followed exactly. Usually, a particular type of grease is recommended except when spindle speeds are very high. Grease is also usually recommended in preference to oil. Often a grease fitting is located outside the housing with a lubricating instruction plate. By rule of thumb, overgreasing is probably more harmful than undergreasing because of pressures built up by heat.

Adjustment of these bearings should be done after the machine has been running sufficiently long for heat to expand the parts. To adjust a cold machine for accuracy is a waste of time and may actually cause the unit to bind when operating. This, of course, can lead to complicated and expensive service problems and parts replacement problems.

FIG. 4-12

CYLINDRICAL ROLLER BEARINGS

The cylindrical or straight roller bearing maintains a rectangular and larger contact with the races than the elliptical ball bearing. Otherwise their general construction, lubrication, and use characteristics are about the same. Because of the larger area of contact, cylindrical roller bearings can handle greater loads than the ball bearing. They are therefore more widely used in machine tools than in power tools, where the more common ball bearing will adequately handle the job. The radial type of needle bearing found in portable tools is actually a kind of cylindrical roller bearing.

FIG. 4-13

NEEDLE ROLLER BEARINGS

These bearings are most often found in portable tools where space is at a premium. Radial needle bearings are well suited to high speeds and lie flat against the races or the outer race and the shaft. In most cases, they have no separator and are held in place by a small retaining lip. Each roller is held in alignment by the close fit of the adjoining rollers (Fig. 4-13).

Care must be taken in removing or greasing these bearings. If one roller comes out or is removed, the remaining rollers will quickly become misaligned and literally fall out. The retaining lip is usually quite small and will not retain the rollers in the case or shell at even a slight angle, or with one roller missing. The tool manufacturer's specifications for the kind and quantity of grease or lubrication should be followed to the letter. The frequency of lubrication is usually stated in hours of operating time and should be adhered to.

Not only should grease be added, but the complete bearing and shaft should be cleaned with solvent and the bearing repacked. Never reinstall a roller bearing with one or more rollers missing. Rollers can easily become cracked while running and can cause permanent damage to the shaft and other parts. If the shaft itself is worn, it will cause short bearing life and should be replaced.

FIG. 4-14

FIG. 4-15

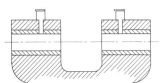

FIG. 4-16

SLEEVE BEARINGS

In contrast to moving parts, sleeve bearings of all sizes or types depend on a thin film of oil to decrease friction. Many types of materials are used, depending on the speed, weight, heat buildup, and other operating factors.

Many of the materials are actually oil-impregnated. The bearings come in a full sleeve (Fig. 4-14) and in half sections (Fig. 4-15). Most applications in the machine field relate to comparatively inexpensive units in the motor, portable electric tool, or small grinding head field. They are occasionally used as spindle bearings in lathes or surface grinders, but this practice is no longer general. Nevertheless, there is probably no bearing more accurate when new and properly installed.

Similar to the sleeve bearing, which is usually bronze, is the so-called poured bearing, which is more often made of babbitt or often soft material. Such bearings are usually poured solid into the opening in the casting or bearing seat, then drilled, bored, or line-reamed to actual size (Fig. 4-16). Line reaming is done when two such bearing surfaces must line up exactly.

Lubrication of the proper type and amount is even more important to sleeve bearings or poured bearings than to the other types discussed. Since antifriction depends entirely on the oil film between the bearing surface and the shaft, lack of oil or lubrication can cause instant failure. The parts involved will have a tendency to bind or at least gall, destroying the bearing and possibly damaging the shaft. Most sleeve bearing units are provided with oil cups (Fig. 4-17), which are usually covered to keep out damaging dust and dirt. Cups with damaged covers should be replaced. Often they are simply pushed into a drilled hole above the bearing area and are held in place by only a tight fit, although some larger cups screw into threaded holes.

FIG. 4-17

Some of the rules given in (Fig. 4-18) pertain to open bearings rather than sealed bearings, but they stress the generally great importance of care and cleanliness.

Keep bearings clean — dirt means damage

Things to Remember

Poor tools, rough bench, plenty of dirt — bad.

Ideal, but work as close to it as you can.

<table>
<tr><td>

DON'TS

1. Don't work in dirty surroundings.

2. Don't use wooden mallets or work on rough or dirty bench tops.

3. Don't use dirty, brittle or chipped tools.

4. Don't handle bearings with dirty, moist hands.

5. Don't spin uncleaned bearings.

6. Don't spin **any** bearings with compressed air.

7. Don't use same container for cleaning and final rinsing of bearings.

8. Don't use cotton waste or dirty cloths to wipe bearings.

9. Don't expose bearings to moisture or dirt at any time.

10. Don't scratch or nick bearing surfaces.

11. Don't remove grease or oil from **new** bearings.

12. Don't use incorrect kind or amount of lubricant.

</td><td>

DO'S

1. Work with clean tools, in clean surroundings.

2. Remove all outside dirt from housing before exposing bearings.

3. Handle with clean, dry hands.

4. Treat a used bearing as carefully as a new one.

5. Use clean solvents and flushing oils.

6. Lay bearings out on clean paper.

7. Protect disassembled bearings from dirt and moisture.

8. Use clean, lint-free rags if bearings are wiped.

9. Keep bearings wrapped in oil-proof paper when not in use.

10. Clean inside of housing before replacing bearings.

11. Install new bearings as removed from packages, without washing.

12. Keep bearing lubricants clean when applying and cover containers when not in use.

</td></tr>
</table>

FIG. 4-18 (Anti-friction Bearing Manufacturers Assoc.)

CHAPTER FIVE
Lubrication

Proper lubrication is vital, not only to the working parts of the machine, but also to ease of operation, correct alignment, and safety. In most cases, it is extremely important to follow the manufacturer's recommendations to the letter.

GREASE AND OIL

Valuable engineering time is spent in determining the materials used, the speeds involved, the heat produced, and all other factors necessary to specify both the type of lubricant needed and the frequency of use. In many cases, "something close" or an all-purpose oil or grease may work almost as well, but on modern high-speed mechanisms using it is really a gamble. The wrong lubricant can easily lead to downtime and expensive service problems. Most manufacturers specify the recommended brands by name (Fig. 5-1).

It is wise to purchase, with the machine or at the same time, the proper and specific lubricants needed. Doing this will eliminate the

POINTS *1 & *2 REQUIRE TEXACO REGAL OIL - BR & O
POINTS *3 REQUIRE TEXACO REGAL STARFAK *2 GREASE OR EQUIVALENT
POINTS *4 REQUIRE TEXACO MARFAK *O GREASE OR EQUIVALENT
FIG. 5-1

temptation to substitute or the necessity to locate a supplier when the need for lubrication is critical. Most portable tool manufacturers supply lubricants under their own brand name (Fig. 5-2).

Although the manufacturer specifies exactly what lubricant should be used, indicates where to lubricate, and even how often, in most cases the quantity of lubricant is not explicit. Overlubrication is definitely a problem, primarily for inexperienced operators. "If two pumps or shots of grease are good, then four should be twice as good" is the normal thinking. In many cases, grease is forced into a closed chamber and the increased pressure only tends to destroy the seals. Oil may run into places which should be dry or clean and lead to either an unpredictable or unsafe operation. To avoid such results, some common sense must be exercised in determining the correct amount of oil or grease necessary to do the intended job.

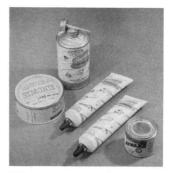

FIG. 5-2

DRY LUBRICANTS

Oil and grease are absolute necessities in the machine shop, but in most cases, modern woodworking equipment would stay in better repair and alignment if liquid lubricants were never used. Most equipment in the price and size class found in the school and cabinet shop is equipped with sealed-for-life ball bearings which do not have to be greased, thereby solving the bearing lubrication problem.

Woodworking machines, in particular, are often overoiled or overgreased. Although this practice, in many cases, may not cause problems in the metal shop, in the woodshop the results are almost always disastrous. Excessive oil and grease, or even the correct amount of these lubricants, accumulate sawdust very quickly, and it eventually turns into a gummy or solid substance which makes the movement of parts practically impossible. This condition is a detriment not only to proper alignment and ease of operation but, in many cases, to safe operation.

A dry lubricant, such as hard wax, graphite, silicon spray, or Teflon spray, is highly recommended for use on trunnions (Fig. 5-3), rack and

FIG. 5-3

pinion gears (Fig. 5-4), variable-speed pulleys (Fig. 5-5), dovetail ways and gibs (Fig. 5-6), jackscrews (Fig. 5-7), and other operating parts which must be lubricated although they do not run or operate at high speeds. In most cases, any movement is for adjustment only.

The primary reason why hard wax is preferred to graphite is that wax is not only an ideal "lubricant" but also a "preservative" for all exposed cast-iron parts on woodworking machines. Cast iron, being porous, will accept quite a bit of hard paste wax. The benefits derived from using hard wax are many. It is an excellent lubricant for facilitating adjustment. Since it does not pick up sawdust, it retains its lubricating qualities, permitting ease of operation for a long period of time. On table tops (Fig. 5-8) or jointer beds, a hard wax surface helps prevent discoloring or rust due to damp conditions or perspiration from the user's hands. Hard wax also contributes to the safe operation of machines because wood does not drag when pushed across the table or against the fence, but instead it slides smoothly and without effort. Incidentally, wax will not discolor light-colored woods such as white pine and maple.

On trunnions, racks, dovetail ways, etc., the wax need not be wiped off or buffed. On table tops and fences, it is necessary actually to push the wax into the porous cast iron, then buff off the excess. Any wax picked up by the wood can make gluing and finishing difficult unless the wood surface is also sanded.

FIG. 5-4

FIG. 5-5

FIG. 5-6

FIG. 5-7

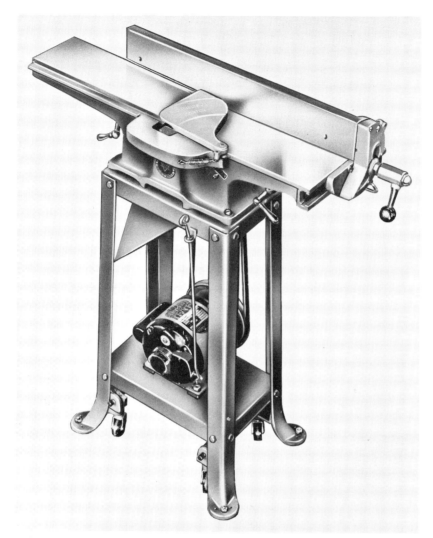

FIG. 5-8

Hard paste wax, floor wax, or car wax should be used. Combination wax and cleaners will not do the lubricating job and can actually increase wear on the moving parts by their abrasive action. Liquid wax is usually difficult to handle except on flat surfaces.

A good rule to follow dictates the use of oil or grease, as recommended by the manufacturer, where high speed or continuous turning and friction are involved; and the use of hard wax on adjustment mechanisms, work surfaces, and exposed cast iron.

Manufacturer's recommendations are usually found in instruction manuals and on lubrication plates fastened to the machines. Figures 5-9 to 5-11 contain sample lists of actual lubrication charts, plates, and lubrication instructions from various manufacturers.

LUBRICATION

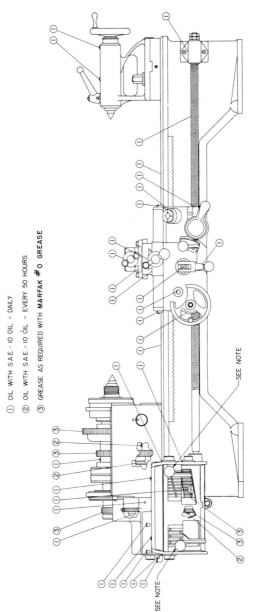

LUBRICATION CHART

① OIL WITH S.A.E.- IO OIL – DAILY

② OIL WITH S.A.E.- IO OIL – EVERY 50 HOURS

③ GREASE AS REQUIRED WITH **MARFAK #O GREASE**

NOTE – TUMBLERS AT EXTREME RIGHT AND LEFT WHEN OILING.

SEE NOTE

SEE NOTE

FIG. 5-9

Before attempting to start your new Metal Lathe make certain that all unpainted machined surfaces are properly cleaned and coated with a film of good machine oil. Then lubricate as required all points shown on the accompanying chart. For the first ten days of use, oil all points indicated as ① twice daily, then once daily thereafter.

Remember that, while your lathe was built to the closest manufacturing tolerances, and thoroughly tested for its ability to reproduce its own built-in precision – it's up to you to maintain that accuracy and prolong the machine's life by your careful attention to its daily lubrication.

LUBRICANT SPECIFICATIONS

OLIVER MACHINERY COMPANY
WOOD AND METAL WORKING MACHINERY

(Refer to Machine Data Sheets)

LUB A Spindle Oil - Viscosity 55/80 SSU @ 100 F.

A high-quality mineral oil containing oxidation inhibitors
to eliminate the possibility of gum and varnish formation.

USE . . . . Ball and roller bearings, Cut spray,
and Oil mist lubrication

American Oil Company	American Spindle Oil A
Gulf Oil Company	Gulf Paramount 37
Shell Oil Company	Tellus Oil 15
Sinclair Refining Company	Cadet Oil D
Socony-Mobil Oil Company	Mobil Velocite Oil 6
Texaco Incorporated	Spindle Oil A (For Cut spray on aluminum and magnesium, use "ALMAG".)

LUB B Lubricating Oil - Viscosity 290/330 SSU @ 100 F.

A High quality turbine type mineral oil containing oxidation
inhibitors to eliminate the possibility of gum and varnish
formation.

USE . . . . Ball and roller bearings, Plain bearings,
friction points, ways, slides, etc.

American Oil Company	American Industrial Oil 31
Gulf Oil Company	Gulf Harmony 53
Shell Oil Company	Tellus Oil 33
Sinclair Refining Company	Duro 300
Socony-Mobil Oil Company	Mobil Vactra Oil Heavy Medium
Texaco Incorporated	Rando Oil HC-C

LUB D Hydraulic Oil - Viscosity 140/160 SSU @ 100 F.

A Premium quality hydraulic oil containing oxidation
preventive, anti-foam agents, and anti-wear additives.

USE . . . . Hydraulic Systems

American Oil Company	Rykon Industrial Oil 15
Gulf Oil Company	Gulf Harmony 43 AW
Shell Oil Company	Tellus Oil 27
Sinclair Refining Company	Duro A-W Oil 16
Socony-Mobil Oil Company	Hydraulic Oil DTE-24
Texaco Incorporated	Rando Oil HD-A

D509 DP-54   1/2

FIG. 5-10

RECOMMENDED LUBRICANTS

MACHINE OIL	GREASE (NLGI Classification)
Gear Oil.........................SAE 140	Heavy...#2 Gear Lube
Heavy..........................SAE 90	Medium..#1 Gear Lube
Medium........................SAE 40	Light...#0 Gear Lube
Light...........................SAE 20-10	Tacky......Sohio EP-110; Mobilplex EP #1; Humble—Lades (Grade 1);
Hi-Grade Spindle Oil or Rockwell #24-812	or Rockwell #999-02-021-5018
	#0 Lithium...............................Sohitran EPO; Multifak EPO;
	or Rockwell #999-02-021-5041

DRY LUBRICANTS—Powdered Graphite, Silicone, Teflon Base, and Hard Wax*

EQUIPMENT AND PARTS TO BE LUBRICATED	RECOMMENDED LUBRICANT	FREQUENCY OF LUBRICATION
DRILL PRESSES		
Quill and Pinion Gear................................	Medium	Occasionally
Splines..	Tacky	Every 3 Months
Outside Surface of Quill.............................	Dry Lubricant	Occasionally
Spindle Return Spring................................	Light Oil	Twice Yearly
Raising Support Collar,		
Elevating Crank, Gears and Column..............	Dry Lubricant	Occasionally
Variable Speed Models—Additional: Spindle and Motor		
Pulley Oil Holes......................................	Medium Oil	Weekly
Pulley Hub...	Dry Lubricant	Occasionally
Ram Type Radial Drill Press		
Additional: Arm Cradle..............................	Light Oil	Daily
Column Guide Key, Feed and Lock Handles......	Dry Lubricant	Occasionally
Power Feed Units		
Clutch Housing Oiler.................................	Medium Oil	Daily
Countershaft Bearing.................................	Medium Oil	Weekly
Clutch Handle Hub and Powerfeed Gears.........	Tacky	Twice Yearly
Foot Feed Units		
Sliding Parts..	Dry Lubricant	As Required
VERTICAL MILLING MACHINE		
Quill and Pinion Oilers; Fine Feed; Wormshaft; Clutch Lock and Hand Feed Lever Hubs; Head Tilting, Knee Elevating and Table Screws; Saddle Oiler...........................	Light Oil	Daily
Spindle Pulley Hub; Saddle, Knee and Column Ways;		
Bevel Gear...	Light Grease	Weekly
Head Tilting Worm Gear.............................	Light Grease	As Required
Upper Spindle Splines...............................	Tacky	Twice Yearly
TOOLMAKER GRINDER		
Vertical Screw and Nut..............................	Light Oil	Weekly
Cross Slide Screw Bearing...........................	Light Oil	Daily
Table and Cross Slide................................	Light Grease	Daily
Cross Slide Screw.....................................	Medium Grease	Every 30 Days
Spindle Ball Bearings................................	Hi-Grade Spindle Oil	Once a Week or as Necessary
Column Bevel Gear...................................	Light Grease	Every 30 Days
10″ METAL CUTTING LATHE		
Quick Change Gear Box..............................	Light Grease	As Required
Gear Train Shaft......................................	Light Oil	Every 50 Hrs.
Head and Tail Stock..................................	Light Oil	Daily
Head Stock Gears.....................................	Medium Grease	As Required
Back Gear Spacing Collar and Extension Oiler..	Light Oil	Every 50 Hrs.
Lead Screw; Oil Cups and Holes; Ball Oilers.....	Light Oil	Daily

70

11″ METAL CUTTING LATHE AND HAND SCREW MACHINE		
Quick Change Gear Box..	Light Grease	As Required
Head and Tail Stocks..	Light Oil	Daily
Head Stock Gears...	Medium Grease	As Required
Head Stock Grease Fitting..	#2 Heavy Grease	Every 200 hrs.
Spindle and Back Gear Oilers......................................	Light Oil	Every 50 Hrs.
Lead Screw; Oil Cups and Holes; Ball Oilers...................	Light Oil	Daily
14″ METAL CUTTING LATHE		
Quick Change Gear Box; Gear Studs; Saddle Slide; Screw Threads and Related Moving Parts.......................	Light Grease	As Required
Headstock and Apron Reservoirs................................	Light Oil (SAE-20 non-detergent)	Maintain Proper Oil Indicator Level
Lead Screw; Oil Cups and Holes; Ball Oilers..................	Light Oil (SAE 20)	Daily
ABRASIVE FINISHING MACHINES		
Moving Parts such as Trunnions..................................	Dry Lubricant	As Required
(Sander/Grinder Motor)..	Light Oil	Occasionally
JOINTERS		
Table Ways and Control Screws; Gibs...........................	Dry Lubricant	Occasionally
TILTING ARBOR SAWS		
Moving Parts such as Trunnions, Racks, Pinions, etc., also Ways and Grooves...	Dry Lubricant	Occasionally
RADIAL ARM SAWS		
Vertical Column and Track Mounting Parts; Gear Rack; Elevating Bevel Gear and Pinion..............................	Dry Lubricant	Occasionally
Elevating Shaft Bearing...	Light Oil	Occasionally
METAL AND WOOD CUTTING BAND SAWS		
Slide Ways of Upper Wheel Bracket; Trunnions and Adjusting Screws..	Dry Lubricant	Occasionally
Variable Speed Band Saw—Above Lubrication Plus:		
Gear Box Grease Level..	#0 Lithium Grease	Every 2,000 Hrs.
Chip Blower..	Light Oil	Every 100 Hrs.
Variable Speed Drive Pulley.......................................	Light Oil	Every 100 Hrs.
Blade Support Bearing..	Light Oil	Periodically
PLANERS		
Raising Gears and Elevating Screws.............................	Dry Lubricant	As Required
Gear Box..	Gear Oil	Once a Year or As Required
18″ x 6″ Model		
Wedgeways; Variable Speed Pulley..............................	Dry Lubricant	As Required
13″ x 5″ Model		
Feed Roller Bearings..	Medium Oil	As Required
Gibs..	Dry Lubricant	As Required
24″ SCROLL SAW—Crank Case.................................	Medium Oil (SAE 30 non-detergent)	As Required
Variable Speed Drive Pulley.......................................	Dry Lubricant	As Required
WOOD SHAPER—Bevel Gears...................................	Dry Lubricant	As Required
12″ WOODWORKING LATHE		
Countershaft Bracket Screw; Variable Speed Drive Screw; Bed Ways; Tailstock; and Quill Adjusting Screw...............	Dry Lubricant	As Required
Variable Speed Pulley Shaft and Tailstock Quill................	Light Oil	As Required

FIG. 5-11

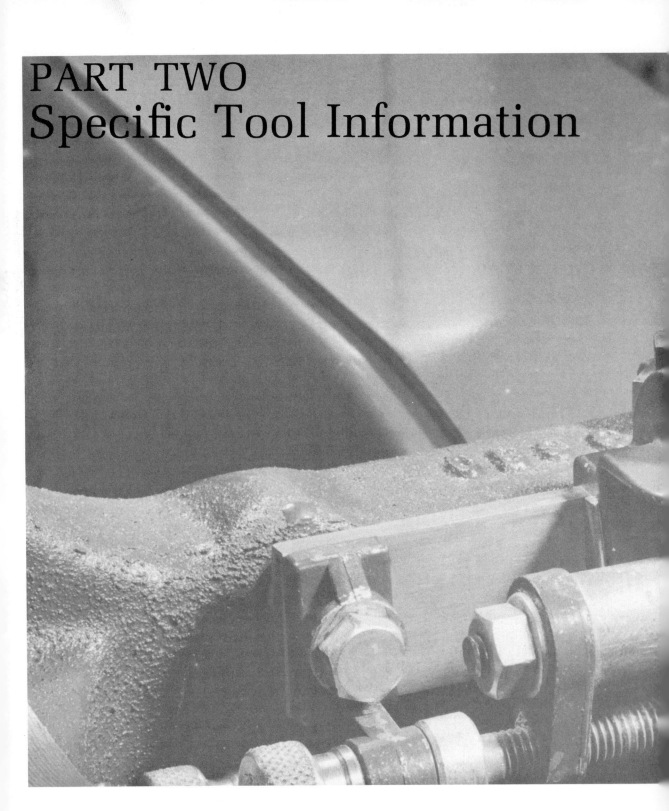

PART TWO
Specific Tool Information

CHAPTER SIX

The Circular Saw

The circular saw, or table saw, obviously got its accepted name from the shape of the saw blade or from its large, flat operating area. Many types and sizes have been built by many manufacturers under many names: variety saw, Unisaw, ripping machine, double arbor and single arbor, sliding table and solid table, cast-iron base and pressed-steel cabinet, belt drive and direct drive, bench model and floor model, tilting table and tilting arbor, motor mounted outside and inside the base, motor tilting with the arbor and motor not tilting. Also a great variety of guide bar, fence, miter gage, and guard designs have been developed through the years. Sometimes new developments were related to a single operation, but usually changes were to provide more production, more accuracy, easier operation, or greater safety.

The typical circular saw (Fig. 6-1) found in today's cabinet shop, school shop, or laboratory is a 10″ or 12″ tilting arbor, belt drive, floor model, with the motor mounted inside the base or cabinet. This typical unit can be divided into two major types of basic construction:

1. Trunnion assembly bolted to the underside of the table (Fig. 6-2).
2. Trunnion assembly hung from (and bolted to) the cabinet (Fig. 6.3).

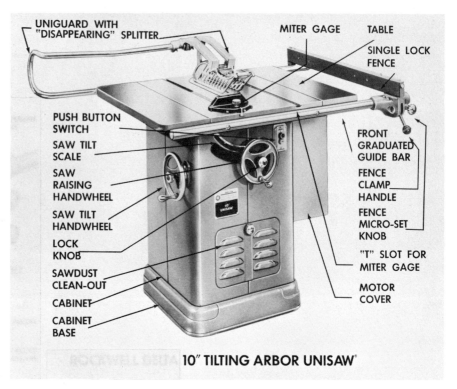

UNIGUARD WITH "DISAPPEARING" SPLITTER

MITER GAGE TABLE

SINGLE LOCK FENCE

PUSH BUTTON SWITCH

SAW TILT SCALE

SAW RAISING HANDWHEEL

SAW TILT HANDWHEEL

LOCK KNOB

SAWDUST CLEAN-OUT

CABINET

CABINET BASE

FRONT GRADUATED GUIDE BAR

FENCE CLAMP HANDLE

FENCE MICRO-SET KNOB

"T" SLOT FOR MITER GAGE

MOTOR COVER

10" TILTING ARBOR UNISAW

FIG. 6-1

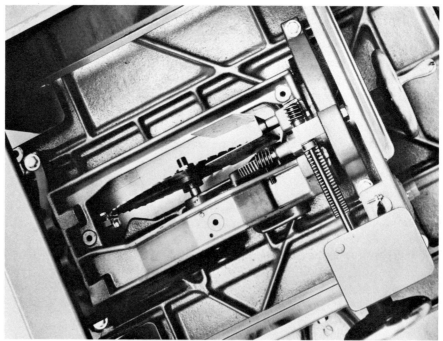

FIG. 6-2

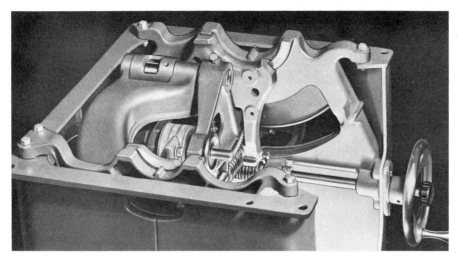

FIG. 6-3

GENERAL MAINTENANCE

The saw should be checked periodically to see that it is not rocking but is seated firmly on the floor. If it is lagged or bolted down, the lag screws or bolts should be checked for tightness and even breakage.

Once a year the cabinet, if cast iron, should be checked for cracks which might cause further problems. Pressed-steel cabinets should be checked at weld points for any sign of weakening or spreading (Fig. 6-4).

FIG. 6-4

All setscrews holding motor or arbor pulleys should be checked for tightness. Correct belt alignment, most important for a smooth-running trouble-free saw, can also be checked at this time. In most cases, the raising and tilting mechanism (primarily the rods that span the cabinet) is held in place with collars and is fastened to the shaft with setscrews, roll pins, or taper pins. These should be checked or tightened.

If the raising and lowering mechanism is stiff, it is convenient at this time to pull the collars back from their bearing seat or boss (Fig. 6-5) and lubricate the area well with hard paste wax, silicone, or graphite. This should be done also to the bearing or sleeve where the shaft or control rod enters the cabinet; i.e., behind the crank handle or wheel. If this is a ball bearing assembly, of course no lubrication is needed.

FIG. 6-5

If the saw is belt driven rather than direct drive, the manufacturer's belt specifications should be strictly adhered to. If driven by a single belt, it is quite possibly special and may even contain wire to ensure correct length and maintain torque transmission. For a three-belt or four-belt drive unit (Fig. 6-6), it is important to purchase matched belts from the original equipment manufacturer. If purchased elsewhere, they should at least meet his specifications. Never replace only one belt of a matched set.

FIG. 6-6

FIG. 6-7

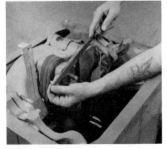

FIG. 6-8

The working surfaces of the trunnions and the rack and pinion should be cleaned of all paint, gum, pitch, and old lubricants. The complete trunnion assembly should then be lubricated with a dry lubricant. This can be done without disassembly by lubricating well all exposed areas when the saw arbor is at 90 deg and again when tilted to 45 deg (Fig. 6-7). If a rack and pinion is used in the raising mechanism, it also should be dry-lubricated.

The rack should be checked for excess wear. If badly worn, the rack or the casting should be replaced. The inside arbor flange should be examined for any irregularities. Nicks or burrs on the inner flange can be carefully touched off with a file in most cases (Fig. 6-8). Burrs on the arbor threads can also be touched off in the same manner. Never attempt this with the saw under power.

The entire table top should be cleaned with solvent and steel wool and given a good coat of hard paste wax. This is also true of the fence, regardless of whether it is cast iron, steel, or aluminum.

The guide rails, fence, and miter gage should be checked for burrs, twisting, or any other irregularity. The guide rails in particular should be cleaned with solvent and steel wool (Fig. 6-9). Lubrication on these assemblies and also on the guide rails should be hard paste wax or a dry lubricant.

FIG. 6-9

The rails should be secure and table slots clean and smooth for ease of operation. If the fence does not clamp tightly in accordance with the particular system used by the manufacturer, it should be adjusted or repaired (Fig. 6-10).

The guard should be checked for proper operation in accordance with the manufacturer's instructions. With a typical "basket" type of guard,

FIG. 6-10

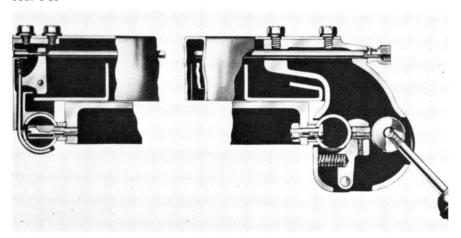

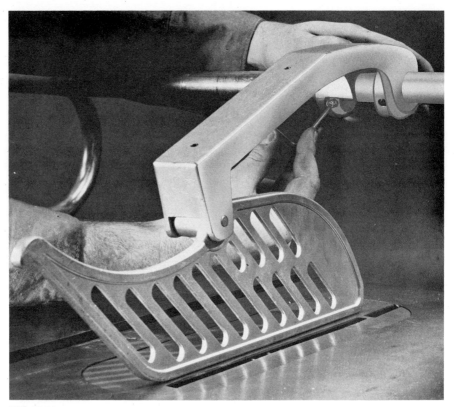

FIG. 6-11

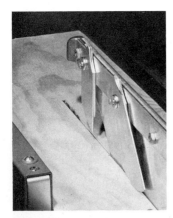

FIG. 6-12

the proper movement of the basket or baskets (Fig. 6-11), the straightness of the splitter (Fig. 6-12), and the free movement of the antikickback fingers or device are necessary. The latter two parts should also be dry-lubricated, preferably with hard paste wax.

All electrical connections, including grounding, should be checked for tightness, and the switch or control itself should be checked for positive fast action.

ALIGNMENT

The object of maintaining alignment in the circular saw is to crosscut square and rip without a taper. The basic accuracy should be preset and not require measuring or adjustments with each change of operation. Most circular saws are manufactured so that accuracy is practically built in, but some intelligent maintenance and initial alignment procedure are always necessary.

Arbor and Table

Generally, in circular saws, the arbor is the "unmovable" or the nonadjustable part, and this is where all alignment must start. It is initially taken for granted that the table slots are straight and parallel as milled by the manufacturer. After this assumption, the table slots must be adjusted so that they are exactly perpendicular to the arbor (Fig. 6-13). To do this, either the entire table or the arbor assembly must be moved, independently of each other.

FIG. 6-13

When the trunnion and arbor assembly is bolted to the underside of the table (Fig. 6-14), this job is more difficult. In most cases, the holes in the table are tapped and the holes through the assembly are slightly oversize. This allows for a slight adjustment when the bolts are loosened, usually enough to obtain correct alignment as required. If taper pins or roll pins have been used for the original (but wrong) alignment, they must be removed. Some caution should be used when retightening this assembly, because all the bolts turn in the same direction. Since tightening can turn the assembly as well, a continuous check must be made during the tightening procedure for the desired perpendicular alignment.

FIG. 6-14

If the trunnion and arbor assembly is hung from the cabinet, the procedure is normally much simpler. The table, in this case, is fastened to the cabinet and is independent of the trunnion and arbor assembly. It is usually held in place by four bolts or cap screws, one at each corner (Fig. 6-15). When the cap screws are loosened, the table can be easily moved into correct alignment. Once again, care must be taken when tightening the cap screws because tightening can cause a shift in the original alignment.

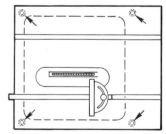

FIG. 6-15

Since the arbor and the table slots are not in the same plane, extension of the arbor must be made. This is most easily done by mounting a blade on the arbor and tightening the arbor nut. This now provides a measuring point perpendicular to the arbor, but even more important, it brings this extension of the arbor parallel to the table slots and above the table surface.

It is now possible to measure accurately the distance between the blade and a table slot. With the blade at maximum height, measurement should be made using the same tooth at both the maximum infeed and the outfeed positions. This "measuring-point" tooth should be "set" toward the slot being used as a reference and can be marked with chalk for easy identification (Fig. 6-16).

FIG. 6-16

By holding or clamping a small piece of wood against the miter gage face (an extension of the table slot) while sliding the miter gage to the front and then to the rear of the blade, the two distances can be equally set (Fig. 6-17). These can be judged very accurately by both feel and sound if the blade is slowly turned by hand against the wood at each position. Either the arbor and trunnion assembly or the table is moved until aligned properly. Depending on how the machine was manufactured, slight

FIG. 6-17

FIG. 6-18

FIG. 6-19

movement is easily accomplished by tapping with your hand or a mallet (Fig. 6-18).

The first step in alignment is the most important because the settings of both the miter gage and the fence are dependent on its basic accuracy. No matter what the manufacturer's or operator's personal "method preference" may be, the basic alignment must be done. There are probably as many proven ways to align a saw as there are good cabinetmakers. The method is really unimportant, but the results are critical.

It is usually a waste of time to attempt to use "precision" measuring instruments because of the various minor but basic inaccuracies inherent in any table saw, in its operation, and in the material being cut. The table slot and the miter gage bar are not usually matched and can have as much as a —.020-in. tolerance. Blade tension is most certainly a factor and can cause a slight difference in actual measurement when running or cutting. A table saw is, by rule of thumb, a *power* tool rather than a *machine* tool, and the real test of accuracy is in squareness or lack of taper of the material being cut.

Miter Gage

Since the error in any angle increases with distance, each measurement should be made for accuracy as far out as practical or possible. This is particularly true of the miter gage. The head of this sliding jig can be "squared" by sliding it upside down against the front guide rail (Fig. 6-19) or by using a square in relation to the miter gage bar, the table slot, or even the saw blade. These methods are usually not satisfactory, and if any degree of accuracy is obtained, it is almost pure luck. The short leg of a framing square should be held tightly against the miter gage head. The long leg can then be lined up parallel to the opposite table slot (Fig. 6-20). The positive stop at 90 deg can now be accurately adjusted and locked.

FIG. 6-20

FIG. 6-21

With the short leg of the framing square still held against the head, it should be turned to the 45-deg position. It is now possible, by sight, to place any number on the inside short leg of the framing square (let's say 10 in.) even with one edge of the same table slot in which the jig is riding. This number should now line up also with the same edge of the table slot on the long leg of the framing square (Fig. 6-21). If it does not, the 45-deg setting should be adjusted and the positive stop locked in place. Exactly the same procedure, in reverse, should be used for the opposite 45-deg positive stop setting.

Fence

The rip fence should be aligned parallel to the most convenient table slot, usually the slot on the right where the fence is normally used. First, it should clamp tightly both front and rear. Second, it must also maintain its parallel alignment to the table slot (actually the blade) regardless of its distance from the blade. Third, it should slide easily and smoothly on the guide rails or bars and be easily adjusted to the desired width of cut. Fourth, the indicator should read as accurately as possible in relation to the scale found on most front guide bars or rails. With the infeed area of the fence aligned exactly with the table slot, the head only of the fence should then be locked or clamped to the front guide bar. This allows the rear of the fence to be moved independently (Fig. 6-22) and to be aligned accurately to the table slot. To do this, different manufacturers may have incorporated different mechanical systems, but the fence body must nevertheless be free to move with the head clamped to the front guide bar. On many units, this is accomplished by loosening two cap screws on the top front of the fence body. The entire fence body should then be aligned exactly parallel to the table slot or open at the rear (to the right for slight clearance) about $1/64$ in. Regardless of the type of control, either single

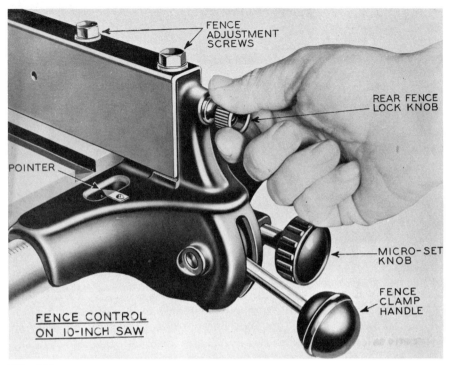

FENCE
ADJUSTMENT
SCREWS

REAR FENCE
LOCK KNOB

POINTER

MICRO-SET
KNOB

FENCE
CLAMP
HANDLE

FENCE CONTROL
ON 10-INCH SAW

FIG. 6-22

lever or separate, the rear of the fence should now be adjusted so that it clamps tightly. The cap screws or other adjustment mechanisms should then be securely tightened to maintain this same relative alignment setting at all fence positions on the guide rails.

If the front guide rail is equipped with a scale, the fence should then be moved to the left, just barely touching the saw blade. The pointer or other visual system can now be adjusted to a zero setting, and will read accurately for width of rip (Fig. 6-23). When the blade is changed, sharpened, or reset, the adjustment must be checked or repeated to maintain continued accuracy.

FIG. 6-23

Most manufacturers incorporate positive stops for both the raising and tilting mechanisms. The most difficult, of course, is the setting for an accurate 45-deg cut, and the parts and instruction manual for the saw in question should be checked for both location and method. It is extremely difficult to "extend" the measurement for this adjustment. Therefore, checking the actual cut with a bevel square on a trial-and-error basis is the best means of accuracy. When the cut is accurate and the positive stop locked or tightened, the tilt scale or pointer should be adjusted to read 45 deg. For the vertical or 90-deg cut, it is comparatively easy to determine the accuracy with a square placed on the table and held against the blade with face spanning the set in the teeth (Fig. 6-24). Once the pointer or tilt scale has been accurately set in the 45- and 90-deg positions, it should read accurately throughout the entire range.

FIG. 6-24

Guard and Splitter

It is imperative that the splitter line up with the saw blade regardless of its length. Manufacturers use many different types of splitters, which are mounted in as many ways (Fig. 6-25). If the splitter is mounted on a bracket in the table, the actual arbor flange should be used as a reference to accurately align the inside face of the clamping mechanism (Fig. 6-26).

FIG. 6-25

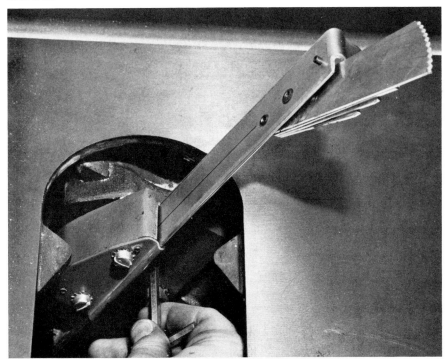

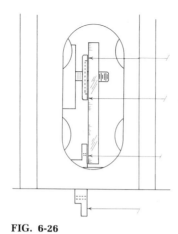

FIG. 6-26

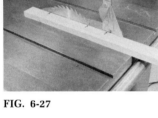

FIG. 6-27

FIG. 6-28

FIG. 6-29

Any outboard holding devices should be adjusted by firmly clamping the inboard device and then placing a straightedge or board against the fully exposed blade and splitter (Fig. 6-27). The splitter can then be held in line while the rear clamp or device is tightened.

Table inserts should be adjusted level with the saw table. Most units in this size class have aluminum or soft metal inserts, adjustable by turning four setscrews on the underside of the insert (Fig. 6-28). On some units these setscrews are adjustable from the top through countersunk or counterbored holes (Fig. 6-29).

The guard itself, regardless of its type, should be adjusted to operate as intended by the manufacturer. Because of the many variations in design, the original instruction manual is definitely the best guide. All hinged or moving parts should be cleaned and lubricated. If any part of the guard rides the material or is raised by the material when a cut is started, it should be freed of all burrs and then lubricated with hard wax (Fig. 6-30).

FIG. 6-30

CHAPTER SEVEN
The Radial Saw

The radial saw is so-named because the arm supporting the yoke, motor, and blade rotates 360 deg around a pivot point while the table and the work remain stationary. This machine is often called an overarm saw because the cutterhead is exposed and is supported from above the table (Fig. 7-1).

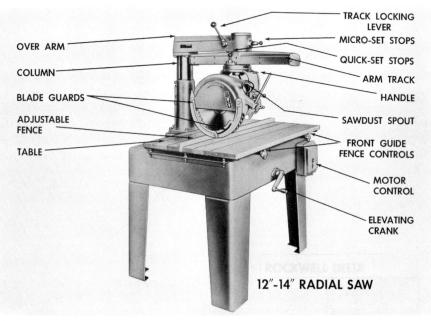

OVER ARM

COLUMN

BLADE GUARDS

ADJUSTABLE
FENCE

TABLE

TRACK LOCKING
LEVER

MICRO-SET STOPS

QUICK-SET STOPS

ARM TRACK

HANDLE

SAWDUST SPOUT

FRONT GUIDE
FENCE CONTROLS

MOTOR
CONTROL

ELEVATING
CRANK

12"-14" RADIAL SAW

FIG. 7-1

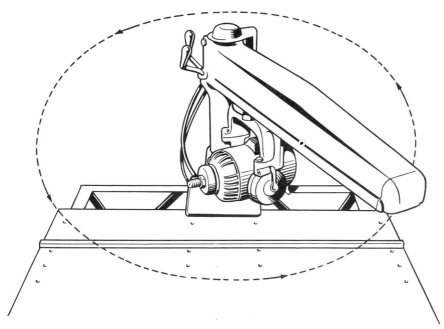

FIG. 7-2

Basically there are three major types of construction or three methods of manufacturing and designing an overarm saw. Each type has its own distinct advantages and disadvantages which must be weighed by the potential purchaser, but fundamentally they all perform in a similar manner.

SINGLE OVERARM

This type of saw incorporates in its design a single arm that pivots 360 deg around the support column (Fig. 7-2). In comparison with other types, fewer connecting, adjustable, and moving parts or assemblies make this type of radial saw both rigid and possibly easier for the normal operator to adjust. The prime disadvantage is that the overarm pivots around the column, limiting the actual cutting angles possible on the table without the use of jigs or fixtures (Fig. 7-3). This is most obvious when cutting left-hand miters. This problem is, of course, easily solved by using a jig, either supplied by the manufacturer or made in the user's shop. The overarm is also always extended over the work.

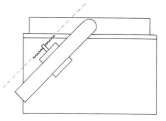

FIG. 7-3

SLIDING OVERARM

This ram type of radial saw eliminates the permanently extended overarm by having it slide through a bearing assembly mounted on the column

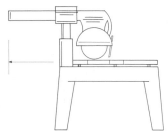

FIG. 7-4

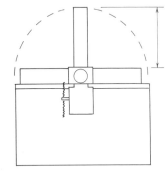

FIG. 7-5

(Fig. 7-4). This requires the operator to pull and push the cutterhead and the overarm during operation. This unit also pivots 360 deg around the column, limiting the actual cutting angles possible on the table. Space must be allowed at the rear of the machine, equal to the total arm travel; therefore it cannot be placed against a wall (Fig. 7-5).

DOUBLE OVERARM

The "turret" arm design has one fixed overarm rigidly fastened to the column. The second or "turret" arm is suspended at its center, at the end of the overarm and rotates at this point 360 deg above the table (Fig. 7-6). This is a definite operational advantage, but it also incorporates one more assembly which must be adjusted. As with the single overarm unit, the arm is always extended when crosscutting or mitering and usually when ripping.

These three major types of radial saws have been built with many

FIG. 7-6

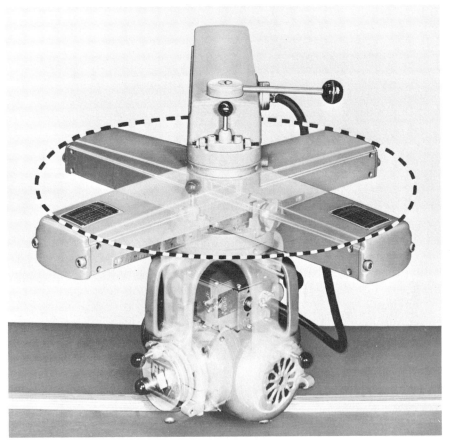

variations in specific design, depending on the manufacturer. The differences are primarily in the ram (sliding overarm), round or tubular versus dovetail ways; the track, outside the arm versus inside the arm; tracks machined in the cast-iron arm versus hardened rods or tracks; the motor as a permanent yoke-hung assembly versus a portable saw attachment; constant speed versus variable speed; as well as many variations in table, size, type, and methods of adjusting.

The swing saw or cutoff saw is a separate unit as compared with the radial saw group. It is intended to perform in most cases a 90-deg crosscut operation completely through the work. If a dado cut is to be made, usually to size the stock in preparation for secondary operations, the work must be taken to a radial or table saw. The swing saw obtained its name from its motion when being operated. The arbor assembly and blade are mounted on a frame which is hinged at the top (Fig. 7-7). Some swing saws can be turned on a pivot at the top of the frame arm to make angle or miter cuts, but compound miters are generally not possible without elaborate jigs or fixtures.

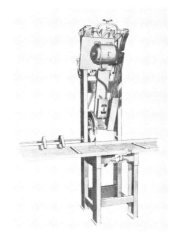

FIG. 7-7

GENERAL MAINTENANCE

The radial saw in particular must be mounted firmly to the stand or cabinet (Fig. 7-8). In many cases radial saws are mounted on legs which are bolted directly to the underframe of the machine (Fig. 7-9). The bolts should be checked periodically for tightness. Lock washers should be added if not originally installed.

All table adjustments should be visually checked, not for accuracy but merely to be sure that all of the parts are there. Some tables have as

FIG. 7-9

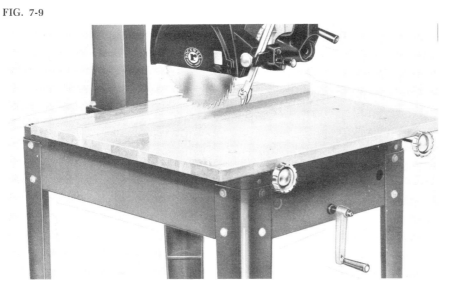

FIG. 7-8
(Fairfield Engineering & Mfg. Co.)

FIG. 7-10

many as three or four separate adjustments, evenly spaced under the table from front to rear at each end (Fig. 7-10). This can mean a total of eight adjustments, each with as many as three parts—a total of twenty-four items which could have loosened, fallen to the floor, and been lost. Needless to say, any missing items should be ordered and replaced.

The raising mechanism should be thoroughly cleaned with solvent and lubricated with a dry lubricant, hard paste wax, silicone, or graphite. Included in this treatment are the gearing (if any), the column, the gib, the jackscrew, and any other moving parts (Fig. 7-11). If collars are involved, they should be pulled back from the boss or bearing surface and dry-lubricated.

Because of the many types of overarm construction, the manufacturer's recommendations for lubrication should be checked. On a sliding ram with dovetail ways (Fig. 7-12), oil is often the mandatory lubricant, although directly contrary to the general rule of thumb concerning the use of dry lubricants on woodworking tools. Many saws with a moving cutterhead use rollers which are actually sealed ball bearings, naturally needing no lubrication (Fig. 7-13). These bearings guide the cutting head by running on tracks cut into the overarm or track arm (Fig. 7-14). The tracks, either inside or outside of the arm casting, should be kept clean and dry-lubricated. Other units with a moving cutterhead use a continuous ball bearing system having a number of independent balls run in a controlled continuous track. The manufacturer's suggestions should be closely followed for cleaning, disassembly, or lubrication of this type of independent bearing assembly.

FIG. 7-11

FIG. 7-12

FIG. 7-14

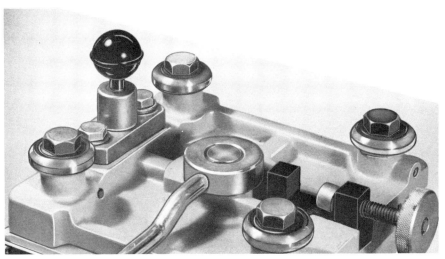

FIG. 7-13

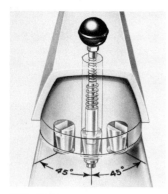

FIG. 7-15

FIG. 7-16

All control areas, surfaces, or mechanisms should be cleaned and checked both for missing parts (setscrews, handles, knobs) and for wear. In many cases where a dog point setscrew is continually moved or changed against a stop, some wear or unevenness will occur. This is true of steel but, of course, more pronounced and more frequent when the control surface is cast iron. The damaged areas should be filed flat and, if need be, a longer adjusting screw installed. Normally these systems are called positive stops; they control continued and repeated accuracy in the overarm or track arm and the cutterhead. Wedge levers, plungers, and eccentric plungers are all commonly used to accomplish the same repeating accuracy. The slots or holes into which these parts mate often show wear and should be corrected with a file or reamer, or should be replaced if possible (Fig. 7-15).

Many of the operating problems related to radial saws can be traced to the fence or the table. If possible, the table itself or the table boards originally supplied with the saw should be covered with a scarfing board (Fig. 7-16). This allows the blade to cut a keft in scrap or an easily replaced surface rather than in an accurate, premachined, and relatively expensive table or set of table boards. Most table boards are dipped or coated to prevent warping, after all necessary machining is done. Other tables are surfaced with a laminate for both appearance and accuracy (Fig. 7-17). Once this sealed surface is cut, moisture can greatly affect the area.

The fence should be carefully picked for flatness (no warp) and straightness. Even though this particular item is normally considered scrap, and always becomes scrap, it can completely nullify good maintenance and accurate mechanical alignment. This is due to the change of cut angle, depending upon the length of the workpiece in relation to the curve in the fence (Fig. 7-18).

FIG. 7-17

FIG. 7-18

The arbor, which in most cases is an extension of the motor shaft, should be at least visually checked for evidence of runout. If the visual check discloses a problem, an indicator should be used for verification. Serious motor problems can be prevented by returning the motor to the motor manufacturer for corrective action immediately.

The inner flange and the shoulder on the arbor or motor shaft should be checked for burrs or nicks, which could cause the blade to wobble and possibly decrease the life of the motor bearings. Any nicks or unevenness should be carefully touched off with a file, with the unit not under power.

Naturally all electricals should be checked. The line running to the motor or cutterhead, which is constantly being flexed, should receive special attention. The connections at each end must be secure, and the fabric or rubber should not be cracked or open. Dust should be blown out of all controls, and they should be checked for positive fast action.

ALIGNMENT

Although the radial saw is basically a contractor's instrument and a cutoff saw, indicating that extreme accuracy is not vital, very acceptable accuracy can be achieved by proper maintenance and careful alignment.

Most radials have a number of critical adjustments simply because of the construction and design. If you think of this saw as being similar to a large C clamp with five or six adjustments between the jaws, you can see the many possibilities of misalignment. Besides these the problems concerning basic rigidity, weight, and the fact that much of this weight is suspended in midair increase the difficulty.

FIG. 7-19

FIG. 7-20

Nevertheless, as in most machines, there is one part or area which is not adjustable. In the radial saw this is the column support, and all adjustments must originate from this point and follow in sequential order until the furthest adjustment point is reached.

Most modern radial saws are built with a circular column which is held in an upright position by the column support. The column support must be firmly bolted or fastened to the frame or base of the machine (Fig. 7-19). The bolts should be checked for tightness periodically because any looseness at the base will make all further adjustments literally useless.

The column support is usually cast iron and is often split about two-thirds of the way down with flanges cast on each side of the opening (Fig. 7-20). This allows the cast to wrap around and hold the column with controlled tightness. The bolts or assemblies used to tighten this casting around the column often have a dual role for they can also be used to open the casting. If gib screws also are a part of the casting assembly, they should be loose or backed off during adjustment of the basic support tightness around the column; otherwise they can actually hold the casting open and nullify the adjustment.

The column support performs other functions also, depending on the manufacturer and the design; often gib adjustments are built into this support. The gib rides against a key, usually bolted to the column, and controls the lateral or rotary movement of the column (Fig. 7-21). The gib should be tight enough to prevent rotary movement, yet loose enough to permit raising and lowering the column to control the depth of cut. The best way to accomplish this adjustment is to snug up all gib screws, then tighten one screw at a time tight enough to stop or restrict vertical movement. The tight gib screw should then be backed off enough to allow the proper feel in the elevating crank, then locked in place with the nut (Fig. 7-22). The same procedure should be followed for the remaining screws.

FIG. 7-21

FIG. 7-22

It is assumed that the tracks or rods are clean and that the bearing outer races or covers are clean; the cutterhead should then be adjusted to the track. In most radial saws the bearings on one side (usually the left) are mounted on a stationary axle or shaft, while the bearings on the opposite side are adjustable to compensate for bearing and track wear, to control accuracy, and to regulate the feel of the moving cutterhead. Various methods are used by manufacturers, but it is common to mount the adjustable bearings on an eccentric shaft (Fig. 7-23). This allows the bearing to move in and out a very short distance as compared to the rotation of the shaft with a wrench. As in most adjustments of this type, it is recommended that both adjustable bearings be reasonably snug or tight against the track and yet allow completely free movement of the cutterhead, in and out. Each bearing in turn should then be tightened against the track by rotating the eccentric shaft until cutterhead motion is impossible, then slowly backed off or loosened until the desired ease of operation is reached. Eccentric shafts are usually equipped with a locking setscrew or other locking system to prevent further movement (Fig. 7-24). Locking is especially necessary.

After long use, tracks which are milled directly into cast iron or even semisteel will begin to show wear. Wear of only a few thousandths of an inch occurs in the most used or center section of track and has a definite effect on the movement of the cutterhead. If the bearings are adjusted to the wear section of track, the head will be too tight at each end of the track arm or overarm. If this condition is too pronounced or serious, the arm must be removed and the tracks ground to match the worn section. There

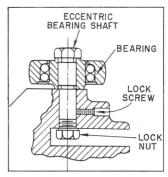

FIG. 7-23

FIG. 7-24

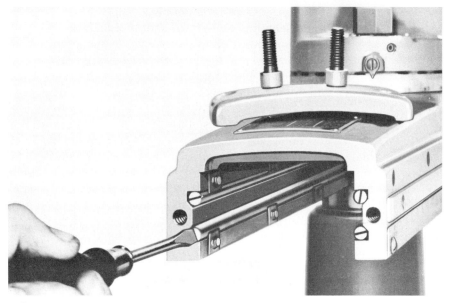

FIG. 7-25

FIG. 7-26

is a limit, of course, to this corrective procedure, depending upon the throw or amount of distance that eccentric shaft will move the bearing.

In some radial saws hardened rods are used as tracks. When the rods (two on each side) begin to show wear, they can be turned or rotated slightly in order to present a completely new track surface to the bearings (Fig. 7-25).

Radial saws with sliding rams, either with circular or with dovetail way assemblies, present a similar problem except that the adjustment is made at the top of the column and controls the ram movement, in and out (Fig. 7-26). Gib screw adjustments or bearing adjustments, depending on the design of the unit, must be made.

If a free-running ball bearing system is used, the manufacturer's recommendations or suggestions should be followed to the letter.

Before alignment of the upper arm or pivot arm is attempted, the fence should be checked to make sure it is true, without warp or wind. It is then possible to adjust the arm slightly right or left until the cutterhead assembly travels exactly perpendicular to the fence, or in a path 90 deg to the fence. This can be done by laying a framing square on the table with one leg against the fence and the other leg slightly to the left of the blade travel line or kerf (Fig. 7-27). With the power off, or disconnected if possible, the cutterhead can be moved in and out and the arm visually aligned. The actual adjustment or movement of the arm is accomplished by as many methods as there are manufacturers; the particular system should be understood before starting the adjustment. Needless to say, the parts and/or instruction manual should be read and followed.

FIG. 7-27

FIG. 7-28*a*

FIG. 7-28*b*

FIG. 7-29

All heeling should now be adjusted out of the cutterhead. Heeling indicates that the blade is not square with the fence (even though the entire cutterhead is tracking square). Heeling can be checked by holding one leg of a framing square against the fence with the other leg lifted far enough to make contact with the blade, just under the arbor nut (Fig. 7-28*a*). The blade can then be aligned parallel to the leg of the framing square by adjusting the cutterhead at its swivel point, once again as recommended by the manufacturer. This adjustment is made with the positive stop engaged or with the positive stop adjustment feature itself (Fig. 7-28*b*). The cutterhead should always return to the same "square to the fence" position after the head is pivoted 90 deg to its rip position.

Care should be taken when checking for heeling to span the teeth of the blade with the framing square. If the square does not lie flat across the face of the blade from gullet to gullet, you may well be adjusting heeling into the assembly. This is also true when checking for blade squareness with the table. In tracking the cutterhead assembly square with the fence, the blade should never actually touch the framing square.

In most saws one adjustment will accurately align the blade and cutterhead, as far as heeling is concerned, for both crosscut and rip positions. If this is not the case and a separate adjustment is required for the rip position, the blade can be aligned parallel to the fence by turning the cutterhead to its inboard rip position and moving the head back until the blade is flush with the fence (Fig. 7-29).

A quick check should now be made to be sure the table height is reasonably the same at all points, possibly within 1/16 in. This can be done easily by swinging the arm over the table in various random positions and moving the cutterhead in and out with the blade about 1/16 in. from the table. The table can now be accurately adjusted, using the table height at the normal starting crosscut position. The blade can now be removed and a dowel rod held between the collars on the arbor or otherwise fastened to the cutterhead; or, for that matter, the rod holding the kickback fingers can be reversed in the guard. The gage or the blade can now be lowered to the table height at the predetermined point and the entire table assembly adjusted to the same plane (Fig. 7-30). In extreme cases a dial indicator may be used, but usually this will not actually increase the accuracy of the saw when making dado cuts, routing, or performing other similar operations.

The blade should now be put back on the arbor and checked for squareness with the table. This can be done with a try square, once again making sure the positive stop is engaged or actually adjusting the stop mechanism, depending on the brand of the unit. This 90-deg adjustment

FIG. 7-30

in most cases will also accurately set the 45-deg positive stop (Fig. 7-31).

Since any part of the mechanism on a radial saw can be quickly misaligned as a result of the normal torque and pressures of cutting, not to mention being misused or struck with a two-by-six in midair, it should be checked often for basic alignment.

Even if a heeling problem becomes obvious, correction should not be attempted without at least a complete check of the normal alignment

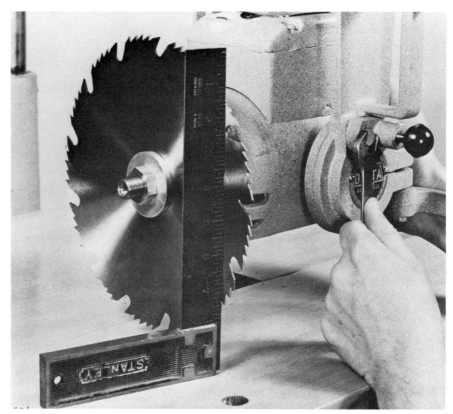

FIG. 7-31

procedure in the proper sequence. Possibly the table leveling step could be excluded, since this is vital only when cutting a dado or performing similar operations.

1. Column support: Is it firmly bolted to the base or frame?

2. Column and key: Is the wraparound casting tight enough to stop side play? Is the key tight?

3. Gibs and screws: Are the gib screws tight enough to stop side play and yet allow for vertical movement?

4. Carriage bearings: Are the bearings adjusted to remove all side play?

5. Fence: Is the fence straight?

6. Tracking: Does the carriage move perpendicular to the fence? Are angle positive stops set accurately?

7. Heeling: Is the blade square with the fence?

8. Vertical: Is the blade square with the table?

9. Table: Is the table level, or in the same plane as the overarm or track arm?

FIG. 7-33

FIG. 7-32

The blade and arbor guard should clamp securely in position, and yet move easily when adjustment for various operations such as ripping is necessary. The flange on the guard and the track or shoulder on the motor housing must be clean and smooth (Fig. 7-32). Special guards for shaping or routing operations use the same clamping system (Fig. 7-33). Leaf guards, which ride the workpiece, should slide and function smoothly (Fig. 7-34). Any roughness should be carefully filed smooth and any possible friction areas coated with hard wax.

FIG. 7-34

CHAPTER EIGHT
The Band Saw

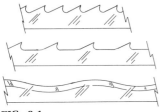

FIG. 8-1

The band saw gets its name from the cutting tool or blade, which is a flexible steel band. This band or blade can have any of an almost infinite variety of tooth shapes or knife edges cut or ground into one edge (Fig. 8-1). The various blades are intended to cut different materials such as wood, ferrous and nonferrous metal, plastic, hard rubber, paper, and even cloth. The width or depth, the thickness, and the length of the blade are all related to the size of the machine, the type of material to be cut, and the actual cut being made.

The upright or vertical band saw (Fig. 8-2) is designed to perform two basic operations. One is curve cutting (Fig. 8-3) and the other is resawing (Fig. 8-4). Straight-line ripping or crosscutting can, in most cases, be done more accurately with a circular or radial saw. Nevertheless, most manufacturers make sliding jigs (miter gages) and fences available as accessories, and band saw tables usually have a milled slot.

Most vertical band saws found in schools and cabinet shops range in size from 14 to 30 in., the most popular being the 14- and 20-in. units. The size is derived from the diameter of the upper and lower wheels, but because the blade must be guarded as it returns upward along the frame, the actual capacity of the unit is usually ¼ in. less than the unit size designation (Fig. 8-5).

Three-wheel vertical band saws have been manufactured in order to increase the throat capacity in small machines, but they are far outnumbered by the more accepted two-wheel units. Band saws normally fall into two general categories:

104

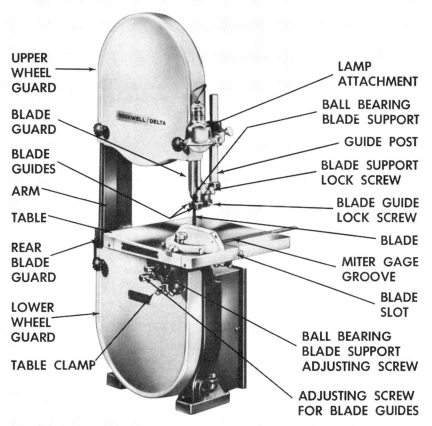

UPPER
WHEEL
GUARD

BLADE
GUARD

BLADE
GUIDES

ARM

TABLE

REAR
BLADE
GUARD

LOWER
WHEEL
GUARD

TABLE CLAMP

LAMP
ATTACHMENT

BALL BEARING
BLADE SUPPORT

GUIDE POST

BLADE SUPPORT
LOCK SCREW

BLADE GUIDE
LOCK SCREW

BLADE

MITER GAGE
GROOVE

BLADE
SLOT

BALL BEARING
BLADE SUPPORT
ADJUSTING SCREW

ADJUSTING SCREW
FOR BLADE GUIDES

14" BAND SAW

FIG. 8-2

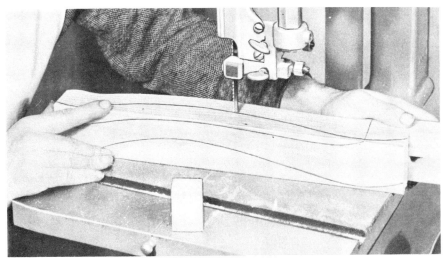

FIG. 8-3

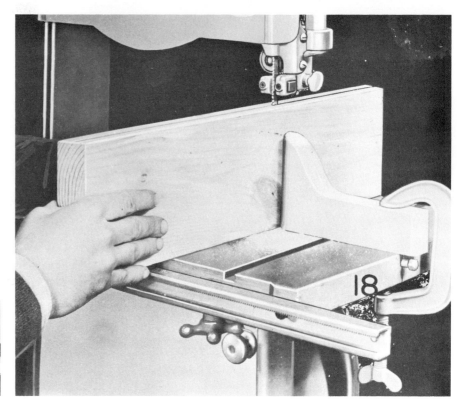

FIG. 8-5

FIG. 8-4

1. WOODCUTTING

3000 to 5000 fpm, one fixed speed depending on the size of the machine; belt drive (Fig. 8-6).

2. METAL WOODCUTTING

40 to 3000 or 5000 fpm, speed range infinite with variable drive or in progressive steps with step pulleys; direct drive or variable speed and backgearing (Fig. 8-7).

FIG. 8-7

FIG. 8-6

Horizontal band saws are designed primarily for straight cutoff of round, flat, or odd-shaped stock (Fig. 8-8). They are used almost exclusively for cutting metal rather than wood or other materials. The machine size is designated by the size of stock or actual capacity rather than the diameter of the wheels, e.g., 6″ round 10″ flat. The stock is held in a vice or clamp with the machine moving down through the work by gravity, often at a controlled rate of fall. Typical speeds for a 6″–10″ unit are 53, 96, and 160 fpm, with a three-step pulley drive. Since curve cutting is normally not possible, blades are somewhat standardized at ½ in. for units of this size.

Combination units are manufactured, i.e., vertical-horizontal; these can be operated in either position for either basic operation. Portable

FIG. 8-8 (KTS Industries, Inc.)

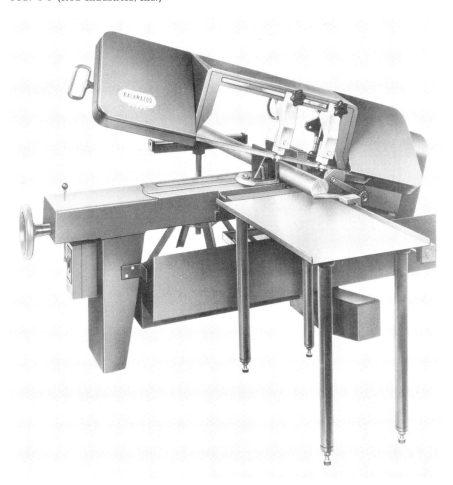

FIG. 8-9

band saws, primarily intended for metal cutting by contractors and maintenance departments, are also available (Fig. 8-9).

GENERAL MAINTENANCE

The cabinet or legs should be checked occasionally for loose bolts, open welds, or other defects which can cause vibration. If the saw is lagged or bolted to the floor, the fasteners should be checked and tightened. Many horizontal units are mounted on casters for portability and should be checked for ease of movement and swivel. Any locking devices should lock firmly when engaged.

All belts and pulleys, whether variable or step pulley type, should be checked for proper alignment, and pulley setscrews should be checked for tightness. The entire table and trunnion assembly must be periodically removed, cleaned with solvent, lubricated with hard wax or other dry lubricant, and reassembled (Fig. 8-10). This is particularly true of a woodcutting machine. The entire area enclosed by the upper and lower wheel guards should be blown out with air or thoroughly brushed out occasionally.

The upper wheel support assembly containing the tensioning and tracking (raising and tilting) mechanism should be removed and cleaned if the action is stiff or erratic. Removal of the upper wheel is, of course, the necessary first step. Dovetail ways, slides, gibs, springs, and all other contact surfaces should be cleaned with solvent and dry-lubricated (Fig. 8-11). In some cases it is possible to do an acceptable job without complete removal, by merely loosening the setscrews and removing the gib. This creates enough open space for cleaning with a brush and solvent.

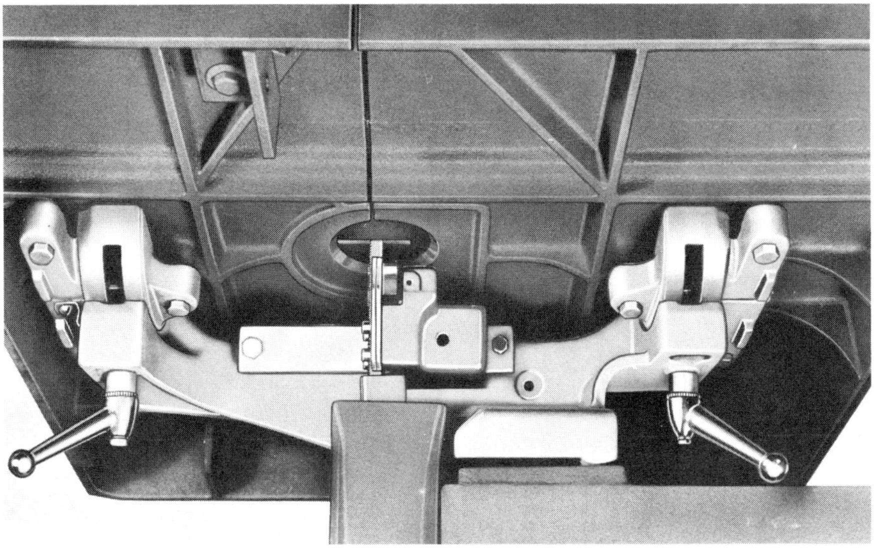

FIG. 8-10

Tires should be checked for both cleanliness and resilience. If they are badly worn, cracked, or cut, they should be replaced with new tires according to the manufacturer's recommendations. Tires must also be crowned (Fig. 8-12) for proper blade tracking. In most modern band saws the crown is automatically built into the wheel or the tire-wheel assembly, and it is no longer necessary that the crown shape be "filed" or ground or otherwise formed.

Cleanliness is vital, for any foreign material embedded in the tires can make tracking difficult and even cause an unbalanced condition of the entire wheel assembly. This not only causes annoying vibration but also can shorten bearing life or in time even bend a shaft. Tires can be cleaned easily with a stiff brush or a block of wood used as a scraper. Solvents can be used also, but some care must be exercised in the case of rubber or plastic tires, which might be destroyed by a chemical reaction.

Replacement tires should be purchased in pairs from the distributor or manufacturer of the machine, and the installation directions should be closely followed. In general, tires fall into three categories as far as mounting or holding to the basic wheel is concerned: tires which are glued on, tires which are stretched on, and those which are actually a snapped-on or locked-on wheel extension.

Glued tires may be rubber, plastic, or even leather; often they must be soaked or even "machined" off the wheel rim. Replacement should be in strict accordance with the manufacturer's recommendations in regard to the tire itself, the glue, and the method to be used. It is often necessary to hand-crown these tires by holding a scraper or a file against the tire and turning the wheel.

Rubber tires stretched around the rim of the wheels are very common in band saws in the 10- to 15-in. size. Most wheel rims which take rubber

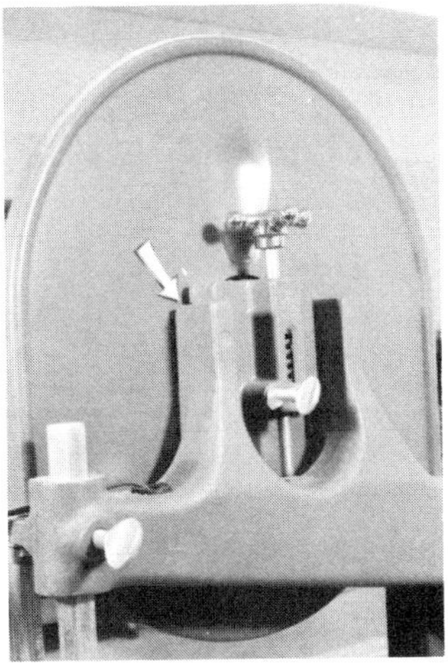

FIG. 8-11

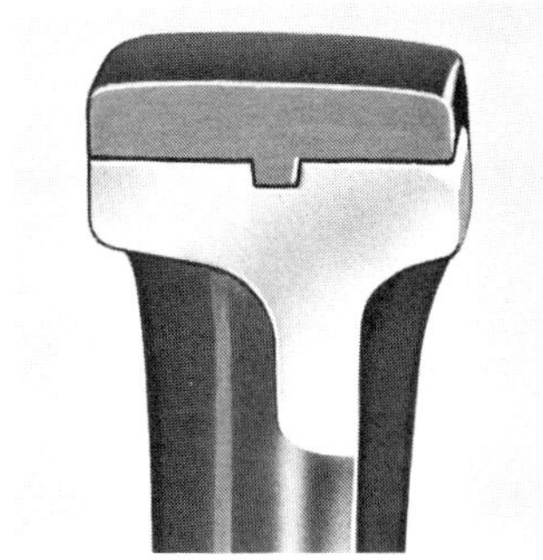

FIG. 8-12

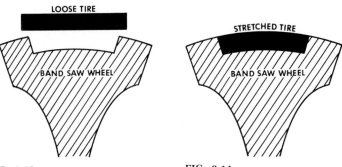

FIG. 8-13 FIG. 8-14

FIG. 8-15

FIG. 8-16

FIG. 8-17

tires are crowned and also have a shoulder on each side or edge. The replacement tire is always smaller in diameter than the rim of the wheel but wider than the distance between the shoulders (Fig. 8-13). When stretched to fit the diameter, the width decreases and the tire fits perfectly between the shoulders. The crown of the machined rim is, of course, reflected in a properly crowned tire (Fig. 8-14).

Care must be taken to equalize the thickness of the rubber around the entire rim. If thicker in one spot, the wheel will be unbalanced and the blade, even if tracking properly, will move from side to side in the guides and in the work. This can be corrected in a number of ways. Rolling the wheel with the new tire installed against the floor or a bench top firmly and with pressure will tend to move the rubber and distribute the tire evenly on the rim. This naturally requires the removal of the wheel. It is usually not difficult to remove the upper wheel, but the lower wheel is usually keyed and/or mounted on a tapered shaft and requires a wheel puller (Fig. 8-15).

Without removing the wheel, a large dowel can be rolled with pressure against the tire, but more time is required. In order to install the rubber tire reasonably even in the first place, it is a good idea to mark the belt with chalk on the edge and the top every 90 deg. This is easily done by holding the loose tire together and marking each end loop; these marks are then matched and the opposite loops marked (Fig. 8-16). The marks are now easily matched to the top, bottom, and each side of the wheel.

By holding a pencil against the frame or rear guard and close to the new tire, a reasonably accurate check can be made regarding tire thickness and a true-running wheel (Fig. 8-17).

On machines 20 in. and larger, the peripheral speed is too great for rubber tires which are not glued to the wheel. Any tire not glued or otherwise held to the rim will actually fly off or eventually work its way off the rim. Because of the gluing problems and the impossibility of using stretched rubber, the Snap-Lock tire was developed. This tire is actually a stiff or rigid band and becomes an extension of the wheel. If it is made of molded rubber, there are usually steel bands inside which keep the tire round and rigid, even when not mounted on a wheel. Precision-molded

FIG. 8-18

plastic tires also are available. They are rigid enough to retain their circular shape without steel band reinforcement (Fig. 8-18). Both types are held on the rim by a tongue molded into the tire which fits into a groove machined into the rim. Tires of the Snap-Lock type are both balanced and crowned, and thus forestall many problems.

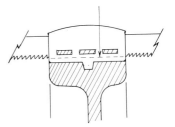

FIG. 8-19

These tires are installed by tapping them on the rim with a wood or leather mallet, starting at any given point and moving slowly around the circumference. The tongue will eventually mate with the groove, producing a loud snap, and will be "locked" on the rim; hence the name Snap-Lock. Installation can be made easier with the use of a dry lubricant or even soap. Some care should be exercised to use no lubricant, liquid or dry, that is harmful to rubber and/or plastic.

The removal of a damaged or worn rigid type of tire is practically impossible without cutting the tire or otherwise destroying it completely. Attempts to pry the tire from the rim usually result in a badly damaged magnesium or aluminum wheel with the tire still firmly mounted. The tire should be carefully sawed across its width with a hack saw or hack saw blade as far through as possible without touching the rim (Fig. 8-19). The tire can be lifted slightly to accomplish the last two or three strokes, and often lifted high enough to cut the tongue or even remove the tire.

Particularly in the case of rubber or nonrigid tires, it is not really necessary to remove the wheel when installing a new tire, but it certainly makes the job much easier and often saves valuable time.

There are probably more types of band saw guides in use than there are manufacturers of machines. This is, of course, because some com-

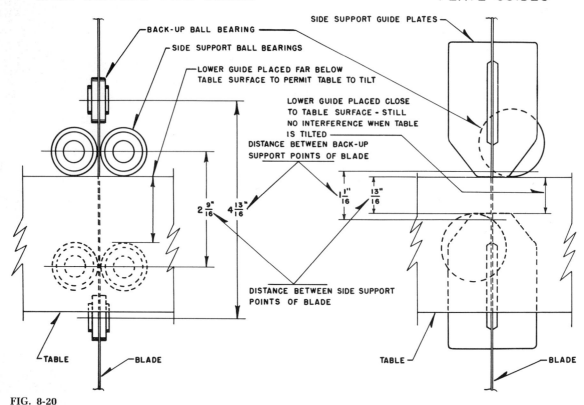

BALL BEARING TYPE GUIDES

PLATE GUIDES

BACK-UP BALL BEARING

SIDE SUPPORT GUIDE PLATES

SIDE SUPPORT BALL BEARINGS

LOWER GUIDE PLACED FAR BELOW
TABLE SURFACE TO PERMIT TABLE TO TILT

LOWER GUIDE PLACED CLOSE
TO TABLE SURFACE - STILL
NO INTERFERENCE WHEN TABLE
IS TILTED

DISTANCE BETWEEN BACK-UP
SUPPORT POINTS OF BLADE

DISTANCE BETWEEN SIDE SUPPORT
POINTS OF BLADE

TABLE   BLADE   TABLE   BLADE

FIG. 8-20

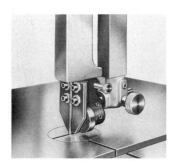

FIG. 8-21

panies will supply guide assemblies of their special design to replace the original guides. In general these assemblies might be divided into two different types: those which are all ball bearing (Fig. 8-20) and those which have a backup bearing and incorporate friction-type guides on each side of the blade (Fig. 8-21). In either case it is essential that the complete assembly be disassembled occasionally and completely cleaned. The bearings are usually sealed and do not require lubrication, but all outboard surfaces should be wiped clean. Any bearing should be replaced if not completely free-running.

All other guide assembly parts can usually be removed from the saw and completely cleaned with solvent or steel wool. On woodworking machines a dry lubricant should be used on all adjustable parts. Oil can be used on a metal working unit although the dry type of lubricant is satisfactory.

The blade guard covering the potentially exposed blade between the upper guide assembly and the upper wheel guard should be checked for proper coverage at all guide heights (Fig. 8-22a). The rear blade guard

FIG. 8-22*a*

FIG. 8-22*b*

covering the moving blade as it returns up along the frame from the lower to upper wheel should provide complete operator protection. Naturally neither guard should touch the moving blade at any time or otherwise interfere with the operation of the band saw.

Operational assemblies, such as built-in clamps, gravity feeds, power feeds, balance mechanisms, blade brushes, and other similar but possibly highly individual items should be checked, cleaned, and restored to proper working order. In most cases the manufacturer's instructions are the best reference. If gearboxes are involved, the instructions must be followed to the letter in regard to possible draining, refilling, correct oil level, or other lubrication questions.

Electrical connections, grounding circuits, and all controls should be checked for both correct operation and safety.

ALIGNMENT

The lower wheel should be the starting point for all basic alignment because in most cases it is mounted on a nonadjustable shaft or axle. This is almost always true in the case of a woodworking machine. Some metal/wood, metal, or large woodworking units have an adjustable gearbox assembly which in effect makes the lower wheel adjustable (Fig. 8-22b). The lower wheel adjustment should never, under normal circumstances, be moved or changed except to compensate for frame twisting due to shipping accidents, extreme changes in temperature, or other external causes. Even then it is advisable to contact the distributor or manufacturer for expert help or advice pertaining to the specific saw. It cannot be stressed too much that the lower wheel should be considered the immovable or nonadjustable starting point.

FIG. 8-23

Before a new blade is installed, the upper wheel tensioning device should be released, lowering the wheel itself (Fig. 8-23). The upper and lower guide assemblies should be both opened up and backed out of the blade path. The table pin or other alignment part can then be removed (if so equipped), and the new blade moved carefully through the blade slot and mounted over the wheels. The table pin should then be replaced.

FIG. 8-24

FIG. 8-25

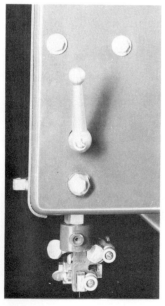

The tracking procedure now begins by increasing the tension and actually raising the upper wheel. The upper wheel should then be turned slowly by hand while a visual check is maintained on the position of the moving blade. It should track or run in the center of the crowned tire. Because of the crown the blade will have a natural or mechanical tendency to climb to the center, as the wheel is slowly tilted right or left. In most cases the tilt mechanism is controlled by a handwheel and needs no locking device (Fig. 8-24).

The tension and tilting adjustments should be alternately increased and changed until the correct tension is reached and the blade is tracking in the center of the crowned tires. When it is certain that the tracking is correct when turning by hand, the final tilt adjustment should be made under power. Since this must be done with the wheel guards removed or open, caution should certainly be exercised. The power can be snapped on, then quickly off several times, for a longer duration each time until with the machine under continuous power the tracking is perfect. Even if a new blade is not being installed, tracking should still be the first checkpoint for accurate adjustment of the machine.

The amount of blade tension needed is very difficult to explain accurately. Many manufacturers provide a scale indicating the correct tension for a given thickness of blade. Such a scale is reasonably accurate only when a new blade and new tires are installed on an older machine or when a completely new machine is adjusted. In most other cases there are too many variables, the thickness of the tires, due to wear; the length of the blade, due to welding; and the thickness of the blade. The type of guide assemblies and the material being cut also may indicate that more or less tension is needed. Experience is really the best teacher, with the scale as a general guide. Too much tension will cause blade breakage, excessive tire wear, tire distortion, bearing failure, and even distortion of the wheel shafts or complete frame assembly. Too little tension will produce mistracking, blade movement in the guides, blade breakage, and inaccurate work. Some happy medium must be maintained.

The upper guide assembly should then be adjusted. Besides having normal blade control, this complete assembly must be adjustable up or down, depending on the thickness of the workpiece, exactly parallel to the blade. In smaller units the parallel movement is nonadjustable and is built into the machine since the actual distance moved is relatively short, usually 6 in. or less. Larger band saws usually have some method to adjust the guides and their supporting member both front to rear and side to side in relation to the blade. One typical method used is the three-point suspension system (Fig. 8-25). The two top cap screws allow for front-to-rear movement of the upper guide bracket by entering the bracket support through oversize holes in the cabinet. The lower cap screw is also threaded into the bracket support but is inserted through a sleeve which is threaded into the cabinet. This acts as a control device and raising mechanism, or in this case allows for adjustment from side to side. The adjustment is made by turning the sleeve, which is tightened or locked by tightening the cap screw.

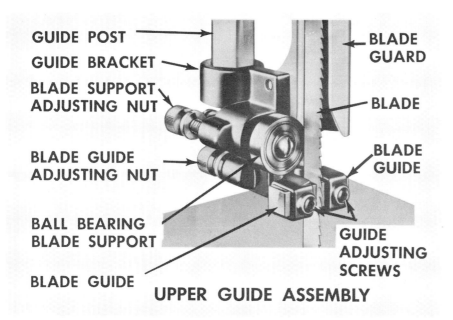

GUIDE POST
GUIDE BRACKET
BLADE SUPPORT ADJUSTING NUT
BLADE GUIDE ADJUSTING NUT
BALL BEARING BLADE SUPPORT
BLADE GUIDE

BLADE GUARD
BLADE
BLADE GUIDE
GUIDE ADJUSTING SCREWS

UPPER GUIDE ASSEMBLY

FIG. 8-26

Regardless of the specific method used, this parallel movement should be carefully checked before starting on the guide itself. This can be done easily by setting the guide assembly reasonably close to the blade at table height. The guide should then be lifted slowly to the maximum depth of cut and visually checked for equal distance from the blade at all heights.

Regardless of the specific manufacturer, band saw guides basically have three adjustable parts, one on each side of the blade and one behind the blade. The two at the sides are intended to keep the blade from twisting during curve cutting. The part behind is to hold the blade firm or literally to keep it from being forced backward as the work is fed into the saw (Fig. 8-26). Because of the continuous friction while actually cutting, the backup part is almost always a bearing. The backup bearing can be positioned to make contact with the blade on its edge or its face, depending on the designer.

The guide blocks or bearings on each side of the blade should be adjusted first, before the backup bearing. Each block or bearing is usually independently movable (Fig. 8-27). They should be set about three or four thousandths of an inch from the blade on each side. This can be done in various ways without gaging equipment. For instance, the guide blocks or bearings can be moved in until they touch the blade, and then the blade is jiggled or moved from side to side rapidly until the guides are moved out the required distance. A piece of paper can be used as a gage while the guide block or bearing is tightened (Fig. 8-28). When the paper is removed, the distance is approximately correct. Actually the guides should be as close as possible without touching the blade.

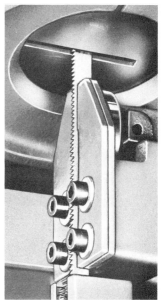

FIG. 8-27

FIG. 8-28

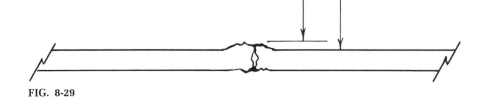

FIG. 8-29

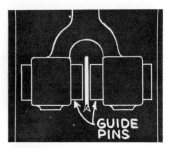

FIG. 8-30

FIG. 8-31

The distance should be checked while the upper wheel is turned by hand to make sure the blade weld is flush with the sides of the blade (Fig. 8-29). Any movement of the blade from side to side instantly indicates badly worn or unevenly installed tires, a bad bearing, or a bent shaft.

Most guide assemblies have provision to move both guides forward or to the rear at the same time with the same adjustment. The blocks or bearings should be adjusted until they are positioned just behind the gullet of the saw teeth or about 1/64 in. behind the point of zero set (Fig. 8-30). In many cases this adjustment has no locking device but uses a close-tolerance National fine thread to prevent accidental creeping or movement.

The backup bearing should now be adjusted to within 1/64 in. or less from the rear edge of the blade (Fig. 8-31). This is true regardless of the exact bearing position or its relation to the blade as used by various manufacturers. Once again this distance should be as small as possible without actually touching the blade. Possibly the best method is to move the backup bearing forward so that it touches the blade and rotates as the blade is moving. It should then be slowly backed off with the adjustment until it stops turning, indicating that it no longer touches, and it is then locked in position. National fine threads on this adjustment can eliminate the need for a positive lock.

Any weaving movement of the blade from front to rear could indicate improper tracking, worn or uncrowned tires, a lack of adequate tension, or an inaccurate blade weld (Fig. 8-32).

The lower guide assembly should be aligned in exactly the same order as the upper guides. This can often be done by removing the table insert for easy visual check. Some care should be exercised, particularly

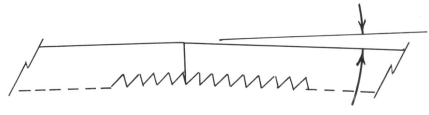

FIG. 8-32

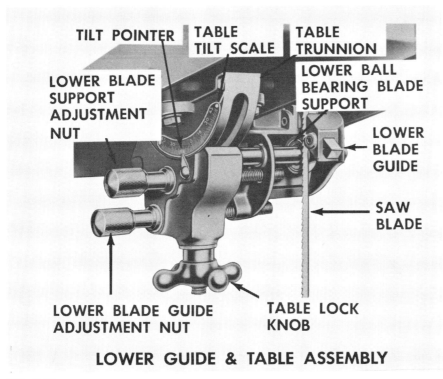

TILT POINTER

TABLE
TILT SCALE

TABLE
TRUNNION

LOWER BLADE
SUPPORT
ADJUSTMENT
NUT

LOWER BALL
BEARING BLADE
SUPPORT

← LOWER
BLADE
GUIDE

← SAW
BLADE

LOWER BLADE GUIDE
ADJUSTMENT NUT

TABLE LOCK
KNOB

LOWER GUIDE & TABLE ASSEMBLY

FIG. 8-33

if the adjustment controls are not extended forward away from the blade (Fig. 8-33).

If all adjustments and alignment procedures have been properly done, the blade will not run true and clear the guide assembly parts by a few thousandths of an inch. The blade will begin to ride against the backup bearing the instant the material to be cut touches the teeth. It will instantly be held straight and true when the operator begins a curve cut. After the material has been cut, the blade should return to the original perfectly aligned relationship to the guides. If it does not, tracking and tension should be checked and the guide assemblies realigned.

In many cases the complete trunnion assembly is mounted on a three-point suspension. Regardless of the specific method used by the manufacturer, the table should be checked for alignment, square with the blade or perpendicular to the blade. It should be checked along the potential kerf line first, then to the side. A combination or try square should be placed on the table with one leg extending up the back of the blade. The basic table mounting can then be adjusted or even shimmed to the point where the table is perfectly square with the blade. If this adjustment is not made, the blade will cut beyond the line (table tilted forward) or not quite to the line (table tilted backward), and an accurate internal square

FIG. 8-34

corner will be an impossibility. This front-to-rear tilting condition will also affect the vertical squareness of any curve-cutting operation. A straight-line through cut would not be affected.

The square should next be backed up against the flat side of the blade behind the teeth (Fig. 8-34). The positive stop can then be adjusted so that the table will return to its square or 0-deg position after tilting (Fig. 8-35). The tilt scale or the pointer should be moved or changed to read 0 deg.

There is really not enough width to the blade to check adequately whether the table slot is parallel; this alignment is usually taken for granted. The miter gage head is then aligned at 90 deg to the table slot (Fig. 8-36) and the fence parallel to the slot. If there is a foot brake, it should be checked and possibly adjusted for proper contact. It should be tested also for stopping ability and a convenient pedal position for the operator.

All adjustable, sliding, or moving parts should be lubricated with a dry lubricant on a woodcutting machine or possibly oil on a metal-cutting unit. All exposed cast-iron surfaces including the table top should receive the same treatment.

FIG. 8-36

FIG. 8-35

Table inserts, if damaged or cut, should be replaced. The insert should fit snugly into place so that the movement of the workpiece will not turn it into the blade. Looseness can often be corrected by center-punching the edge in several places or hitting the flat surface—close to the edge with a hammer. Either method will add a slight amount of metal to the diameter and correct the loose fit. Some manufacturers now provide a locking feature to keep the insert from rotating.

Figure 8-37 may be of help in diagnosing both blade and band saw problems.

CUTTING PROBLEMS · BAND SAW BLADES

PROBLEM	POSSIBLE CAUSE	SUGGESTED REMEDY
TEETH STRIPPAGE	Too Few Teeth per inch	Use finer tooth blade
	Loading of gullets	Use coarse tooth blade
	Excessive feed	Decrease feed
	Work not secured in vise	Clamp material securely
BLADE BREAKAGE	Teeth too coarse	Use a finer tooth blade
	Misalignment of guides	Adjust saw guides
	Dry cutting	Use cutting lubricant
	Excessive Speed	Lower speed
	Excessive feed	Reduce feed pressure
	Excessive tension	Tension blades to mfr's recommendation
RUN-OUT AND RUN-IN	Wheels out of line	Adjust wheels
	Guides out of line	For a straight and true cut, realign guides, check bearings for wear.
	Excessive Pressure	Conservative pressure assures longer blade life and clean straight cuts.
	Support of blade, insufficient	Move saw guides as close to work as possible.
	Material not properly secured in vise	Clamp material in vise, level and securely
	Blade tension, improper	Loosen or tighten tension on blade, check back of blade for excessive wear due to stress of metal
BLADE TWISTING	Blade not in line with bearing guides and rollers.	Check bearings for wear and alignment
	Blade too narrow	Use wider blade
	Excessive blade pressure	Decrease pressure & blade tension
	Blade binding in cut	Decrease feed pressure
DRY CUTTING	Premature tooth wear	*Use lubricant on all materials, except cast iron
	Blade too coarse	Use finer tooth blade
	Not enough feed	Increase feed so that blade does not ride in cut
	Excessive Speed	Decrease speed

*Lubricant can be safely used on all materials. For best results, cut dry on cast iron, or use a good quality stick wax, applied to the blade before, and during cutting.

FIG. 8-37

CHAPTER NINE
The Scroll Saw

The intricate scrollwork which can be done on this machine accounts for one of its two popular names, scroll saw (Fig. 9-1). It is also called a jig saw, possibly because of its fast, almost dancing movement up and down, and is responsible for the term "jigsaw puzzle." The scroll saw, depending on the blade, can cut extremely small or tight curves, often turning a radius the thickness of the blade used. By installing the blade through an opening or predrilled hole in the workpiece, inside cutting is possible.

The typical scroll saw in today's school shop, craft shop, or sign shop has a throat opening of 24 in. and a thickness capacity of 2 in. The scroll saw, in comparison with other power tools, has the most violent and instant motion change in the most confined space. The mechanical change from rotary to reciprocal action is accomplished by various methods depending on the manufacturer.

GENERAL MAINTENANCE

Although they can be bench-mounted, most scroll saws are mounted on an open stand, often with casters. In most cases the stand, either open or cabinet type, is merely supporting the saw at the correct height and contains no working mechanism. If equipped with casters, the unit is reasonably portable and can be moved to any location in the shop (Fig. 9-2).

The bolted or welded stand should be checked for loose bolts or open welds. Cabinet doors and casters should be checked for proper operation. Doors should latch tightly for safety, and hinges should be firmly

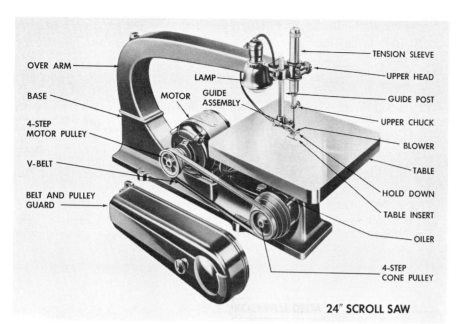

OVER ARM

BASE

4-STEP
MOTOR PULLEY

V-BELT

BELT AND PULLEY
GUARD

LAMP

MOTOR

GUIDE
ASSEMBLY

TENSION SLEEVE

UPPER HEAD

GUIDE POST

UPPER CHUCK

BLOWER

TABLE

HOLD DOWN

TABLE INSERT

OILER

4-STEP
CONE PULLEY

24" SCROLL SAW

FIG. 9-1

FIG. 9-2

fastened to both the door and the cabinet. Casters should turn and roll easily when extended and should lock in this position. When these casters retract, the four legs of the stand should meet the floor firmly with full weight. If any rocking is evident, it is often possible to loosen the stand bolts and allow the stand to adjust itself before the bolts are retightened. Naturally the unit must be on a level floor.

The entire cast frame of the machine should be checked for cracks or other damage. If the overarm is a separate casting (Fig. 9-3), the bolts holding the parts together should be tight. In most cases the alignment is controlled by steel pins or roll pins which should be replaced if they are missing. They are usually found in opposite corners of the mating parts.

FIG. 9-3

On a four-speed or step pulley unit the motor should be firmly mounted to the base of the machine or to the stand shelf. The pulley alignment should be checked before and after tightening the motor mounting bolts. The setscrews holding the pulleys on the drive shaft and the motor shaft should also be checked and tightened after proper alignment is obtained. A variable-speed unit is similar except that the motor should be firmly bolted to the sliding plate, and the plate assembly in turn should be firmly bolted to the frame of the saw (Fig. 9-4). The shaft which moves the sliding plate and the plate should be thoroughly cleaned and waxed for easy movement. The limit of the movement, forward and backward, should be checked and all collars on the shaft tightened. The guides also should be tightened, including the setscrew in the crank handle.

The variable-speed pulley or expanding sheave should carefully be

FIG. 9-4

FIG. 9-5

FIG. 9-6

FIG. 9-7

FIG. 9-8

removed from the motor shaft (Fig. 9-5). The spring is extremely powerful but also has a very short range, just enough to control the sheave movement. This entire unit should be cleaned with solvent and well lubricated with hard wax or other dry lubricant. Never oil this sheave (Fig. 9-6). Oil causes a buildup of dirt, pitch, and dust, causing the sliding parts to freeze and often causing permanent damage.

Most scroll saws are lubricated by a splash system. The oil reservoir should be checked both for foreign material or dirt and for correct oil level or capacity. In most cases No. 20 weight oil is light enough to be splashed through the crankshaft area and heavy enough to stick to moving parts and resist being pumped up the lower plunger. Under normal operations, even in a school or cabinet shop, there is no need to change oil after any specific time interval. If the oil filter cap is kept closed during operation of the machine, the oil will stay reasonably clean. Occasionally small amounts of oil may be needed to maintain the correct level, but a complete oil changing is not normally necessary even after years of continuous use.

One condition which may require complete draining and cleaning is a collection of broken blades in the oil sump. If these build up high enough to interfere with the internal mechanism, they must be removed. Often they can be reached by removing a cover plate. The broken blades drop through the hollow lower plunger and into the sump if they are not held when the lower chuck jaws are loosened.

The operating mechanism can usually be inspected or even replaced without draining the oil (Fig. 9-7). The change from rotary to reciprocal action is usually accomplished by an eccentric shaft and cross slide or a crankshaft and connecting rod (Fig. 9-8). Whatever the type of action used, the parts are subject to more than average wear because of the violent and instant changes in movement. They should be checked for possible wear or looseness every few months if the unit is in daily use. All setscrews, bolts, nuts, or other fasteners should be checked for proper tightness or adjustment. Care should be taken to check the bottom setscrew when two are used for locking purposes. Any major adjustments should be done in accordance with the manufacturer's recommendations.

The lower chuck, upper chuck, and upper guide assemblies should be cleaned and made easily adjustable. A combination of oil, gum, pitch, and dirt tends to lock the adjustments in one spot. If necessary these assemblies should be removed from the machine, washed or soaked in solvent until clean and free-moving, and coated with a dry lubricant.

The table should be removed and the trunnions cleaned and lubricated with hard wax or a dry lubricant. The locking device or method used to turn the table 90 deg should also be checked (Fig. 9-9). While the table is off the machine, the lower plunger bushing assembly should be checked for proper height and also for its relationship to the lower plunger. This should be a firm sliding fit and is often controlled by a felt sleeve or insert bushing. The felt not only provides smooth friction-free movement up and down, but also tends to lubricate. If damaged, it should be replaced with a new felt sleeve, presoaked for a few minutes in oil. The bronze or metal bushing usually screws into the saw housing and is held at the proper height by a setscrew (Fig. 9-10). This locking setscrew is often covered with dirt or paint and is easily missed. If the bronze bushing insert is turned with a spanner wrench or rotated with a hammer and punch without releasing the setscrew, permanent damage will be done to the threads.

FIG. 9-9

In many units the upper plunger assembly is adjustable for both tilt and side-to-side movement where it is mounted on the arm (Fig. 9-11). This entire area should be cleaned, but not necessarily lubricated.

All electrical controls and connections, including the grounding system, should be checked. Belt guards should be properly installed and should cover the belt-drive system completely. It is vital to both safety and proper machine operation that the exposed motor shaft be equipped with a small handwheel. The switch should be at the front of the machine for operator convenience and safety (Fig. 9-12).

FIG. 9-10

ALIGNMENT

The upper guide assembly should be moved back so that the blade can be installed without interference. It is important to adjust the guide to the correctly installed blade, not the blade to the guide assembly.

If you are not sure of the alignment of the upper plunger assembly, it is necessary first to make sure that the upper and lower plungers will be moving in exactly the same plane. This can be done by clamping a saber blade or any small stiff piece of metal in the center of the lower chuck jaws. Make sure the blade is in the flat jaws, not the V jaws (Fig. 9-13), and is held upright as perpendicular to the table as possible. The upper plunger should then be pulled down to meet the top of the blade, with the upper chuck open. If they mate exactly, the plungers are probably in line; otherwise the entire upper assembly should be moved until they mate. Even when this is done and the upper chuck is clamped to the blade, a visual check should be made to be sure the upper assembly is not heeling

FIG. 9-11

FIG. 9-12

FIG. 9-13

or tilting to one side. It must be vertical, 90 deg to the table, and exactly in the same plane as the lower plunger. The test blade should now be removed.

A normal or jeweler's blade should then be clamped firmly in the center of the flat jaws of the lower chuck and also in the center of the upper chuck jaws. To ensure that the blade is perpendicular to the table, a square can be placed against the teeth of the blade with the other leg extending forward, flat on the table (Fig. 9-14). The blade may now have to be moved forward or backward in either chuck to match the upright leg of the square. At this time the table itself can be squared with the blade by extending the table leg of the square to one side (Fig. 9-15). The table should be clamped square and the scale or the pointer changed to read 0 deg of tilt.

Blade tension should be increased beyond the point where the upper chuck will hit the plunger assembly. Exactly what tension is correct is impossible to gage because too many factors are involved; i.e., the type of teeth, the blade thickness, the blade width, the type of material to be cut, the thickness of the material, and the extent and tightness of the curves to be cut. A general rule of thumb is: the heavier the blade, the less tension is needed. Most saws have a scale of some type for quick reference (Fig. 9-16).

The saw mechanism should now be turned over by hand, using the handle or wheel on the motor shaft, to check for any unusual noise or tightness. If there are problems, the drive should be rechecked and corrected for belt and pulley misalignment, setscrew looseness, cross slide wear, lack of oil, bushing tightness or misalignment, chuck looseness, or lack of proper tension.

The guide assembly (Fig. 9-17) should now be adjusted to the blade.

FIG. 9-14

FIG. 9-15

FIG. 9-16

The guide is designed to keep the blade from twisting and supports it at the rear under cutting pressure—the same as a band saw guide. The main differences are purely mechanical and in size. Because the jeweler's blade used in a scroll saw, even a relatively wide blade, is narrow compared with the normal band saw blade, twisting is not usually controlled by separate blocks or bearings. Most often a precut slot is used with the depth and width of the slot related to the dimensions of the average blades. The various slots are either individually cut into separate guide arms (Fig. 9-18) or symmetrically cut into a disk which can be rotated to match the appropriate slot with the blade being used (Fig. 9-19).

Regardless of the specific type, the correct slot should be chosen primarily because of width. The blade should clear each side and run completely free (Fig. 9-20). Next the backup mechanism, usually a hardened roller, should be brought forward to touch the blade, then backed off slightly so that it does not turn when the blade is moving but not cutting. This could be only a few thousandths of an inch.

Most scroll saws also have a hold-down which is spring-loaded or actually is a spring itself (Fig. 9-21). It should be checked for smoothness and for equal height of each leg which spans the blade. The entire guide assembly should then be lowered until the hold-down touches the table, to ensure squareness, and the hold-down adjustment tightened.

FIG. 9-17

FIG. 9-19

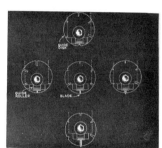

FIG. 9-20

FIG. 9-21

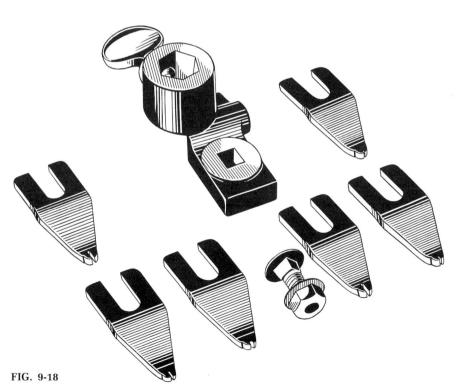

FIG. 9-18

If the scroll saw is equipped with a blower, it is usually driven by a cam or other mechanical method directly from the crankshaft. Most of the problems involve a cracked or stiff diaphragm in the pump, or a leaking base or base connections. The diaphragm should be replaced if old or broken after the chamber has been cleaned out with solvent. The control is usually a ball bearing which is forced to move in both directions by the air pressure. At one end of the track, air is allowed to be pumped through the base; at the other end the steel ball is pulled into the opening and stops any reverse pressure. This happens extremely fast, and in most cases coincides exactly with the stroke of the saw. This tube or track area must be clean for proper operation. Normally no adjustment is provided.

Hose connections are usually the slip-on type and have no clamping mechanism. Until the hose is too short, small ½-in. pieces can be cut from either end to provide a good tight connection. If the hose is too short or is old and cracked, it should be replaced.

The finger guard, belt guard (Fig. 9-22), and any other safety features should be checked, adjusted, and in place for operation.

FIG. 9-22

CHAPTER TEN

The Drill Press

The drill press (Fig. 10-1) is probably the most versatile power tool manufactured and is found in almost every woodworking and metalworking shop. If it is considered a stationary tool primarily intended to produce accurate holes, the type of shop where it is used or the kind of material drilled is practically unlimited. The primary sizes used in school shops, cabinet shops, and metal job shops range from 14 to 20 in., although both larger and smaller sizes are available. The variety of models is extensive but available usually by a catalog designation from any one of a number of manufacturers. The following is a sampling of the types or combinations which are available:

Floor model	Full guard
Bench model	Spring-loaded guard
Tilting table	Cantilever guard
Nontilting table	Top belt guard
Production table	Mechanical power feed
T slot production table	Air hydraulic power feed
With table-raising mechanism	Split head casting
Five-spindle bearing	Solid head casting
Four-spindle bearing	Four-step pulley
1/2" arbor hole spindle	Five-step pulley
Bonnet guard	Planetary gear spindle pulley

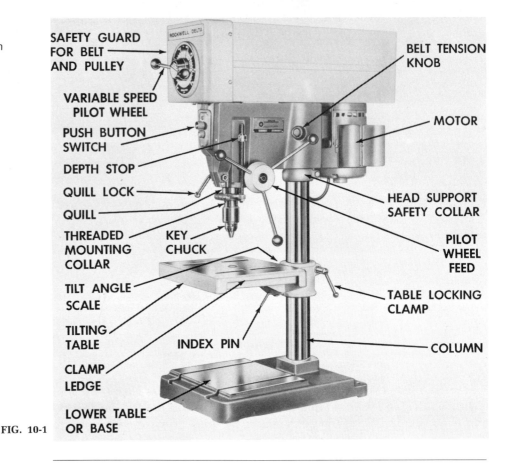

SAFETY GUARD FOR BELT AND PULLEY

VARIABLE SPEED PILOT WHEEL

PUSH BUTTON SWITCH

DEPTH STOP

QUILL LOCK

QUILL

THREADED MOUNTING COLLAR

KEY CHUCK

TILT ANGLE SCALE

TILTING TABLE

CLAMP LEDGE

INDEX PIN

LOWER TABLE OR BASE

BELT TENSION KNOB

MOTOR

HEAD SUPPORT SAFETY COLLAR

PILOT WHEEL FEED

TABLE LOCKING CLAMP

COLUMN

FIG. 10-1

High speed	6″ stroke
Slow speed	5″ stroke
Variable speed	4½″ stroke
With head-raising mechanism	Sixteen-spline spindle
With counterbalance mechanism	Fourteen-spline spindle
Pilot wheel	Two-spline spindle
Two-spoke wheel	Foot feed
Preloaded cartridge	V-belt drive
Spindle adapters with collars	Poly-V-belt drive
One-piece spindle and holder	Flat belt drive
No. 2 MT spindle	Geared head
No. 1 MT spindle	Self-belt tensioning
No. 3 MT spindle	Tilting/rotating head
Drill chuck	Multispindle
Head-mounted push buttons	Solid table
Floor or foot controls	Sectional table
Long column	With jackshaft
Short column	

In this incomplete list we have not considered the accuracy of various units or the many variations in electricals available. All these factors show that the common production drill press can be almost custom-ordered to match the user's exact requirements.

Some of the many jobs a drill press will do include the following:

Drill	Mortise	Grind
Rout	Plug-cut	Sand
Shape	Surface	Press

Although some specific models and related uses are by far the most popular, large distributors often carry not only complete drill presses, but also component assemblies. Columns, heads, tables, and electricals are individually stocked both for replacement sale and for assembly into complete presses. Within a few minutes some distributors can assemble from these components almost any specific model or catalog number listed, as well as a great many others.

GENERAL MAINTENANCE

Drill presses are usually lagged to the floor for absolute stability, for even a slight rocking motion of the base is greatly exaggerated at the work level. The lag screws should be checked for tightness. At the same time the column could be checked for tilt with a carpenter's level and, if necessary, shims added between the uneven floor and the base (Fig. 10-2).

All castings should be checked for cracks or other damage. In addition to the base, table, table bracket, and head, the motor mounting plate and even the guard may be made of cast iron. On a step pulley press, the guard should be checked for ease of opening (Fig. 10-3). Hinges, sup-

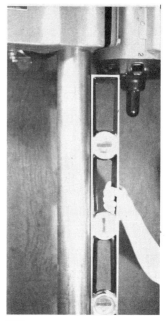

FIG. 10-2

FIG. 10-3

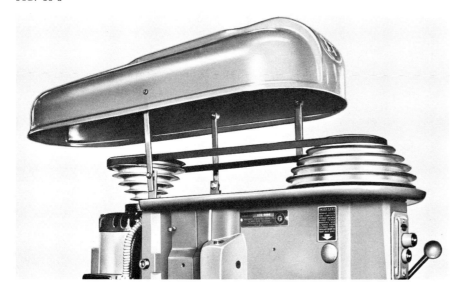

FIG. 10-4

ports, stops, latches, springs, and other working mechanisms should be cleaned and lubricated.

Pulley setscrews should be checked for tightness and the pulley itself checked for excessive wear or cracked flanges. In most cases a bad pulley must be replaced; it cannot be repaired (Fig. 10-4). By slowly turning the pulleys separately, by hand, a bent shaft or bad bearing can often be detected. Once again replacement is usually the only cure for a worn bearing or a bent shaft. This is often expensive, particularly if a motor shaft is bent, because the shaft is almost always an extension of the rotor assembly.

The quill should be removed from the press and also all parts of the upper spindle assembly. The tension on the quill return spring must be released or the spring unwound (Fig. 10-5). The individual manufacturer's directions should be followed to the letter to avoid damage to the drill press or physical injury because this spring is under a great deal of tension. The depth stop, and in many cases the collar holding this stop, should also be removed (Fig. 10-6). The pinion shaft and feed handle can then be removed or pulled out so that the quill assembly is allowed to fall

FIG. 10-5

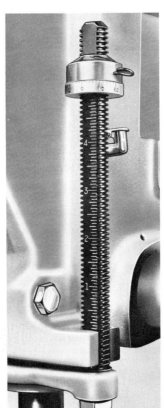

FIG. 10-6

130

(Fig. 10-7). In most cases both the unwound spring and the spring housing can then be removed as a unit. The quill should be clamped in the press by tightening the locking handle, or it should be held in the left hand while the pinion shaft is removed with the right. If this is not done, it is quite possible that the quill assembly will slide out of the head casting, damaging the quill or breaking the table.

FIG. 10-7

The end of the pinion shaft is usually slotted or split. It mates with a straight flat section on the internal end of the clock spring (Fig. 10-8). Care should be taken when reassembling the press that the slot and the spring mate correctly; otherwise the spring could be pushed out of its housing and instantly expand to a diameter of 2 ft or more. The outboard end of this spring is hooked and fits into a precast slot in the housing (Fig. 10-9). If a broken spring must be replaced, most manufacturers recommend purchasing the complete assembly of housing and enclosed spring as a unit. If only the spring is purchased, extreme care must be taken when removing the broken spring and inserting the new one in the housing. The replacement spring is usually compressed with a heavy hog ring (Fig. 10-10). The spring should be slowly tapped into the case or housing. Slowly the housing or case takes over from the retaining ring, and the ring is literally pushed off by the case.

FIG. 10-8

If there are bearings in the quill assembly, they can usually be checked without removal; they should not be removed except to be replaced if defective. In removing them, care should be taken with threaded collars, snap rings, wave washers, or other small parts. Some bearings have a different type of seal on each side, and this should be carefully noted (Fig. 10-11). Many bearings are damaged by removal or installation; therefore great care should be taken not to damage the seals by prying or tapping them. Only the inner or outer races should be pulled or pushed. All disassembled parts and assemblies should be cleaned with solvent, checked for wear, burrs, or other evidence of wear, lubricated, and reassembled. The internal parts and quill bearing surfaces of the head casting also should be cleaned and lubricated.

FIG. 10-9

Light machine oil should be used as the lubricant on most moving or sliding parts. Grease should be used on spindle splines (Fig. 10-12), not only for more permanent lubrication, but also to take up any wear or error space and eliminate backlash. This also stops any objectionable noise caused by backlash. All quill and spindle parts, particularly the splines, should be cleaned and handled carefully to avoid nicks, burrs, or other damage. On units with a replaceable or slip spindle (Fig. 10-13), the spindle should be checked for straightness. This can be done in a number of ways, but slowly rolling it on a flat surface, possibly the drill press table, is reasonably accurate and requires no special gages or equipment.

When the quill is reassembled into the head, the splines will often be tighter than normal, possibly too tight. The quill should then be lowered until the splines separate. The spindle or the upper drive pulley assem-

FIG. 10-10

131

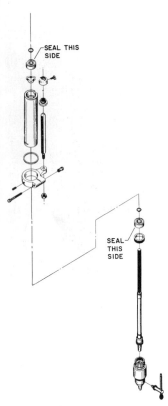

SEAL THIS SIDE

SEAL THIS SIDE

FIG. 10-11

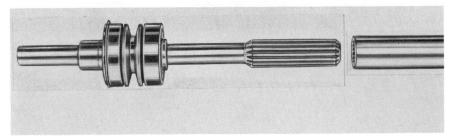

FIG. 10-12

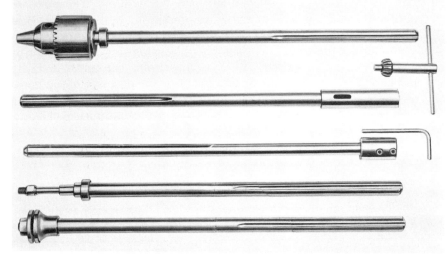

FIG. 10-13

FIG. 10-14

FIG. 10-15

bly should be turned slightly and reengaged until the correct feel is obtained. This condition is sometimes due to slight inaccuracy in the male or female splines but more often due to a normal wear pattern caused by continuous use.

The table bracket should be checked for proper tightening on the column. If this bracket is a split casting, and particularly if it is old, enough wear may have occurred to prevent any clamping action even when the kerf is closed tightly. This is true of most collars. In most cases the condition can be corrected by filing a slightly larger kerf, giving the casting more space to close (Fig. 10-14). The wear is almost always in the cast-iron bracket or collar rather than the steel column. Shims also can be used between the table bracket and the column, but this method is not recommended because it may tilt the table out of proper horizontal alignment.

If the table bracket has a built-in raising mechanism, the gears should be checked for wear, cleaned, and properly lubricated (Fig. 10-15). Ball or sleeve bearings also should be checked and/or replaced. The crank handle should fit tightly on the shaft. Any burrs on the flat of the shaft should be filed until the flat is smooth.

Clamping mechanisms on head castings and nonsplit casting brackets should be removed, cleaned, and checked for proper clamping action. In most cases the clamping parts are shaped to match the curve of the column. Care must be taken in reassembly to assure proper mating with the column.

The flat mating surfaces of a tilting table and bracket should be free from burrs, cleaned, lubricated, and capable of being clamped tightly in any position.

The column should be checked for nicks or burrs which could damage the head casting or table bracket. They should be carefully touched off with a file, and the entire column cleaned with steel wool and solvent. The column should be lubricated with a dry lubricant or even a light coat of oil, to prevent rust and make table raising both easier and safer. A good rule of thumb is: in a woodshop use a dry lubricant such as hard wax; in a machine shop use oil.

The motor bracket, regardless of the type or style, should be removed and cleaned (Fig. 10-16). In most cases it is not necessary to remove the motor as a separate unit or entity. All moving and adjustable parts of the bracket, including the connecting or mating part of the head casting, should be cleaned. This is particularly important if the drill press is equipped with a self-tensioning type of mount. All moving, sliding, or hinged parts should be lubricated with a dry lubricant.

FIG. 10-16

ALIGNMENT

Belt and pulley alignment is vital for proper operation, accuracy, and long assembly or part life. This is accomplished on a drill press more easily than on most other tools, since raising or removing the guard usually exposes completely the belt and pulleys. A straightedge (a jointed board is excellent) should be placed, front to rear, across the pulleys as close to the center as possible. The step pulley with the largest sheave at the top, usually the motor pulley, should be used as the basis for the initial check because the span from one edge to the other is greater. When the straightedge is held tightly against the rim of the motor pulley, it should also touch exactly the top of the spindle pulley (Fig. 10-17).

FIG. 10-17

If the pulleys do not line up, the following adjustments should be checked in this order:

1. Make sure the spindle pulley is properly installed. This pulley is often a part of an assembly including bearings and is seated and locked into the head casting.

2. Make sure the motor pulley is mounted as low as possible on the motor shaft.

3. Make the actual adjustment for pulley alignment by raising or lowering either the motor mount or the motor itself on the mounting bracket.

It is obvious that this basic alignment could be accomplished also by raising or lowering the pulley on the motor shaft or possibly even the spindle pulley, but other complications soon occur. These can include excess vibration, short bearing life, bent shafts, pulley damage, and even guard problems.

While this alignment is being checked, care should be taken to make sure the motor and motor pulley are not tilted. The two pulleys not only must be level as far as height is concerned, but also must run in the same plane.

Whatever the method used by various manufacturers or even by one manufacturer on various drill presses, original belt tension should be adjusted. The motor mounting assembly should be moved to the rear until the center of the belt can be moved, with the fingers, about $1/2$ in. on a 14- or 15-in. drill press, and slightly more on larger units (Fig. 10-18). The proper tension allows the belt to run as loose as possible, yet to pull without slipping under full drilling torque or load.

Play or movement between the quill and the head casting should be checked with the quill extended. By grasping the extended quill or the chuck with the left hand and attempting to move it back and forth, you can easily feel or even see wear or inaccurate adjustment (Fig. 10-19).

Two methods are used to correct or eliminate this movement. One is to squeeze the wraparound or split head casting if this particular type of basic construction is used (Fig. 10-20). Another way is to increase the

FIG. 10-18

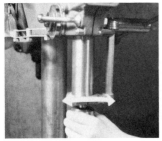

FIG. 10-19

FIG. 10-20

pressure on the plug or quill adjuster (Fig. 10-21). Both of these two basic methods have various systems for adjusting and locking, usually quite easy to figure out.

In the case of a split casting head, the casting is usually closed or squeezed together with a special nut and bolt system. Usually this does not operate as a visual check might indicate. An open hole, slightly larger than the bolt or fillister head screw, is drilled in the right section of the casting. The fillister head screw is inserted through this hole and threaded into a tapped hole in the left section. The casting is drawn together, around the quill, by tightening the screw with a screwdriver. The nut on the exposed end of the screw is used only to lock the adjusting screw (Fig. 10-22). Tightening this nut will not squeeze the casting. Continued turning will destroy the threads on the nut and the screw or even snap off the screw.

Drill presses with a solid head casting are equipped with a quill adjuster system, usually employing a bronze plug. The plug is held against the quill, forcing the rear surface of the quill against the casting and thereby eliminating any play or looseness. The plug itself is very short and is driven or held in place and adjusted by a threaded shaft inserted into a tapped hole in the head (Fig. 10-23). A locking system incorporating a special washer and round head screw is usually a part of this assembly.

In any of the systems used, there must be no play between the quill and the head casting, and yet the quill must move in and out of the casting

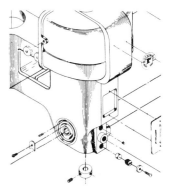

FIG. 10-21

FIG. 10-22

FIG. 10-23

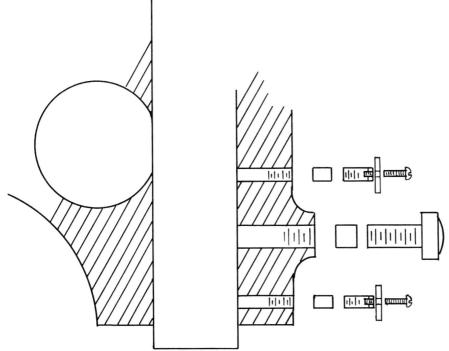

135

with comparative ease. This indicates that some happy medium must be reached between these two requirements. Attempts to adjust from "loose to tight" are usually unsuccessful because it is impossible to guess how close the adjustment is to being really tight. For this reason the quill should be extended and the adjustment tightened until the quill is locked in this position. The split casting should then be allowed to open slowly, or the plug should be slowly backed out until the return spring will draw the quill back up in the head (Fig. 10-24). In most cases the actual area of adjustment between being locked tight and the correct adjustment is very small. Care should be taken to avoid being hit by the possible quick movement or spin of the pilot wheel or feed lever. The locking nut or screw should be tightened while the adjustment is held in the final correct position.

FIG. 10-24

Failure to remove side play or looseness between the quill and the head casting by this normal adjustment procedure is probably due to excess casting wear. This can, of course, be corrected by replacement of the head casting or even the entire head assembly. Short of this extreme, many manufacturers will supply upon request an oversize quill. Usually .002-in. oversize is adequate to take up the excess wear and make normal adjustment possible, although .004-in. and .006-in. oversize quills are also available.

The mounting of the chuck should be checked because it is a definite contributor to the accuracy or inaccuracy of the drill press. Most key chucks are mounted on a No. 33 chuck taper, which is really the bottom or lower end of the spindle. If the press is to be tested for accuracy or runout with a dial indicator, the external male taper (Fig. 10-25) is the correct place to check. If the check is made on a steel dowel held in the chuck, you are then really checking the press and the chuck as an assembly, including the straightness of the dowel and the accurate mating of the taper.

FIG. 10-25

Many modern small drill presses use a threaded collar to draw the chuck on the taper in a straight line. The threads and, even more important, both the male press taper and female chuck taper must be perfectly clean in order to maintain accurate alignment (Fig. 10-26). Since the No. 33 chuck taper ground on the spindle is usually machined, using the quill assembly and the actual machine's bearings as a fixture, this taper is usually more accurate than the female taper in the chuck. Different chuck adapters (Fig. 10-27) will usually show different runout readings even on the same drill press. On a slip spindle or solid spindle unit, the chuck is forced on the nonreleasing No. 33 chuck taper and literally becomes a permanent part of the spindle. If the chuck must be removed, it should be done carefully with a set of steel wedges, making sure that it is driven straight off the spindle (Fig. 10-28). If tapped crooked, both tapers could be permanently damaged or the spindle could be bent. If the spindle or the chuck is replaced or even if the original parts are reassembled, this should be done by using straight-line pressure, not by tap-

FIG. 10-26

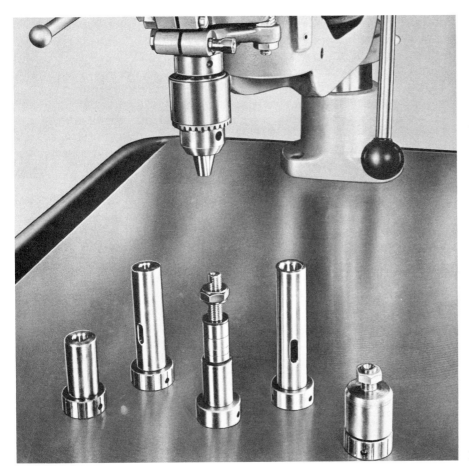

FIG. 10-27

NOTE: WEDGES TO BE TOUGH BUT
NOT HARDENED. SUGGEST USING CHISEL STEEL

SCALE: ½ SIZE

1 OF EACH REQ.

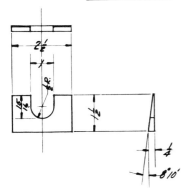

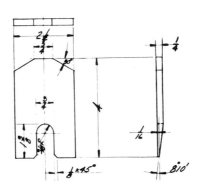

FIG. 10-28

ping, because of the necessity for accurate in-line alignment. This can be done on an arbor press or even by using the drill press itself for in-line pressure. A simple jig can be made to hold the chuck, or even a flat board can be used to protect the table while applying pressure with the quill.

Caution should be used when adjusting the quill return spring tension. Many manufacturers now use a method of adjustment controlled with a wrench or screwdriver (Fig. 10-29) rather than manually winding up the spring. In older presses this was done by pulling the spring housing away from the retaining lugs and progressively turning the assembly until it once again matched the lugs (Fig. 10-30). If the assembly starts to slip, you should release it immediately and let it unwind. Attempting to stop or hold it will result only in skinned fingers. The more modern housing and spring assembly is usually mounted in a recess or cavity in the drill press head. It is often turned or tensioned by a pinion shaft which mates with a rack in the outer rim of the housing (Fig. 10-31).

Most tilting drill press tables have a positive stop at the 0-deg or level position. This stop is usually a taper pin inserted in a hole which has been drilled and taper-reamed through both the table and bracket (Fig. 10-32). With the pin inserted and the clamp tightened, the table should be checked to make sure it is exactly perpendicular to the spindle. This can be done accurately with a dial indicator and an extension held in the chuck. You should get within .0005 in. of the same reading while making a 6-in.-diameter circle on the table. This allows for slight runout of the spindle and chuck, and slight inaccuracy of the machined table. A greater difference from front to rear could indicate dirt between the table and the bracket, or even a bent column. A greater difference from left to right can be corrected by removing the taper pin, adjusting the table to read level, and slightly reaming out the hole to match the correction. If the pin and the hole are not tapered, a larger hole should be drilled and a new oversized pin made and inserted. It is a good idea to chain this pin to the underside of the table. If a tilt scale is included with the machine, the pointer or the scale should be adjusted to read 0 deg.

FIG. 10-29

FIG. 10-30

FIG. 10-31

FIG. 10-32

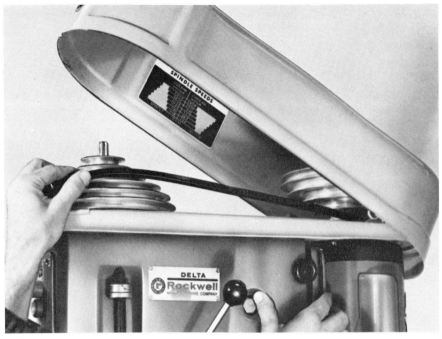

FIG. 10-33

FIG. 10-35

All guards should be checked for ease of opening and closing in addition to proper guarding. Proper basic positioning of the motor mount should be checked, not only for tension, but for ease of changing belts (Fig. 10-33). Although the tension and alignment of variable-speed units are preset by the manufacturer, they also should be checked (Fig. 10-34).

Typical construction of a variable-speed split head casting drill press is shown in Fig. 10-35; that of a five-bearing five-step press with a bearing support above the spindle pulley is shown in Fig. 10-36.

The column, table top, and base surfaces can be protected with hard wax.

FIG. 10-34

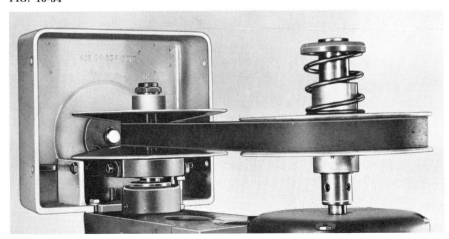

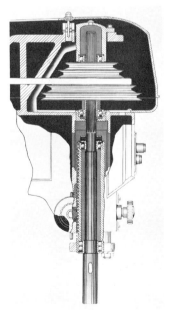

FIG. 10-36

CHAPTER ELEVEN
The Mortiser

FIG. 11-1

The name "mortiser" is directly related to the prime purpose of this unit, which is to cut the mortise half of a mortise and tenon joint. The tenon may be easily made by any of various methods on such machines as the saw, jointer, or router, but the hollow chisel mortiser (Fig. 11-1) is unique in that it "drills square holes" or actually drills round holes and cleans out the corners in one machining operation. The same operation can be done on a drill press with a mortising attachment (Fig. 11-2) but not as conveniently or easily.

Most mortisers found in school or cabinet shops are of the hollow chisel variety. Chain mortisers also are available, but they are usually larger and intended for production work. They also limit the minimum size in length and depth of the mortised hole produced. The ease and safety of the hollow chisel mortising unit, as well as such extra conveniences as a moving or sliding table, make this a popular machine for schools and custom cabinet shops.

GENERAL MAINTENANCE

All cast-iron parts should be checked for cracks or other possible damage. In most cases the base and column are cast as an integral part, not manufactured as two castings bolted together. Lag screws or bolts holding the unit to the floor should be checked for tightness and breakage.

The flat and V ways machined into the front of the column should be cleaned with solvent and lubricated according to the manufacturer's recommendations. If the ways are extremely dirty or nicked, the motor assembly, hold-down and fence unit, and table assembly should be removed from the machine to be thoroughly cleaned and checked for nicks. Any small burrs or other roughness should be carefully touched off with a file. Care should be taken in removing the table assembly not only because it is heavy, but also because the pull line from the foot pedal lever must be disconnected. This lever is either spring-loaded or under constant pull by a counterweight (Fig. 11-3).

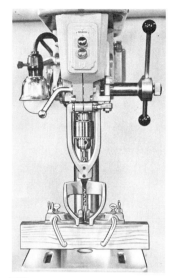

FIG. 11-2

FIG. 11-3

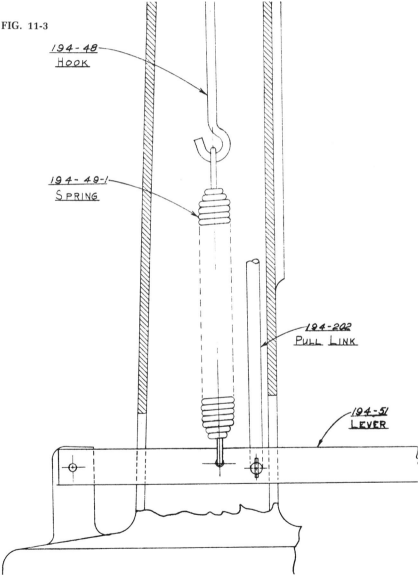

194-48
HOOK

194-49-1
SPRING

194-202
PULL LINK

194-51
LEVER

FIG. 11-4

Gib screws can be loosened and the gib carefully removed. On reassembly, after lubricating the ways, replace the gibs exactly as they were originally.

The screw and the ways controlling the horizontal movement of the table should be cleaned and lubricated. In some cases the table itself can be removed for cleaning while the table bracket is still on the column. Thus the weight can be cut down by separating the total assembly into two subassemblies (Fig. 11-4).

Bearings, sealed ball bearings, or sleeve bearings should be checked. Collars, setscrews, washers, drive screws, and other items should be checked, cleaned, and lubricated before reassembling.

All pivot points and linkage points on the foot lever and pull bar mechanism should be cleaned with solvent and lubricated. If this mechanism is disassembled, it should be reassembled in exactly the same adjustment positions as when taken apart.

Replaceable wood tables should be replaced if they are damaged or have been mortised into often enough to affect the accuracy of the machine.

All electrical connections should be checked for tightness, and the controls for positive and fast action. The unit should be checked for proper grounding.

ALIGNMENT

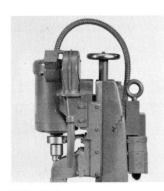

FIG. 11-5

Basically the alignment of the mortiser is controlled by the ways machined into the front of the column. There is usually a combination of V and flat surfaces, all machined or ground in exact relationship to each other. This indicates that if the gibs are properly tightened, the table, motor slide or back plate, and all other assemblies clamped to these ways will line up properly.

By rule of thumb the gib screws on the motor plate assembly can be adjusted tighter than on the table because the necessary movement is slower and is controlled by a screw (Fig. 11-5). The table must move more freely in response to the foot lever and should be not quite as tight. The motor plate gib screw adjustment might be compared to adjusting the gibs on a jointer table. In either case, all gib screws should be drawn up snug; then one screw should be tightened until movement is stopped. It can then be backed off until the desired feel is obtained at the control. Then all other gib screws should be adjusted by the same process.

The same gib tightening process should be followed for the horizontal movement of the table. The rack and gear or other operating system should be clean, lubricated, and adjusted for complete freedom of movement. This is also true for the in-and-out movement of the table. Whichever system is used, tubular knee or ways, the mating parts must be clean and the locking device firm regardless of the position.

If the table tilts, positive stops can be set by using a square placed on the table in relation to the chisel.

142

The spring tensioning device should be checked for tension, possibly with a typical piece of work clamped to the table. Spring tension can usually be increased or decreased by turning or adjusting a tensioning nut on the outside top of the machine (Fig. 11-6). A turnbuckle type of adjustment is sometimes located inside the column as part of the spring and tensioning assembly. If a counterweight or counterbalance system is used, the weights may have to be changed to assure proper table return. This system is usually a little slower or more sluggish than the spring system.

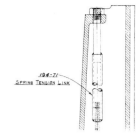

FIG. 11-6

The motor, which is bolted to the sliding base or motor slide, and the bracket supporting the chisel must be in perfect alignment (Fig. 11-7). In most cases any slight misalignment is from side to side rather than from front to rear (the latter position is controlled by the original machining process). The chisel holding bracket can be hit out of line by a careless operator and will instantly cause vibration, noise, and burning between the chisel, held by the bracket, and the bit, held by the motor and chuck. Possibly the best alignment procedure is to insert the bit up through the chisel and check visually whether it enters the chuck in exact alignment. If it does not, the bracket should be slightly loosened and tapped into line. You should be able to turn the chuck and bit by hand easily, with no binding between the chisel and bit.

Most hollow chisel mortisers will serve also as very accurate boring machines, with no changes except for removing the chisel holder and

FIG. 11-7

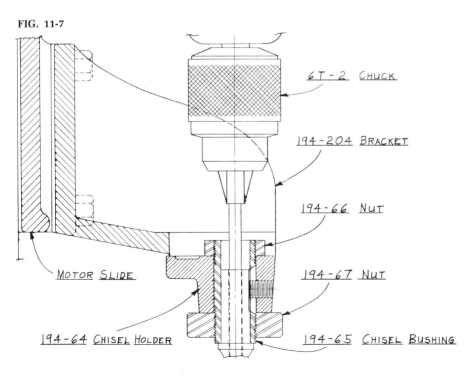

143

FIG. 11-8

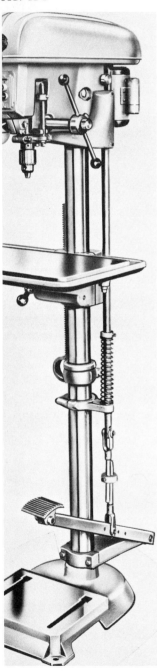

bushing. Manufacturers sell this unit also specifically as a boring or drilling tool.

When a normal drill press is adapted for mortising, an accessory unit is fastened to the press in place of the regular stop collar. This incorporates the chisel and bushing holder. The total accessory package also usually includes a fence and various hold-down attachments. In this case the original machining of the manufacturer must be depended upon to guarantee perfect alignment. Most drill presses which will accept a mortising attachment will accept a foot feed attachment made by the same manufacturer (Fig. 11-8). The foot feed is adjustable and is usually spring-loaded. The original return spring on the pinion shaft of the press and the extra spring on the foot feed combine to pull the bit and chisel out of the work. The foot feed is usually attached directly to the pinion shaft instead of the normal drill press pilot wheel or handle. Since the quill moves instead of the table as in an actual mortising machine, the operation is different but basically similar.

Any guards or guarding equipment should be adjusted and installed to operate as intended by the manufacturer.

Leveling of the machine is not vital to the accuracy of work produced by the mortiser. Nevertheless, it is usually desirable to bolt or lag the unit to the floor. It has a tendency to tip or be unsteady, particularly if long work is being mortised without additional support.

CHAPTER TWELVE

Abrasive
Finishing Machines

With the belt finishing unit (Fig. 12-1), also called a belt sander, accurate finishing to size is both easier and faster than by hand. Metal finishing or wood sanding depends primarily on the type of belt installed on the machine. In most cases this unit is used for finishing flat surfaces and externally curved work. Any internal curved finishing work is limited in diameter by the size of an exposed drum (Fig. 12-2) except on machines using a very narrow belt. The 1-in. belt units fall into this category (Fig.

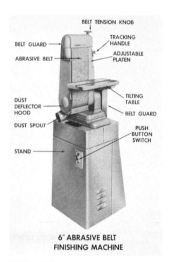

6" ABRASIVE BELT
FINISHING MACHINE

FIG. 12-1

FIG. 12-2

145

FIG. 12-3

12-3). The standard platen is usually flat, but formed or shaped platens for woodworking are available from edge sander manufacturers (Fig. 12-4). On a stroke sander (Fig. 12-5) the platen is actually held in the operator's hand (Fig. 12-6). Whatever the size or type, the actual method of stock removal and the purpose are the same. The basic sizes found in a metal job shop, cabinet shop, or school shop are 1 in., 4 in., and 6 in., indicating the width of the belt. The length varies greatly, depending on the size of the machine.

The disk finishing unit (Fig. 12-7) is used primarily for fast stock removal of either wood or metal. Since the disk does not move in line with the grain, final sanding or finishing, particularly of wood, should be done by hand or with a belt machine. The final accurate pass across a miter or compound miter, after sawing, is a typical disk finishing machine operation. The platen is actually the disk on which the abrasive is mounted. Internal curves cannot be finished on this unit, and in most cases it is advisable to use only the downward portion of the disk. This tends to hold the work safely on the table, but it also restricts the size of the area which can be sanded or finished. It should be remembered that although the rpm is the same, the cfm (cutting feet per minute) increases noticeably from the center to the outer edge of the disk. This can greatly affect the finish and rate of stock removal and, when working with wood, can increase the possibility of burning or discoloring the material. The

FIG. 12-4

STRAIGHT PLATEN

FORM PLATEN

FIG. 12-5

FIG. 12-6

FIG. 12-7

FIG. 12-8

sizes most frequently found in small industrial shops and school shops are 10, 12, 14, and 16 in., indicating the diameter of the disk.

The oscillating spindle sander (Fig. 12-8) is unique primarily because it oscillates or moves up and down while rotating. Spindle sanding or metal finishing can be done easily on a lathe or a drill press (Fig. 12-9), but the oscillating movement, which helps prevent burning and provides a smoother finish, must be made by moving the workpiece. This unit is intended for sanding or finishing inside or outside contours, but it can also finish straight edges. Work can easily be lowered over the spindle for sanding inside areas. The average oscillating spindle sander operates on a basis of 27 to 30 revolutions for every oscillation stroke. Most units found in a cabinet or school shop have interchangeable spindles ranging from ¾ to 3 in. in diameter, the smaller sizes predominating. The appropriate size of abrasive sleeve is slipped over the spindle or holder. It is usually held tight by a squeezing or expanding action controlled by a nut on top of the spindle.

FIG. 12-9

FIG. 12-10

The spindle sander and stroke sander are usually separate units. The belt and disk units are quite often combined into one combination belt and disk finishing machine powered by one motor (Fig. 12-10).

GENERAL MAINTENANCE

All castings should be checked approximately once a year for cracks, especially near bearing seats. Pressed-steel stands, cabinets, guards, and dust spouts should be inspected at the weld points. Guards in particular should be free from distortion or any other damage which might cause them to be ineffective. The mounting bolts, nuts, and lock washers used to secure either the unit to the stand or various major assemblies together should be checked for tightness. All fasteners, regardless of the type, used to hold guards in their proper place, should be checked. Any parts found to be too badly damaged should naturally be replaced.

In general any finishing machine is liable to shaft or bearing damage due to the fine dust created by the sanding or finishing operation. For this reason alone, dust collection is almost mandatory for long bearing life. The efficiency and correct operation of the dust collector should be checked, no matter what type is used: a full shop system, a separate external floor model, a separate (Fig. 12-11) attached unit, or a "built-in" collector.

FIG. 12-11

Belt Finishing Machine

The raising and tilting mechanism should be disassembled and cleaned in solvent. The ways, flats, keys, and other parts of the upper drum support assembly and the main casting also should be thoroughly cleaned. Any burrs or marks on these adjusting parts should be filed smooth (Fig. 12-12). If keys are used, they should be reassembled on the same side of the casting and in exactly the same position as when originally assembled. Because of abrasive grit and continuous adjustment, each key and its related slot have a different and definite wear pattern. It is vital to accurate belt tracking that this identical relationship be maintained. All parts should be lubricated with hard wax or a dry lubricant.

FIG. 12-12

Bearings should be checked by holding the idler drum and slowly turning the shaft by hand. If they are found to be satisfactory, the drum, shaft, bearing, and casting assembly should not be taken apart or disturbed, but merely cleaned. If the bearings, the drum, or the shaft must be replaced, an arbor press should be used to force the shaft out of the drum. The drum itself is often made in two matching halves (Fig. 12-13) and can be damaged by pounding or sudden shock.

Ball bearings which are sealed cannot be repaired but must be replaced if found defective. In most cases the bearings used in abrasive machines are double-sealed at least on one side with both plastic or felt and a metal seal (Fig. 12-14). Care should be taken when removing the defective bearing to note which side is different or double-sealed. The new or replacement bearing should be installed in exactly the same manner. In this specific application it is also advisable to buy the same brand or at least order by the manufacturer's part number.

FIG. 12-13

The drive or lower drum, drive shaft, and bearings should be checked, disassembled if necessary, and reassembled in the same general manner as the upper or idler drum assembly. In many cases washers or spacers of specific thickness are used; the faces on the two sides may be different. It is therefore a good idea to lay out the parts, on removal, in the correct order. The manufacturer's parts or instruction manual should be followed closely (Fig. 12-15).

Both the upper and lower drums are usually crowned to ensure correct and constant tracking of the abrasive belt. Because abrasive grit or dust slowly but surely finds its way behind the belt, the drums and the platen eventually show excessive wear. When the wear becomes critical on the idler and drive drum, the slight crown is literally ground flat. This condition must be corrected. A good temporary solution is to make about two revolutions of 1-in. masking tape around the center of the drum (Fig. 12-16). This raises the center of the drum, and the belt will usually track easily. A second solution is to file the drums, under power, carefully taking some metal from the edges and none from the center. This is rather easy on the drive or lower drum because it is powered. A ¼-in. strip of abrasive belt can be used to drive the upper or idler drum on one side of the face while filing the opposite side (Fig. 12-17); care should be taken to

SHIELD

FELT SEAL

DOUBLE SEAL

FIG. 12-14

6" ABRASIVE BELT FINISHING MACHINE

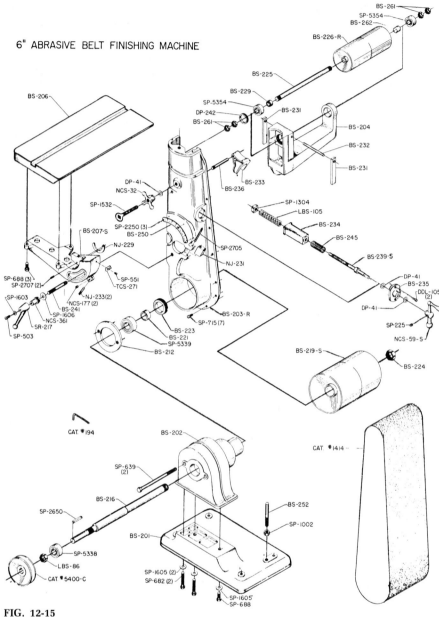

FIG. 12-16

FIG. 12-17

FIG. 12-15

remove as little material as possible because the drum or drum halves are hollow and quite thin. Naturally the final solution is to replace the drums. Because of the tilting and raising mechanism involved, the idler drum is the controlling factor in accurate tracking. For this reason also the required crown is more critical for the idler drum.

The platen (Fig. 12-18) should be flat and smooth because it both backs up the pressure of forcing the workpiece against the belt and controls a great deal of the accuracy built into the machine. Dirt and grit eventually get behind the belt and act like a grinding compound. The wear is much greater on the platen than on the drums because the movement of the workpiece increases the pressure at the table level. The platen is stationary, not moving or revolving with the belt.

The dirt and grit eventually cause or grind a convex indentation in the platen across its entire width, usually from the table level to 1 in. above. This is true regardless of the material used for the platen. Hard chrome or other platings are excellent, but even they only delay this action.

It is obvious that no matter how carefully the table is aligned perpendicularly to the platen or belt, accurate work cannot be done if the platen is curved. The workpiece will be finished with exactly the same curve or shape, not square or flat. This fault can be corrected quickly by increasing the table height. A piece of formica with any type of ¾- or 1-in. backing, clamped to the regular table, will usually raise the work enough to be backed up by a flat area on the platen (Fig. 12-19). This will eventually wear a new groove 1 in. higher and can eliminate the miter gage slot, but it is an instant and easy solution, although a temporary one. The worn platen can be removed and reground also, but this is more expensive and takes time. Since the relationship between the cast-iron webbing and the original thickness of the platen is engineered to eliminate warping, care should be taken to grind off as little of the original surface as possible. The final solution, of course, is to purchase a new platen from the manufacturer. Platens which are made of heavy-gage sheet metal cannot be reground in most cases.

The table, table trunnion, and mating base casting area, including positive stop assemblies, should be cleaned with solvent (Fig. 12-20). Burrs and nicks should be carefully filed off and the assemblies lubricated with hard wax or a dry lubricant.

On edge sanding machines (Fig. 12-21) formed platens are available, usually custom-made, to conform exactly to a specific piece of molding. These are easily replaceable (Fig. 12-22).

Setscrews should be checked for tightness in both the motor pulley and drive shaft pulley. All nuts and bolts holding the unit to its stand should be checked. Handle or control assemblies for tracking, unit tilting, table tilting, or tensioning should be cleaned and tightened.

Electrical controls and connections, including grounding, should be checked for safety and fast proper operation.

Stroke Sander

Maintenance suggestions for the stroke sander are similar to those for the belt sander or finishing machine. The crowned drive drum or idler drum

FIG. 12-18

FIG. 12-19

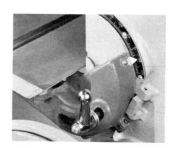
FIG. 12-20

FIG. 12-21

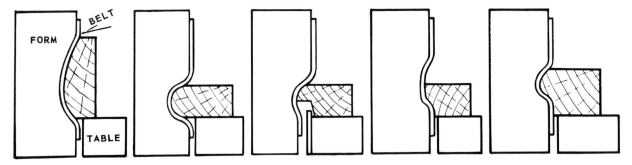

Special forms are easy to make. First roughed out on shaper or saw -- belt is then turned inside out, and moulding pressed against it to sand final pattern into form block. Cloth-backed belts are 2-1/4" x 80", light-weight, flexible, economical, come in grits from 1/2 to 6/0.

FIG. 12-22

assembly which contains the tracking mechanism should be disassembled and cleaned with solvent. Rough spots or burrs should be carefully filed off the parts lubricated, with a dry lubricant, and the assembly reassembled. The lift mechanism also should be cleaned, checked, and lubricated. Any looseness will seriously affect tracking of the belt (Fig. 12-23).

FIG. 12-23

The tracks or rails for the sliding table should be cleaned and possibly lubricated. If nylon or similar slides are used on the table, cleanliness is important and lubrication is often not necessary.

1″ Belt Finishing Sander/Grinder

This unit is similar to, but mechanically much simpler than, the belt finishing machine and the stroke sander. All parts and assemblies should be cleaned in solvent. Tracking is even more important, for these are three-wheel machines. The wheels or drums are one piece similar to a pulley but crowned and equipped with their own bearing (Fig. 12-24). The tension is not usually adjustable, but is spring-loaded. The spring

FIG. 12-24

should be checked to make sure the tension is adequate for belt tracking. If obviously weak, a new spring should be installed. A worn or damaged platen should be replaced.

Disk Finishing Machine

It is vital that the disk or revolving platen run true. The use of a dial indicator is not really necessary. A true-running disk will eliminate vibration, producing a more accurate finish and increasing bearing life. Safety is an important consideration because the distance between the table and the abrasive disk must be both close and constant.

If the disk is found to be wobbling or running out, it should be removed from the motor shaft and checked. The fit of the hub on the shaft and the setscrew should be checked for looseness. Also cracks can appear near the hub, and even separation of the hub and the disk can occur in some cases. Disks in this condition should be replaced. The motor shaft also should be checked for runout. The runout condition can often be corrected by replacing the motor bearings or actually straightening the shaft if it is really bent. It is best to have this done by a motor repair station.

FIG. 12-25

A slightly bent disk can be recut on the machine itself, using a jig and a carbide lathe tool bit. Extreme care should be taken when attempting this operation. One method is to C-clamp a toolholder and bit to the face of the miter gage (Fig. 12-25). In the 90-deg or perpendicular position the bit should extend beyond or past the face of the disk. When the head is turned, the depth of cut can be controlled. A series of very light cuts should be taken in a complete pass across the half of the disk which is rotating downward until the surface is flat, smooth, and true-running.

The thickness of the disk must be checked to make sure there will be enough material left after resurfacing. The fact that the disk is not parallel to the miter gage slot indicates a need for table or motor adjustment only, rather than correction for wobble or runout.

The trunnion assemblies should be cleaned with solvent and lubricated with hard wax or other dry lubricant. Positive stop parts

FIG. 12-26

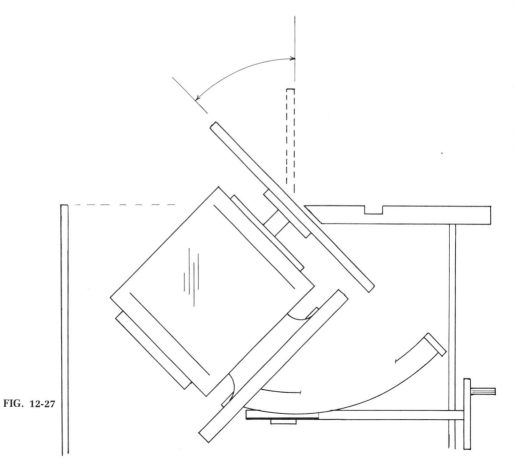

FIG. 12-27

should be cleaned and lubricated to make adjustments easy to accomplish. The trunnions could be a part of the table assembly on a tilting table unit (Fig. 12-26) or a part of the frame on a tilting disk and motor unit (Fig. 12-27). If the leading edge of the table is seriously damaged, it should be reground parallel to the table slot. Make sure to duplicate the original angle because clearance is necessary when the table is tilted. This is true of both belt and disk finding machines.

Spindle Sander

In most spindle sanders the drive gears, bearings, and drive assembly parts run in an oil reservoir, owing to the speed of the unique oscillating-rotating action (Fig. 12-28). The oil level should be maintained with the type of oil recommended by the manufacturer. Oil changes are not normally necessary even after years of use, unless the oil is definitely contaminated or extremely dirty.

Racks, table trunnions, worm gears, and other parts should be cleaned with solvent, and dry-lubricated positive stop assemblies should be cleaned, lubricated, and made easy to adjust. Table inserts, often the nesting type, should be clean and fit snugly into the proper opening.

FIG. 12-28

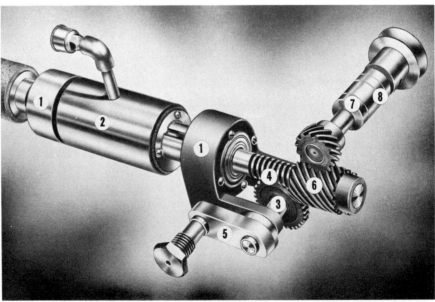

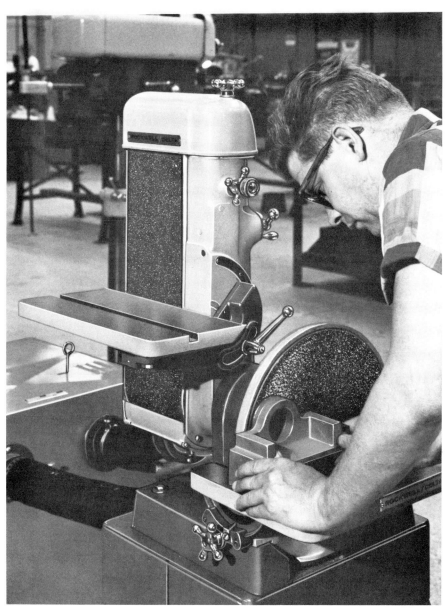

FIG. 12-29

Combination Belt and Disk Finishing Machine

The normal combination unit (Fig. 12-29) is simply two machines driven by one motor and controlled by one switch or starter. All maintenance suggestions for the separate machines apply to the combination. A dust collector unit is sometimes built into the stand or cabinet, and in this case the motor, usually of a higher horsepower than that of a separate machine, is driving three machines. Proper belt alignment and tension are vital because any loss of power will affect all the units involved.

If a cloth dust bag is used, it should be definitely separated from the drive mechanism or belts and pulleys.

ALIGNMENT

Belt Finishing Machine

The platen should be positioned about $1/64$ in. beyond the top of the crown of both drums. This can be checked by placing a straightedge vertically on the center of the platen (Fig. 12-30); this causes the belt to lie or move tight and flat on the platen. The top and bottom edges of the platen are usually chamfered but should be checked for any roughness, nicks, or burrs. These should be carefully filed off until smooth; otherwise belt ripping or excess wear may occur.

The abrasive belt should be the exact length recommended by the manufacturer. Even $1/4$ in. shorter or longer can cause tension or tracking problems. It is advisable to purchase the belt from the machine manufacturer or his distributor by catalog number.

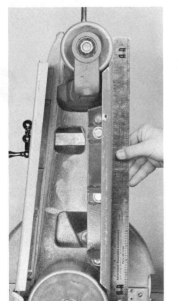

FIG. 12-30

As tension is slowly increased, it is advisable to rotate the belt by hand. In this way the idler drum tilting or tracking mechanism can be checked and adjusted. Tension should be increased until it is extremely difficult to put your fingers between the belt and the platen. There is no exact measurement for this adjustment, but the abrasive belt must lie flat and tight against the platen. It should not move left or right during any finishing operation.

After the abrasive belt is tight and tracks properly when rotating by hand, the final tracking check and adjustment must be made under power. One hand should be used to adjust the tracking mechanism and the other to snap the power quickly on and off. This gives the operator a chance to track the belt perfectly under power without cutting into the casting or the guard with the abrasive belt (Fig. 12-31). This adjustment should then be locked.

The miter gage slot in the table should be parallel to the abrasive belt or the platen. The table should also be positioned as close to the belt as possible. About $1/16$ in. will usually allow it to be tilted and returned to its 90-deg position without touching the belt. This closeness is obviously related to safety and accuracy in operation, giving full support to the workpiece, yet preventing foreign objects being caught between the table and the moving belt.

The table is usually supported by one trunnion bracket, and some adjustment is possible between the table and the bracket (Fig. 12-32). The hex head screws holding this assembly should be loosened to allow table movement. The table can then be held against the abrasive belt with a

FIG. 12-31

^{1}/₁₆-in. spacer between the belt and the table. Holding this firmly in while retightening the screws ensures both the correct spacing and a parallel miter gage slot. Two or three thicknesses of cardboard or show card stock make an excellent spacer or gage (Fig. 12-33).

By placing a square on the table with one leg against the abrasive belt, it is possible to adjust the positive stop for 90 deg. A piece of scrap lumber cut on a saw can be used as a gage for 45 deg. The pointer or the tilt scale should then be set to match these settings (Fig. 12-34).

FIG. 12-32

Most vertical belt finishing units can be used also in a horizontal or tilted position (Fig. 12-35). It is vital to recheck the belt tracking each time the main assembly is moved or tilted. Quite often the belt will not track exactly as it did when adjusted in the vertical position, but will lead off to the right or left, damaging the main casting or the guard.

This procedure is exactly the same for a belt finishing machine which is part of a combination unit. All belts and pulleys should be in alignment and all setscrews tight.

On special-purpose units the manufacturer's recommendations should be followed although the same general principles apply.

Stroke Sander

Because of the belt length tracking is often more difficult than on smaller units, but the adjustments and the procedures are similar. The tension must be reduced to some extent because the method of operation is quite different and does not require the belt to be held snugly to a permanent platen. Tracking problems seem to be directly related to the amount of crown on the drums. Many new units have high-crowned drums that al-

FIG. 12-33

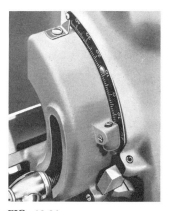

FIG. 12-34

FIG. 12-35

most eliminate this problem. They are almost self-tracking. On older units the idler drum can be recrowned, replaced, or even taped as an emergency solution.

1″ Belt Finishing Sander/Grinder

All the adjustments found on the larger machines are usually found also on the 1-in. belt units. The main difference is in the simplicity or lack of sophistication in the mechanical parts or mechanisms. The tension is normally spring-loaded and not adjustable. Either the spring is adequate or it must be replaced. Tension is not nearly as great or as important on the 1-in. unit.

Tilting of the main idler drum or wheel is done by tilting the whole shaft. This is mechanically accomplished by loosening and tightening two opposing cap screws at the inboard end of the shaft (Fig. 12-36). Adjustment should be made by first moving the belt by hand and finally under power, as with all belt finishing units. Tracking should be rechecked when changing the position of the belts from one pulley or drum arrangement to another.

FIG. 12-36

The platen should be adjusted parallel to the belt, and the belt should ride it snugly during operation. The platen is usually sheet metal, not cast iron, and can literally be bent or twisted to the proper position if other adjustment is impossible (Fig. 12-37). The table should be aligned at 90 deg to the belt, using a square on the table with one leg extending up the belt. The trunnion mechanism is usually a very simple bracket with no positive stops or scale.

Disk Finishing Machine

The disk should be positioned about 1/16 or 3/32 in. from the table. In the case of individual units with tilting tables and on tilting disk machines, this is done by moving the motor. With the four bolts loosened, a piece of stock of the proper or desired thickness can be placed between the disk and the table as a gage. A sanding disk should be installed on the machine when this adjustment is made. Unless the edge of the table is extremely worn, this will also ensure that the miter gage slot is parallel to the disk. The motor mounting bolts should be firmly tightened after this adjustment is made.

FIG. 12-37

The table can be adjusted at 90 deg to the disk, using a square. The positive stop should be set, and either the scale or the pointer adjusted to read 0 deg (Fig. 12-38).

If the belt finishing machine is a part of a combination unit, the table or trunnion assembly must be moved to obtain proper alignment. The holes in the table are usually oversized to allow for this slight adjustment. If not, they can be carefully enlarged with a file.

The disk can be adjusted on the shaft to some extent, but it is recommended that the disk be tightened on the shaft as far back as possible. Any adjustment for alignment should be made by moving the motor or the table.

The upper guard is a separate part and can usually be tilted. It should be adjusted so that it does not project beyond the face of the disk and yet covers the edge (Fig. 12-39).

The miter gage used on either the belt or disk finishing unit can be adjusted easily by using a try square. With the head of the square held against the miter gage and the leg extending along the flat surface of the belt or disk, a true 90-deg adjustment is possible. A bevel gage can be used to set the 45-deg stops, or an accurate 45-deg gage of scrap wood can be cut on the saw. It is imperative that the table or the miter gage slot be first aligned parallel with the disk or belt; otherwise heeling will occur.

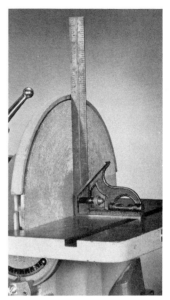

FIG. 12-38

Spindle Sander

As in the case of all belt-driven units, it is important that proper pulley alignment be checked. Both pulleys should be positioned as close to the base of the shaft as possible. This could require moving the motor to avoid positioning the motor pulley at the end of the shaft, just to maintain alignment.

The table should be adjusted 90 deg to the spindle by placing the head of a try square on the table with the leg against the spindle (Fig. 12-40). If a limiting or positive stop is provided, it should be locked. The tilt scale or pointer can now be set to read accurately.

Since the table tilts from front to rear, any lack of squareness with the spindle as checked from either side must be corrected by raising or lowering one of the trunnion assemblies. If this is not possible, shims must be inserted between the table and one of the trunnions.

FIG. 12-39

General

All guards, cast iron or sheet steel, should be properly installed and adjusted to guard as intended by the manufacturer. The manual supplied with each individual machine is the best guide. All exposed cast-iron surfaces should be coated with hard wax for ease of operation and as a rust preventive. Waxing the entire machine not only improves and protects the appearance, but also makes the unit easier to clean.

FIG. 12-40

CHAPTER THIRTEEN
The Jointer

FIG. 13-1

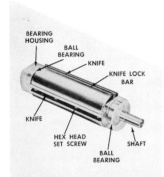

BEARING
HOUSING
BALL
BEARING
KNIFE
KNIFE LOCK
BAR
KNIFE
HEX HEAD
SET SCREW
SHAFT
BALL
BEARING

3-KNIFE CUTTERHEAD

FIG. 13-2

The jointer is used primarily to dress lumber to an exact size. The name jointer comes from the use of two straight and square edges in order to ensure a good glue joint. This machine will surface lumber accurately and can be used to remove warp, wind, or twist (Fig. 13-1). Rabbeting, tapering, beveling, stop beveling, chamfering, and stop chamfering can be done on the jointer.

There are various types and sizes, but basically a jointer consists of a front infeed and rear outfeed table, a cutterhead, and a fence. In most cases the tables, base, and fence are made of seasoned, ribbed, and machined cast iron. The front or infeed table is always adjustable to control the depth of cut. The rear table may be adjustable or actually can be an integral part of the base casting. In the latter case the head itself will be vertically adjustable. Most jointers found in school shops, cabinet shops, and home shops have a three-knife cutterhead (Fig. 13-2).

The fence may be either end- or center-mounted, depending on the manufacturer or the size of the unit, but in both cases it performs the same function.

The typical jointer (Fig. 13-3) found in the school, cabinet, or home shop is usually a 4-, 6-, or 8-in. unit. The size is designated by the length of the knives, which also determines the maximum capacity for surfacing material.

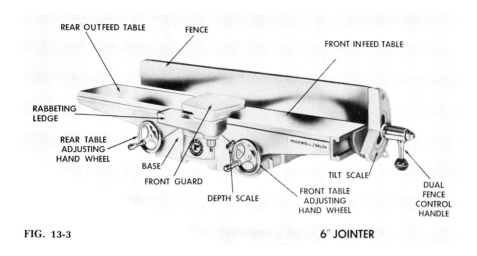

REAR OUTFEED TABLE   FENCE

FRONT INFEED TABLE

RABBETING LEDGE

REAR TABLE ADJUSTING HAND WHEEL

BASE

FRONT GUARD

DEPTH SCALE

FRONT TABLE ADJUSTING HAND WHEEL

TILT SCALE

DUAL FENCE CONTROL HANDLE

FIG. 13-3   6″ JOINTER

GENERAL MAINTENANCE

A periodic check should be made for cracks in all cast-iron parts. The webbing should be carefully inspected for any cracking or separation that could indicate serious table warpage. This condition is rather rare and usually indicates that in manufacturing, a green casting, rather than an aged or normalized one, was used. There is no real solution to this problem except replacement of the defective table and complete regrinding.

Broken castings, either front infeed table, rear outfeed table, or the base, cannot be individually replaced in the field with any guarantee of accuracy. Most manufacturers will require that the original castings be returned to their plant. A new casting is then assembled to complete the unit, and the entire machine literally put back into the production line. The two tables are then reground, with the base casting used as fixture. This assures original accuracy and guarantees table alignment.

The stand or cabinet should be checked for cracks in cast iron, open weld joints, or loose fasteners. The fence should be removed and the unit itself removed from the stand. The jointer should be placed face or table side down on a workbench and completely disassembled.

It is wise to note the position of the gibs when removing the tables and to keep the infeed gib with the infeed table and the outfeed gib with the outfeed table. The outside flats of the gib are usually easily discernible by the indentations matching the gib screw positions (Fig. 13-4). In many cases the indentations are drilled into the gib prior to assembly. This tends to hold the gib in its proper position when moving the jointer table. Otherwise it could slowly shift its position over a period of time. If new gibs are to be installed, they should be purchased from the

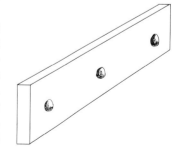

FIG. 13-4

manufacturer or should be carefully indented with a drill point at each screw position.

Loosening the gib screws and removing the gibs first will usually make removal of the adjusting mechanism easier, owing to the allowable table movement in all directions. In most cases the tables will have to be removed by sliding them along the complete dovetail, not by merely lifting straight up.

All table adjusting mechanisms should be removed and cleaned with solvent; these include handwheels or cranks, shafts, bushings, threaded shafts, washers, pins, and table screw nuts. The jointer tables can then be completely removed (Fig. 13-5). All dovetail ways on both the base and the tables should be cleaned with solvent. Any burrs or nicks should be carefully filed off. Steel wool is usually necessary to remove the hard deposits of pitch, gum, dirt, and oil.

The base dovetail is usually all one continuous track, but the table dovetail has a pad at the top and bottom of the track.

In most cases also the head must be removed from the unit. In many jointers with two movable tables, the head is easily removed by loosening

FIG. 13-5

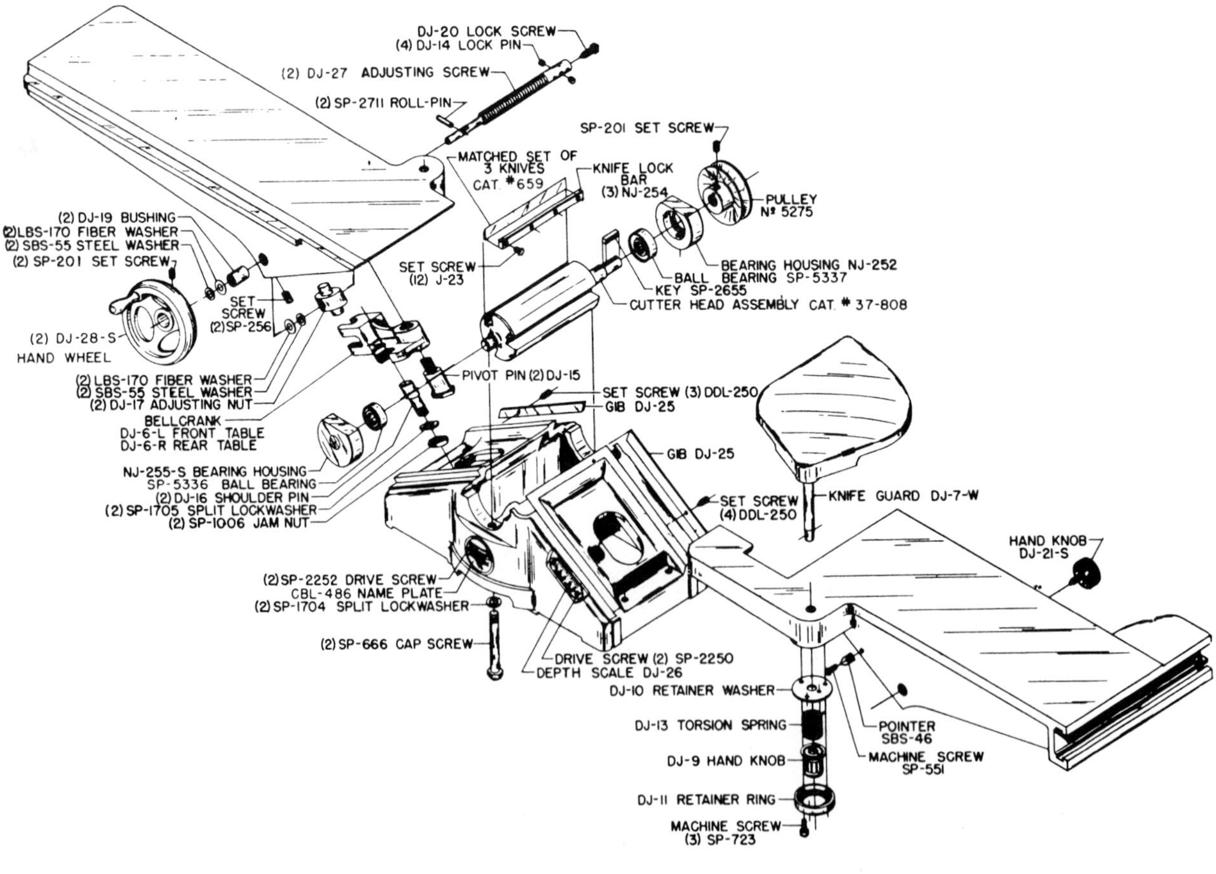

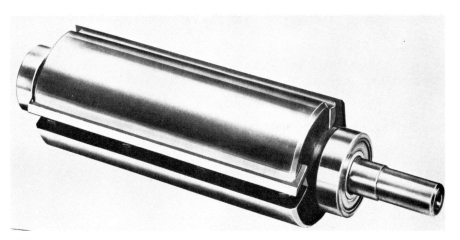

FIG. 13-6

the hollow head cap screws under each pillow block. This type has no alignment parts and can be lifted straight out, up or down, after the screws are removed. Care should be taken to hold each pillow block on its own end of the head. Because the block or the bearing can be damaged by falling off, they should be reassembled in the same relative positions, left or right. In most cases they are interchangeable as made by the manufacturer and even have the same part number, but in an older machine they are "worn in" and should not be switched.

The jointer head should be removed carefully and never held vertically by hand if the blades are in the head. It is wise to wrap a rag around the entire assembly when lifting it out of the jointer.

The pillow blocks, including the bearings, should be removed, and the complete head cleaned with solvent (Fig. 13-6). Most dirt and foreign material can be removed with a brush from the lock bar, setscrews, or other holding devices. Unless the knives are to be replaced, it is not necessary to remove them just to clean the head. The inner face of the bearing, the face and bottom of the pillow block, and the shaft ends should be cleaned. If new bearings are to be installed, the entire inside of the pillow block should be cleaned with solvent.

Hard wax or other dry lubricant should be used on all disassembled parts, and the jointer should be reassembled. The gibs can be moved slightly while turning in one screw until the indentation is found; then all screws can be tightened snugly. Gibs and dovetails should receive an extra coating of dry lubricant.

The jointer should now be placed back on the stand or cabinet, bolted tight, and the V-belt installed or the direct-drive motor should be reconnected. If the rear table is cast as part of the base, care should be taken to reassemble any head-raising mechanism exactly as it was removed.

All fence holding and adjusting parts, either center- or end-mounted, should be cleaned with solvent and dry-lubricated, preferably with hard wax (Fig. 13-7). The fence should then be mounted and tightened.

Pulley alignment and belt tension should be checked for correctness.

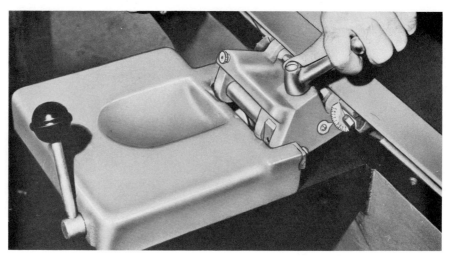

FIG. 13-7

ALIGNMENT

Most problems of table alignment are caused by dirt in the dovetail ways or loose gibs and setscrews. Squirting oil into the top of the ways will of course make the tables move more easily but it also enables dirt and dust to build up. This dirt, only a few thousandths of an inch in thickness, causes the table ends to drop $1/16$ in. or more. Even tightening the gib screws will not correct this condition (Fig. 13-8).

If the ways are clean, and dry-lubricated, the gib screws should be adjusted as tight as possible, yet allowing for table adjustment. After all gib screws are snug enough and the gib is in its proper position, the top gib screw should be tightened until the table cannot be moved. While you continually attempt to move the table up and down with the handwheel or crank handle, this top screw should slowly be backed off until the cor-

FIG. 13-8

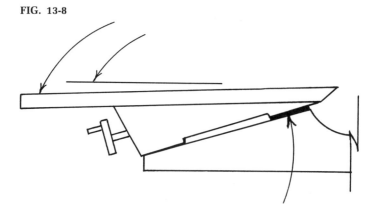

rect feel is obtained and the table will move (Fig. 13-9). The same method of locking the table, then backing off the setscrew, should be used to adjust both table gibs, starting at the top and working screw by screw down the length of the dovetail way.

Because of the method of manufacturing, perfect table alignment in the same plane is practically a certainty.

Very possibly the best way to be certain that the knives are set at the correct (equal) height in relation to the head is to have the knives sharpened in the head. This is no doubt the easiest way and can be done in the jointer with a sharpening attachment. It can be done also by removing the head and sharpening the knives in a tool and cutter grinder. With either method the head itself is used as a fixture, guaranteeing height accuracy.

FIG. 13-9

Depending upon size of the jointer and the manufacturer's choice of engineering, there are two major ways to make this critical height adjustment a little easier. One is by spring-loading the knives. This is usually done by drilling shallow holes in the head directly under each end of the knives. The holes act as seats or retainers for the springs (Fig. 13-10). This machining can be made in the field if the depth of the drilled holes is accurately controlled. They should all be exactly the same depth and in

FIG. 13-10

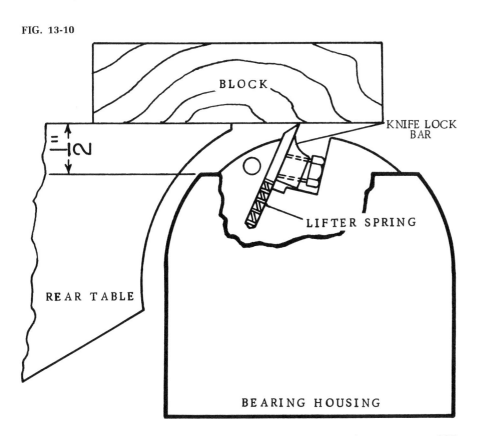

167

exactly the same places, relative to each knife, in order to maintain perfect head balance. The machining should be done on a drill press or even a vertical milling machine, using a fixture to hold and position the head accurately.

The other method is to supply raising screws at each end of each knife. These screws usually have an extended shoulder, which fits into a slot in the knife, or are located partially under the knife. By raising or lowering the screw, the knife is easily positioned.

If the knives are not ground in the head or are not spring-loaded, or if raising screws are not incorporated in the head, the adjustment is much more difficult. There are probably as many methods or systems for accomplishing this as there are operators, but in all cases the rear table is used as the basic reference point.

The rear table should be locked about $1/32$ in. from its top position, or even in the highest position; dropping down this slight amount may decrease the maximum depth of cut, but it is usually a more accurate position for knife adjustment. Each knife must be raised or adjusted until its arc is exactly the same as the outfeed table height. This can be checked by slowly rotating the head back and forth while holding a straightedge or piece of hardwood on the rear table extending over the knife area (Fig. 13-11). When each end of the knife just touches the gage, it should be tightened in the head.

If the head can be positioned with a jig in the same relative position for each knife, the process is simplified. Edge distance can be set for accurate rabbeting. This is often done by inserting clips in symmetrically located holes drilled in the end or side of the head (Fig. 13-12). With the head locked, the knives can now be moved to meet the gage. A magnet can be used to pull the loose knife up to its proper height if the head is not spring-loaded or supplied with raising screws.

If the wooden gage is cut out to expose the center of the knife (Fig. 13-13a), the center locking nuts can be tightened enough to hold the knife in position. After the gage is slid back on the rear table, the locknuts should be tightened at random, e.g., 1, 3, 5, 2, 4 or in a similar system, depending upon the number of locknuts. This pattern should be repeated, tightening a little more each time, until the knife is locked in the head. The entire process is then repeated for each knife.

It is important not to tighten each end first or to progress in order from one end to the other. A jointer knife as short as 4 in. can be noticeably bowed if this is done; an 8- or 12-in. jointer knife can be arced high enough to measure with ease.

When the knives are raised and tightened, care should be taken to see that they are even at the outboard edge. This is necessary for the rabbeting operation; otherwise the rabbet will be cut with only one or two knives, and a rough corner will result.

There are many commercial products, gages, magnets, and jigs available from manufacturers, designed to help solve this difficult knife adjusting problem (Fig. 13-13b).

FIG. 13-11

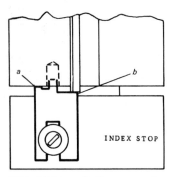

FIG. 13-12 *a* Knife gage positioned in head, *b* knife positioned flush with gage.

FIG. 13-13*a*

FIG. 13-13*b*

The fence, which rides on the front or infeed table and clears the outfeed table, should be squared with the infeed table. This can easily be done by placing a try square on the front table with the blade extending up the fence surface (Fig. 13-14). The fence should now be adjusted to its square or 90-deg position. The 45-deg inboard tilt position can be adjusted to match a 45-deg try square head. A bevel square can be set at 135 deg and the fence set to match. The adjustment of a center-mounted fence is slightly different from that of an end-mounted fence. The manufacturer's instructions should be followed in adjusting the positive stop positions (Fig. 13-15).

FIG. 13-14

Test for Accuracy

Guards should be checked to make sure they cover the cutterhead properly. The so-called pork chop type (Fig. 13-16) should ride on the infeed table and never, regardless of the table adjustment or fence position, touch the knives. The spring should be adjusted for adequate re-

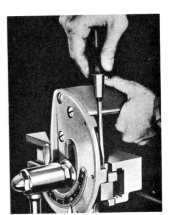

FIG. 13-15

FIG. 13-16

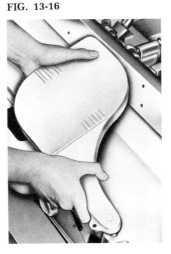

FIG. 13-17

turn. The internal clock spring type can be adjusted by turning the knurled knob which is a part of the table assembly with the guard removed. The guard can then be reinserted, with the split shaft slipped over the spring pin (Fig. 13-17). External spring assemblies (Fig. 13-18) should be repositioned, even by drilling a new hole in the table casting, or replaced if too weak to be effective. The rear guard also should be checked on jointers with an end-mounted fence. The center-mounted fence assembly adequately guards the exposed rear areas when properly installed.

Extended arm-type guards (Fig. 13-19) should be checked for smooth operation, all moving parts lubricated with a dry lubricant, and spring tension adjusted. All guard parts should slide smoothly against the jointer table and the material being cut. Nicks and burrs should be carefully filed smooth.

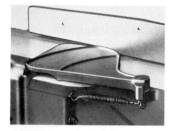

FIG. 13-18

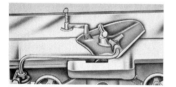

FIG. 13-19

Straightedges, dial indicators, surface gages, and other such precision equipment are not necessary, required, or even recommended for a jointer accuracy check. There are many methods which can be used, but an actual cut is undoubtedly the best check. We are more interested in an accurate cut—smooth, straight, and square—than in merely checking the unit itself. The basic jointer problem and complaint, hanging tables, is almost always eliminated by proper cleaning and gib adjustment.

The rear table should be lowered at least ⅛ in. A 1- by 4-in. board as long as both tables should be started through the jointer, with about 1/16-in. depth of cut. It should be held firmly against the fence and against the infeed table only. When the wood extends well over the rear table, possibly three-fourths of the way, it should be held in that position and the unit shut off (Fig. 13-20). The outfeed table should now be raised to match the

FIG. 13-20

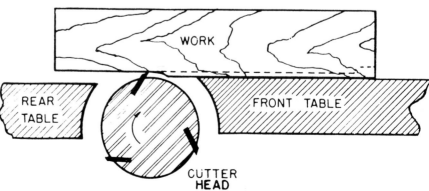

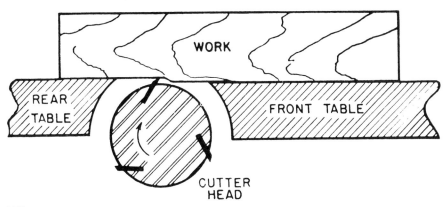

FIG. 13-21

cut exactly (Fig. 13-21). This method of positioning the arc of the knives and the rear table in the same plane is easy and extremely accurate.

The squareness of the wood should also be checked and the fence readjusted if necessary.

The tables and fence should be coated with hard wax. The scale or the pointer should be moved to indicate the depth of cut accurately.

CHAPTER FOURTEEN
The Planer

Most thickness planers (Fig. 14-1) found in cabinet shops and school woodshops are really single surfacers. They will plane to a controlled thickness one side of the material at one time. The material is usually wood, but it could be hard rubber, plastic, or other similar and rather soft material.

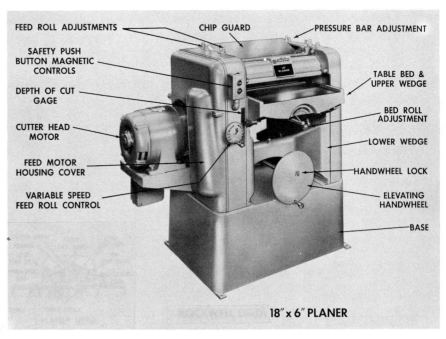

FEED ROLL ADJUSTMENTS — — CHIP GUARD — PRESSURE BAR ADJUSTMENT
SAFETY PUSH BUTTON MAGNETIC CONTROLS
DEPTH OF CUT GAGE
CUTTER HEAD MOTOR
FEED MOTOR HOUSING COVER
VARIABLE SPEED FEED ROLL CONTROL

TABLE BED & UPPER WEDGE
BED ROLL ADJUSTMENT
LOWER WEDGE
HANDWHEEL LOCK
ELEVATING HANDWHEEL
BASE

18" x 6" PLANER

FIG. 14-1

The planer will not remove warp, wind, or twist from a board. This work must be done on a jointer. The planer will reduce the thickness and plane smooth, but the warp or twist will remain.

Planers are usually described by two dimensions: the maximum width and maximum height or depth of material which can be planed; for instance, a 13″ × 5″ or an 18″ × 6″ planer. Often the maximum width designation is used alone, e.g., 13″, 18″, 24″, and 36″. Most school or cabinet shop planers are in this general size range (Fig. 14-2).

There are many types of rolls, drives, and adjustments, but most planers are classified, after the size designation, as either of two major types of basic construction:

1. SCREW BED CONSTRUCTION
This indicates that the table is raised or lowered usually with twin screws which turn simultaneously with one control (Fig. 14-3).

2. WEDGE BED CONSTRUCTION
This indicates that the wedge-shaped bed is supported by a reverse wedge which, when moved in or out, raises or lowers the table (Fig. 14-4).

FIG. 14-2

FIG. 14-3

FIG. 14-4

173

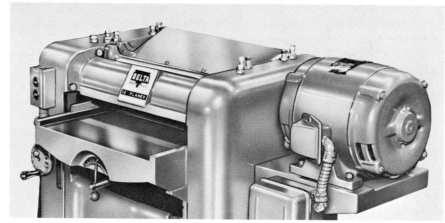

FIG. 14-5

FIG. 14-6

FIG. 14-7

Both types are common.

Planers are designated also as direct-drive (Fig. 14-5) or belt-drive (Fig. 14-6) units. In some small planers the same motor is used through a gear, chain, or belt system, to drive both the cutterhead and the feed rolls (Fig. 14-7). In larger units separate motors are used (Fig. 14-8). Types of infeed rolls vary greatly, depending on the manufacturer, the purpose, the size of the machine, and the cost, but they can usually be designated as sectional (Fig. 14-9) or solid (one piece) (Fig. 14-10). The latter is usually also serrated. The outfeed roll is normally smooth and solid.

By rule of thumb a planer is not a power tool, but in every sense a machine tool. It can easily produce work accurate to thousandths of an inch. Therefore adjustments, preventive maintenance, and alignment procedures must be approached with this fact in mind.

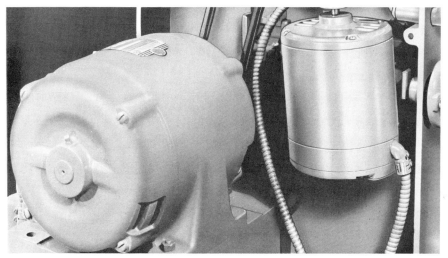

FIG. 14-8

FIG. 14-9 Sectional top infeed roll showing construction and two of the fluted sections and springs.

FIG. 14-10

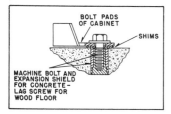

FIG. 14-11

GENERAL MAINTENANCE

Castings should be checked closely for cracks, nicks, or burrs at least once a year. Even a slight defect can seriously affect the performance and accuracy of the planer. Lag screws or bolts should be checked for tightness or breakage. Shims between the base and the floor should be firmly in place because the machine must be perfectly level (Fig. 14-11).

All internal holding parts or structural supports such as the rods should be tight. Feed roller tensioning springs should be checked for breakage and proper operation (Fig. 14-12). Belts should be checked for wear and proper tension. Pulleys or sheaves must be checked for alignment on all drive systems. Worn belts or sheaves should be replaced, following the manufacturer's recommendations. Because of the high torque transmission necessary for a positive drive, many planers use a matched set of drive belts, or a belt with a wire or steel core. It is imperative to duplicate this system exactly.

The chip guard and all other easily removable guards or side plates should be taken off the machine and the entire unit thoroughly cleaned (Fig. 14-13a,b). The cutterhead, infeed and outfeed rolls, table rolls, and table should be washed with solvent to remove dirt, pitch, and gum. A brush or even a sharp stick covered with a solvent-soaked rag can be used safely to clean the head and serrations on the infeed roll. Steel wool is often necessary. The lower edge of the chip breaker and pressure bar should be checked for straightness and smoothness.

FIG. 14-12

FIG. 14-13*a*

The table rollers and even the pillow blocks supporting the rollers should be removed and cleaned (Fig. 14-14). The pillow block adjusting and support areas in the table must be free from chips, gum, and pitch.

All exposed cast-iron parts and steel rollers can be given a good coat of hard wax as a lubricant and rust preventive. Wax or other dry

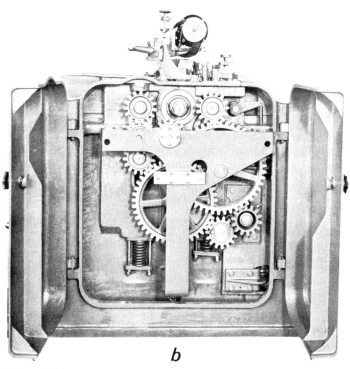

b

FIG. 14-13*b*

FIG. 14-14

FIG. 14-15

lubricant will make most adjustments work more smoothly and decrease the buildup of dust and dirt. Sealed ball bearings, used for most cutterheads, of course need no lubrication. Wax or a dry lubricant is good also for elevating screws, gib ways, and even table roll bearing surfaces. Gear oil or grease, as recommended by the manufacturer, must be used for gearboxes. The level should be checked periodically and the oil or grease drained and replaced about once a year if the planer is used constantly (Fig. 14-15). In a school shop this might indicate that the oil should be changed every three years under normal use.

All electrical connections, in many cases including wiring to more than one motor from one or more control stations, should be checked for tightness and proper insulation. The controls should be checked for fast positive action.

ALIGNMENT

With many machines, particularly woodworking units, it is possible to begin checking the alignment if the unit is steady enough not to rock on its base or stand. The planer adjustments, being more critical, require that

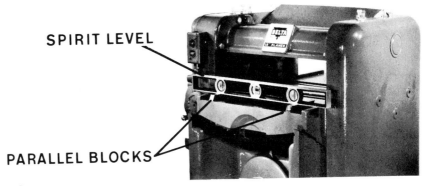

SPIRIT LEVEL

PARALLEL BLOCKS

FIG. 14-16

the machine be bolted or lagged to the floor. The floor should be concrete or extremely solid to prevent rocking or vibration.

After the machine has been snugly lagged to the floor, a spirit level should be placed across the front or infeed table. The table surface itself must be used as the reference area even if parallel blocks are needed to raise the level above the table shoulders or edges. This is necessary because the shoulders, whether cast with the table or bolted on, are not necessarily the same height and often are not even machined. All other precision adjustments will be affected by any twisting in the major frame or assembly. Therefore it is vital that the planer be leveled, just like any machine tool (Fig. 14-16). Hardwood wedges can be used as shims, and any excess shim stock can be cut off. This makes it easy to watch the level while tapping the wedge slowly under the machine. Metal shim stock or various commercial leveling devices designed specifically for this purpose can be used. The results are important, not the method. While the lag screws or bolts are being tightened firmly, watch the level and compensate with shim stock for any change in reading.

Every working, turning, sliding, or adjustable part of the machine must be immaculate. For instance, it would be ridiculous to attempt adjusting the table rolls in thousandths of an inch when they are covered with pitch and gum as thick as $1/64$ in.

The knives should be adjusted in the head in strict accordance with the manufacturer's directions or recommendations. Most planer heads have raising screws or lifters built in, making the job a little easier. The same general suggestions which apply to the jointer cutterhead and knife adjustments apply to the planer head. (See Chap. 13, "The Jointer," p. 168.) The major difference is the point or area of reference for alignment. The rear table is used for the jointer, but the cutterhead itself is used for the planer. In most cases the manufacturer supplies a knife gage with the machine as standard equipment (Fig. 14-17). The distance the knives extend out of the head is a controlled and vital adjustment. The diameter of the cutting circle is directly related to the speed. The rake angle of the

FIG. 14-17

knives and the proper or even possible adjustment of the chip breaker, pressure bar, and infeed and outfeed rolls are also related.

If the knives are ground or jointed while locked in the head of a jointer, it is a simple matter to match the rear table to the arc of the reground knives. When the knives are ground or jointed in the head of a planer, the knives must be loosened, raised to match the knife gage, and retightened. This is necessary if a sharpening attachment (Fig. 14-18) was used directly mounted to the machine, or even if the head was removed (Fig. 14-19) and the sharpening done on a tool and cutter grinder.

If only one spot on the blades is nicked, a temporary solution is to move one knife slightly to the left or right. This can be done on a jointer

FIG. 14-18

FIG. 14-19

also except that the knife should be moved to the rear of the unit away from the rabbeting ledge. This trick of not removing or regrinding all three knives will usually produce a smooth cut, saving both time and knife stock.

The planer table must now be aligned exactly parallel to the knives or to the cutterhead. This can be done by making a gage block out of hardwood (Fig. 14-20). The gage can then be used to check the distance from the table to the head or knives at the extreme right and left of the table surface (Fig. 14-21). This measurement or check can be made also with two boards of the same width and with parallel edges. The table rolls must be below the table surface. The manufacturer's directions should be followed to adjust the table if it is not parallel to the head. On a screw bed unit there is usually an adjustable collar at the top of the screw; this can be raised or lowered independently of the screw. On a wedge bed unit the actual bed and upper wedge are usually separate castings and the table can be adjusted independently (Fig. 14-22).

If the table is not moved up or down after being adjusted parallel to the knives, and if the arc of knives was used as the reference point, the same gage or boards can be used to check the pressure bar. This part of the planer is often spring-loaded or mounted with rubber gaskets that allow it to move or give slightly. Its purpose is to hold the wood or stock down as it comes from the cutterhead, preventing vibration or chatter. It must be adjusted tangent to the cutting arc and parallel to the knives or the table (Fig. 14-23a). If the stock will not feed or stops suddenly, the pressure bar is probably too low (Fig. 14-23b). If the stock is rough and has chatter marks, the pressure is too high (Fig. 14-24). Misalignment of even a few thousandths of an inch will cause these problems.

The chip breaker is self-adjusting and usually requires no adjustment. It is normally weighted to provide a uniform light drag as the material is fed through the machine. It must have a smooth edge, be tangent to the cutting arc, and be parallel to the knives or the table. Nicks or rough

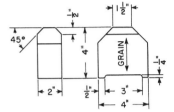

FIG. 14-20

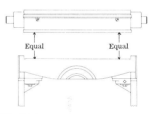

FIG. 14-21

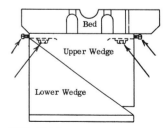

FIG. 14-22

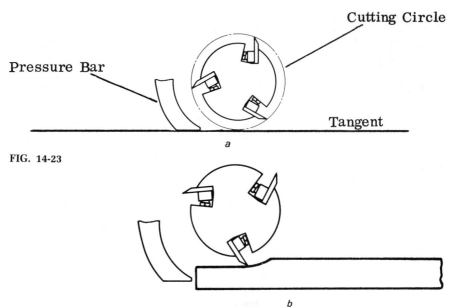

Cutting Circle

Pressure Bar

Tangent

a

FIG. 14-23

FIG. 14-24

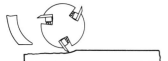

b

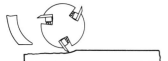

FIG. 14-25

spots on the edge should be lightly touched off with a file. If the entire casting is warped, it must be remachined or replaced. The purpose of the chip breaker is to break or curl the chip as it is cut by the knives and prevent the cut from splitting back into the stock (Fig. 14-25).

Both the pressure bar and the chip breaker are positioned very close to the cutting circle and often move or are adjusted around a larger concentric circle, rather than actually moving straight up and down. This in itself indicates the importance of proper knife height, in addition to the exact setting of the pressure bar.

Most outfeed rolls are smooth; infeed rolls are corrugated or serrated and often sectional. Also available are special infeed rolls made of hard rubber or other materials. These rolls are powered and turn at exactly the same speed, even though the speed or rate of feed may be variable. They are often powered by a separate motor and drive (Fig. 14-26) in larger planers.

Both rolls should be adjusted parallel to the table about $1/32$ in. lower than the arc of the knives (Fig. 14-27). The position can be checked with the same homemade gage if the table is lowered $1/32$ in. or slightly less from its original gaging position. Each roll should then be checked and adjusted at each end in relation to the table. Note that the center of the base of the gage was cut out in order to span the gap in the table and the table roller (Fig. 14-28).

In some planers the pillow blocks supporting the upper rolls actually bottom out and are not really adjustable. The distance is preset in relation to the correct arc of the knives. This is one more reason to set the

FIG. 14-26

Cutting Circle

Smooth outfeed roll

Corrugated infeed roll

Feed rolls set 1/32" below cutting circle

FIG. 14-27

knives accurately with the gage supplied by the manufacturer. If the rolls
are not adjustable, the spring tension can usually be controlled. The least
possible tension which will still feed the material through the machine is
a good rule of thumb. Also it is more important to have the tension on the
right and left side equal than to have any specific amount of pressure;
otherwise the material or stock will have a tendency to turn as it moves
through the planer. Without actually measuring the pressure with instruments, equal pressure can be easily judged by inserting a 4-ft two-by-
four in the planer and actually lifting the roller and spring on one side

FIG. 14-28

FIG. 14-29

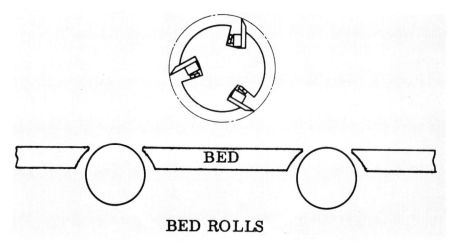

BED ROLLS

FIG. 14-30

(Fig. 14-29). The right and left sides can be compared, and also the outfeed roller spring tension can be compared with the infeed roller spring tension.

The table rolls in small planers (Fig. 14-30) must usually be adjusted manually at each end of the rollers, depending upon the height desired. This height is often indicated as low for smooth stock, medium for normal or average work, and high for rough lumber; .002 in. might be considered low, .005 in. medium, and .010 in. high, although each manufacturer, and for that matter each operator, has his own opinion on the correct setting.

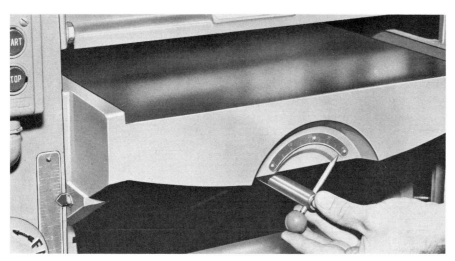

FIG. 14-31

Even in larger planers, where the bed roll height is controlled by an external lever, with a scale indicating the height, the original setting must be made at each end of each roll (Fig. 14-31). This is to ensure that the roll is not only the correct height but also parallel to the table surface or bed.

There are many commercial gages, supplied or sold by the original equipment manufacturer and also by other companies. Dial indicators also can be used, but they are not really necessary. By laying a straight-edge or even the blade from a try square across the rollers (Fig. 14-32), the height can be checked with a feeler gage, or even with various thicknesses of paper. The same end of both bed rolls can be checked in this manner. Be sure to adjust both sides with the same system to assure the same height. If the planer has an exterior control lever and scale, the pointer should be set at a specific height; then the rolls are adjusted with a feeler gage to match the indicator.

FIG. 14-32

Most bed roll adjustments under the pillow blocks have both an adjustment screw and a locking nut. Different types and styles of mechanical adjustment systems are used by various manufacturers, but they are all intended to accomplish the same purpose. The manual supplied with the unit is the best guide.

The best gage or the best test of any machine adjustment is to check the work it produces. The depth of cut scale can be set accurately by adjusting it to match the thickness of a finished piece.

All guards should be in operating order and properly installed. If an exhaust hood is attached, it should not interfere with the normal operation of the planer, particularly the upper part of the pressure bar or chip breaker.

The accompanying troubleshooting chart (Fig. 14-33) applies to planers of any size, even those larger than normally found in a school or cabinet shop; it could be extremely valuable in diagnosing problems.

FIG. 14-33

TROUBLESHOOTING IN PLANING

IF CLIP or SNIPE APPEARS AT BEGINNING OF BOARD:

1. Pressure bar may be set too low.
2. Chipbreaker may be set too high.
3. Upper infeed sectional roll may be set too high.
4. Lower infeed roll may be set too high.
5. Spring tension may be too light on pressure bar.

IF CLIP OR SNIPE APPEARS ON END OF LUMBER:

1. Pressure bar may be set too high—not even with cutting circle.
2. Lower outfeed roll may be set too high.
3. Upper outfeed roll may be set too low.
4. Lumber may not be butted.
5. Grain may be running against knives.

IF KNIVES TEAR OUT LUMBER:

1. Feed may be too fast.
2. Joint on knives may be too heavy.
3. Moisture content may be too high.
4. Head may be running too slowly.
5. Cut may be too heavy.
6. Cutting angle may be too large.
7. Grain may be running against knives.

IF KNIVES RAISE THE GRAIN:

1. Joint may be too heavy—a light joint is the best.
2. Feed may be too fast.
3. Cutting angle may be too large.
4. Head may be running too slowly.
5. Moisture content of lumber may be too high.
6. Cut may be too heavy.

IF CHIP MARKS APPEAR ON LUMBER:

1. Blower system may not be strong enough.
2. Feed may be too fast.
3. May be loose connection in blower system—no suction.
4. Exhaust pipe may join at too large an angle to main blower pipe.

IF PANELS ARE TAPERED ACROSS THE WIDTH:

1. Center table may not be set parallel with body of cylinder.
2. Grinding rail may not be set parallel with body of cylinder.
3. Center table may be worn.

IF UNDESIRED POUNDED GLOSSY FINISH APPEARS:

1. Knives may be dull.
2. Feed may be too slow.
3. Joint may be too heavy.

IF WASHBOARD FINISH APPEARS:

1. Knives may have been driven back into the head.
2. Machine may be completely out of adjustment.
3. Joint may be too heavy.

IF REVOLUTION MARK SHOWS UP:

1. Knives may be ground poorly.
2. Knives may need jointing.

IF LINES APPEAR AT RIGHT ANGLES TO THE KNIFE MARKS:

1. Knives may have checkered and nicked up by over grinding and taking temper out of steel.
2. Chips may have wedged between rolls and tables.
3. Pressure bar may be dragging.

IF STOCK TWISTS IN MACHINE:

1. Pressure bar may be cocked.
2. Upper outfeed roll may be cocked.
3. Upper outfeed roll may have uneven spring tension on it.
4. Lower rolls may be cocked.

IF KNIFE LIFTERS MUST BE REPLACED FREQUENTLY:

1. Jack screws may not be tight in slots and knives drive back, shearing the lifters.

IF MACHINE SQUEALS:

1. Pressure bar may be dragging on stock.

IF STOCK STICKS OR HESITATES IN MACHINE:

1. Pressure bar may be set too low.
2. Lower rolls may be set too low.
3. Upper rolls may not be set low enough.
4. Cut may be too heavy.
5. Coaxer board may help lumber through machine.

IF MACHINE IS NOISY AND VIBRATES AND POUNDS:

1. Knives may be too dull.
2. Machine may not be leveled correctly.
3. Machine may not be on solid foundation.
4. Pulley belt may be jumping on pulley.
5. Pressure bar may be set too low.

IF MOTORS KICK OUT:

1. Knives may be dull, thus overloading motors.
2. Pressure bar may be set too low, putting drag on motors.
3. Motor may be drawing high current because other machinery in use in the plant has pulled down the voltage.
4. Machine may be out of adjustment.
5. Lower rolls may be set too low.

IF POWER HOIST SLIPS:

1. Nut may be too loose on friction gear.
2. Oil may have gotten into fiber discs.

CHAPTER FIFTEEN

The Uniplane

The uniplane (Fig. 15-1) is a unique woodworking tool intended to joint or surface material with machine tool accuracy. The cut is made with eight specially ground ¼-in. tool bits positioned symmetrically on an 8-in.-diameter cutterhead (Fig. 15-2). The head is placed vertically in the fence of the machine. The front fence moves in and out to control the depth of cut, in the manner of the front table on a jointer; the center and rear fences merely pick up the cut, in the manner of the rear jointer table. The table of the uniplane acts like the fence of a jointer. The maximum size of work is 6 in.; the minimum is "extremely small" (Fig. 15-3).

Since the actual cutters or tool bits are exposed only in a ⅜-in. slot, both short and small stock can be safely finished. The position of the work, moving past the cutting head while lying flat on the table, and the downward force of cutting action contribute to both safety and accuracy. The depth control is marked in .005-in. increments indicating the precision control possible (Fig. 15-4).

Because of the fixed rear table and fixed cutterhead, stop chamfering and rabbeting operations are not possible. This new type of machine, actually an assembly of old concepts, is not intended to, and will not, replace other woodworking tools.

GENERAL MAINTENANCE

All cast-iron parts of the machine table and fences should be checked for cracks or other imperfections—particularly the webbing (Fig. 15-5),

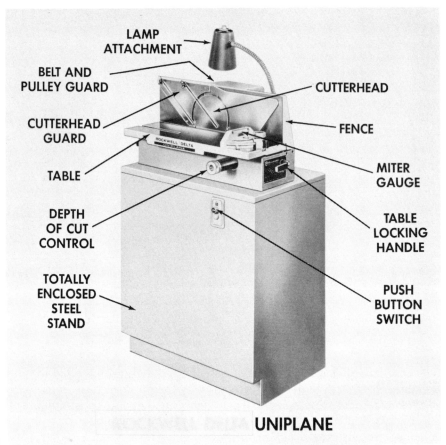

LAMP ATTACHMENT

BELT AND PULLEY GUARD

CUTTERHEAD

CUTTERHEAD GUARD

FENCE

TABLE

MITER GAUGE

DEPTH OF CUT CONTROL

TABLE LOCKING HANDLE

TOTALLY ENCLOSED STEEL STAND

PUSH BUTTON SWITCH

UNIPLANE

FIG. 15-1

FIG. 15-2

FIG. 15-4

FIG. 15-3

FIG. 15-5

FIG. 15-6

FIG. 15-7

which prevents warping of the relatively long, wide, yet thin castings.

The cabinet should be inspected for open weld joints, twisting, or other defects. The motor mounting bracket or plate should be firmly bolted to the cabinet. Lag screws or fasteners holding the unit to the floor should be tight to prevent rocking or tipping.

The unit itself can easily be removed from the stand or cabinet although this is not necessary in most cases. Set screws in the motor pulley and the arbor pulley should be checked for tightness, and belt alignment should be checked at the same time. The motor should be firmly bolted to the motor plate in the correct position to provide both alignment and proper belt tension. The belt should be inspected for wear, cracks, or damage to the outside cover (Fig. 15-6).

After the plastic guard is removed (Fig. 15-7), all table and fence working surfaces should be cleaned with solvent and possibly steel wool.

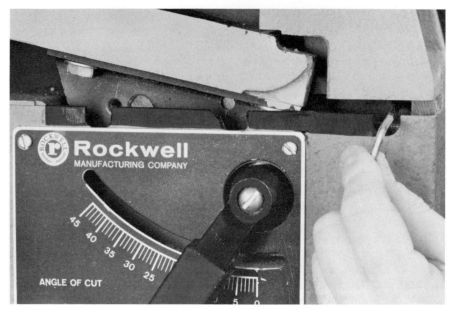

FIG. 15-8

FIG. 15-9

Complete removal is not recommended unless necessary for further maintenance on the cutterhead.

By tilting the table, it is possible to remove the two screws holding the threaded block to the underside of the slide. After the gibs are loosened, the front fence and slide can be removed. The rear and center gib screws are easily accessible from the side of the machine with the table in its 90-deg position. The front gib screw is located through a hole in the trunnion (Fig. 15-8) when the table is tilted about 13 deg.

The dovetail ways of the slide and the base should be cleaned and lubricated with a dry lubricant. The block and the screw shaft also should be thoroughly cleaned with solvent and dry-lubricated. Care should be taken to replace the gib exactly in its original position. It is not normally necessary to remove the front fence from the slide.

The cutterhead should be cleared of all chips and dirt. If gum or pitch has collected on the surface or in the cutter bit holes, it should be removed with solvent. The buildup of foreign material can destroy the balance of this highspeed head and lead to vibration, inaccuracy, and excessive bearing wear.

If the bearings or shaft is found to be defective, the entire shaft and preloaded bearing assembly must be removed and replaced as a unit (Fig. 15-9). Before this project is attempted, the machine should be disconnected from the power source or the belt removed. The tilting table can then be removed by unbolting it from the trunnions. The center fence can be pulled straight out and away from the cutterhead by removing the two cap screws holding it to the base casting (Fig. 15-10).

FIG. 15-10

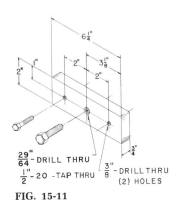

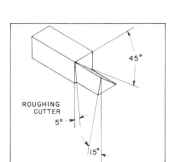

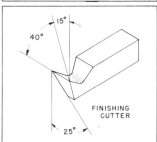

$\frac{29"}{64}$ - DRILL THRU
$\frac{1"}{2}$ - 20 - TAP THRU

$\frac{3"}{8}$ - DRILL THRU
(2) HOLES

FIG. 15-11

ROUGHING CUTTER

45°
5°
15°

FINISHING CUTTER

15°
40°
25°

FIG. 15-13

A steel wheel puller must be used to remove the cutterhead from the tapered arbor or shaft (Fig. 15-11). The hole dimensions should be reasonably accurate to avoid head or shaft damage. After removal of the nut and washer from the shaft (Fig. 15-12), the wheel puller can be used to break the taper by inserting two ⁵⁄₁₆-18 × 1¼″ hex head cap screws through the puller into the tapped holes provided in the cutterhead. A ½-20 × 1½″ hex head cap screw should then be threaded into the puller and forced against the end of the shaft. This will break the taper, and the puller can be removed.

After the retaining plate is removed, the bearing and shaft assembly can be removed from the rear by tapping lightly on the tapered end of the shaft. This should be done with a wood or plastic mallet. The cutterhead can be removed by sliding it through the opening in the rear of the fence.

The cutters should be removed from the cutterhead and the head completely cleaned before installing a new cartridge assembly. This is a good time also to touch up or sharpen the cutters according to the manufacturer's directions (Fig. 15-13). The cutters should be reinstalled in the head after the complete machine is cleaned, lubricated, and assembled, for otherwise they can easily be damaged during assembly. They must be set with a gage for proper depth in relation to the rear fence surface.

FIG. 15-12

FIG. 15-14

All machined cast-iron surfaces should be waxed. Wax is an excellent preservative and lubricant also for the screw shaft, the block or nut, and the dovetail ways on the infeed table slide. Trunnions and all related sliding and mating surfaces also should be coated with wax or other dry lubricant.

The electrical connections and controls, including the grounding of the unit, should be checked.

ALIGNMENT

First the gib controlling the movement of the infeed slide dovetail ways should be adjusted to a snug fit. With the table tilted at about 13 deg, the outboard screw can be adjusted. The two end screws should be tightened first, so that the table will still move, but rather tightly along the ways. The feel should be obtained by locking one end screw so the table will not move, then backing the adjusting screw out until the table will move. This adjustment is made while the depth control knob is turned (Fig. 15-14). The same procedure should be followed for the other end screw, then the center screw.

The table stop for 90 deg can be set by placing a square on the table surface with the blade extending up the outfeed fence (Fig. 15-15). An adjusting screw, built into the unit, can be turned up or down with an Allen wrench. The scale should then be moved to read 0 deg (Fig. 15-16). The locking mechanisms at each end of the table should be adjusted until they tighten with the handle below the table surface.

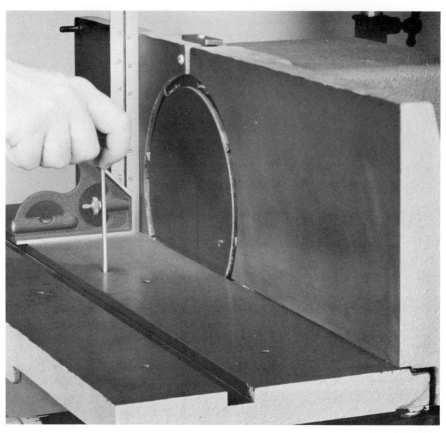

FIG. 15-15

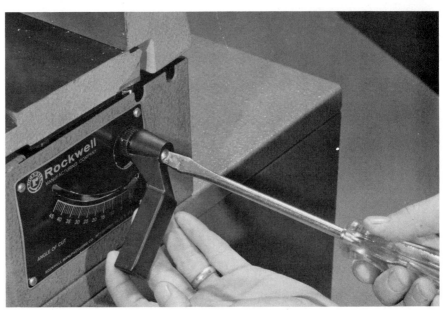

FIG. 15-16

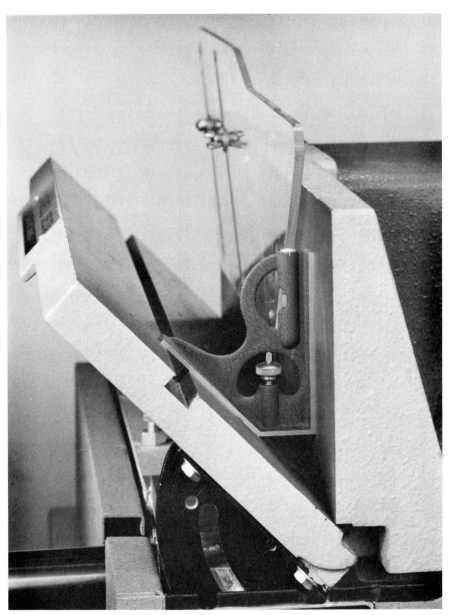

FIG. 15-17

The 45-deg positive stop can be set by holding the head of a try square between the fence and the table (Fig. 15-17). The relationship between the miter gage slot and the fence should be checked to make sure they are parallel. This can be done by holding a framing square or a straight jointed edge tightly against the outfeed table. The infeed table can then be moved with the depth control to match the rear fence exactly. The distance can then be remeasured from the miter gage slot to the fence at each

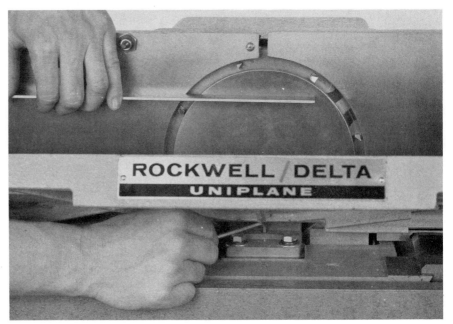

FIG. 15-18

FIG. 15-19

end of the machine. Any adjustment needed can be made by slightly loosening the bolts holding the table to the trunnions.

The center fence must be adjusted to match exactly the fixed rear or outfeed fence. This center section can be tilted in or out by turning the setscrew in the center of the base or support casting (Fig. 15-18). The two hex head cap screws should be loosened very slightly to allow for this movement. The base can be tapped slightly with a soft-faced hammer to turn the entire center fence until it is in surface alignment from right to left. These two critical adjustments should be made and checked alternately, including the retightening of the cap screws, until the fence is locked in perfect alignment in all respects with the outfeed fixed fence. Since the cap screws both tighten by turning clockwise and are held tight by lock washers, some care must be taken not to move the fence in the same direction when the final tightening is done.

Blacklash can be removed from the depth control screw by turning an adjusting screw. This screw is reached through a hole in the slide with the table tilted at 45 deg (Fig. 15-19). The adjustment should be made carefully while turning the control knob back and forth. It is not possible to remove all of the blacklash, regardless of the adjustment. This feature is primarily intended to compensate for wear over some extended period of time.

The front fence should now be moved with the depth control knob, exactly in line with the center fence. This can be gaged by placing a straightedge across the rear and center fence, extending over the front fence, and then bringing the front fence up to match this surface (Fig. 15-20). The graduated collar can then be rotated to read zero and the setscrew tightened (Fig. 15-21).

The four roughing cutters and four finishing cutters are positioned in equally spaced broached square holes in the cutterhead and held by a setscrew (Fig. 15-22). The cutters are alternated in the head with the holes marked with an *R* and an *F*.

Supplied with the machine is a gage which acts also as a guard between the top of the infeed and outfeed table (Fig. 15-23). The gage is used to set the tool bits to the correct depth in relation to the rear fence. It can be fastened to the rear fence, rotated 180 deg, and is preset with a .003-in. step on one end for setting the roughing bits and a .005-in. step on the other for setting the finishing bits. On some units this is done from the top by inserting the Allen wrench into the setscrew between the fence sections (Fig. 15-24). Other units are supplied with a long special Allen wrench that allows the cutter bit to be set in position close to the table surface (Fig. 15-25).

All four roughing cutters should be set first, in every other hole. Next the gage should be reversed and the finishing cutters set. Care must be used to insert the cutter bit in the correct position when sliding it into the head. Each bit should be held or forced lightly into the gage while tightening the setscrew. This can often be done with a small stick or even another Allen wrench (Fig. 15-26).

The rollers, studs, and washers holding the plastic guard to the outfeed fence should be clean and lubricated with wax. The slots in the

FIG. 15-20

FIG. 15-21

FIG. 15-22

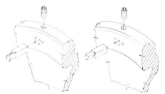

FIG. 15-23

FIG. 15-25

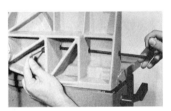

FIG. 15-26

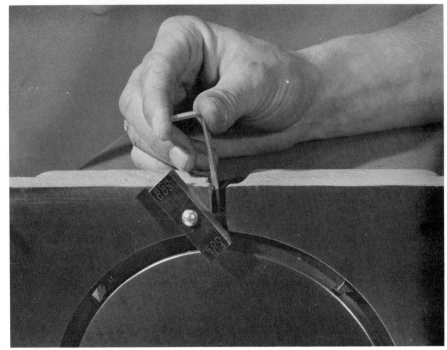

FIG. 15-24

FIG. 15-27

plastic guard must be clean and smooth so that the guard can ride up onto the work being moved into the machine. It should be adjusted free enough to slide or drop back instantly over the cutting area after the work passes through. This adjustment is made by tightening or loosening the hex nut on the outboard stud (Fig. 15-27). The leading edge and bottom edge of this guard must be completely free from nicks or burrs. It should be lightly filed or sanded and coated with hard wax for safe and proper operation.

Because of the precision settings involved and the extremely accurate work which can be produced by this unit, it is advisable to level the machine and anchor it to the floor. This can be done by placing a spirit level on the table and shimming between the cabinet and the floor until levelness is obtained. This precaution can help to eliminate future inaccurate work due to misalignment of the fences and the table.

CHAPTER SIXTEEN

The Shaper

The shaper (Fig. 16-1) is designed primarily to cut moldings or grooves in the edge of the work. This changing of "shape" led naturally to the name shaper. External, internal, curved, straight, or irregular edges can be shaped or molded on the same machine. The technique may be slightly different for various operations, such as using a fence for depth of cut control (Fig. 16-2) rather than a collar and starting pin (Fig. 16-3), but the basic cutting method is still the same.

The overarm router or shaper (Fig. 16-4) is similar to a portable router, except that the horsepower is usually greater and the typical shaper control surfaces such as tables and fences are evident. Basically the stationary overarm unit and the portable router are directly driven by a universal ac dc motor and hold the bit (Fig. 16-5) or cutting tool in a chuck or collet. The traditional shaper uses a three-lip three-wing cutter (Fig. 16-6) or cutterhead mounted on a spindle which is belt driven by a constant-speed motor. On the overarm unit the table is vertically movable (in addition to the spindle above the work), whereas the spindle is vertically adjustable below the work on the normal floor model shaper.

GENERAL MAINTENANCE

All cast-iron tables and all cast parts in the drive mechanism should be cleaned and carefully checked for cracks in the surface or webbing (Fig. 16-7). Steel cabinets should be checked for open welds. If the unit is

FIG. 16-2

FIG. 16-3

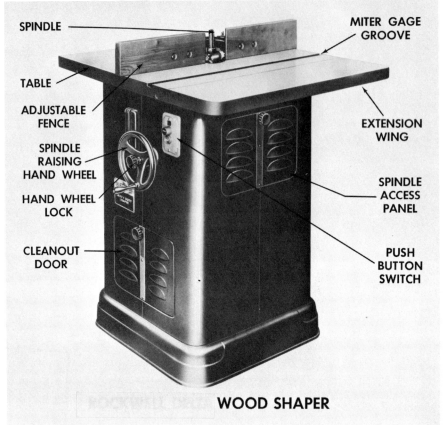

SPINDLE

MITER GAGE
GROOVE

TABLE

EXTENSION
WING

ADJUSTABLE
FENCE

SPINDLE
RAISING
HAND WHEEL

SPINDLE
ACCESS
PANEL

HAND WHEEL
LOCK

CLEANOUT
DOOR

PUSH
BUTTON
SWITCH

WOOD SHAPER

FIG. 16-1

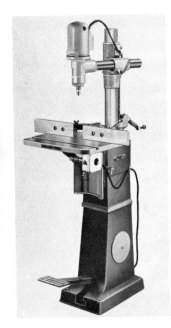

FIG. 16-4

lagged or bolted to the floor, lag screws, studs, and nuts should be checked for tightness.

The entire operating or drive assembly should be firmly bolted to the underside of the table. Most table model or cabinet model units in the cabinet shop or school shop size are designed with a self-contained assembly (Fig. 16-8a). If the assembly is extremely dirty or if the raising nut or other parts must be replaced, it is often advantageous to remove it from the table and cabinet. In most cases this can best be done by turning the entire shaper upside down (Fig. 16-8b). If the bolts holding the assembly to the table and the spindle adjustment handwheel or shaft are removed, the entire mechanism can be lifted out of the cabinet.

The elevating screw, cam nut (Fig. 16-8c), slides, columns, ways, collars, and other raising parts should be thoroughly cleaned with solvent and dry-lubricated. Dovetail ways on overarm movable table units and table-raising mechanism also should be cleaned with solvent and dry-lubricated.

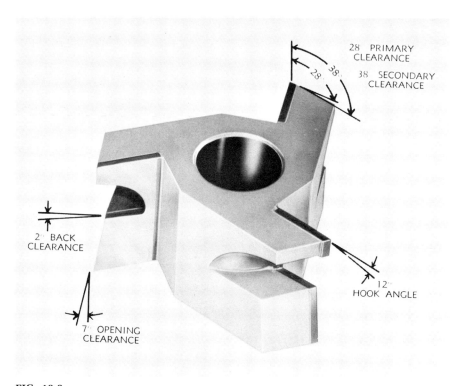

28 PRIMARY CLEARANCE

38 SECONDARY CLEARANCE

2° BACK CLEARANCE

7° OPENING CLEARANCE

12° HOOK ANGLE

FIG. 16-6

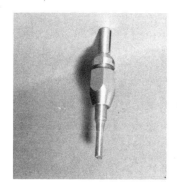

FIG. 16-5

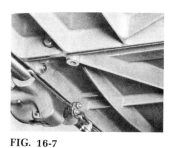

FIG. 16-7

FIG. 16-8a

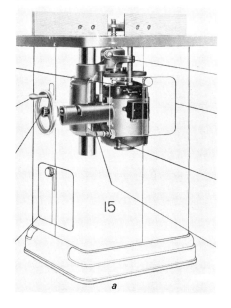

FIG. 16-8b

FIG. 16-8c

Pulley alignment should be checked and motor mount bolts tightened. Pulley setscrews should be checked for tightness and sheaves checked for excess wear.

All spindles, spindle tie rods, washers, screws, nuts, collars, and lock washers should be soaked in solvent and wiped clean. Pitch or gum deposits can greatly affect the delicate balance necessary for high-speed accurate shaping. An unbalanced condition will shorten bearing life to a great extent. Particular attention should be paid to the taper at the base of the actual spindle and the opposing taper in the bearing assembly. The sleeve and bearing assembly is often a preloaded cartridge and should not be disassembled unless absolutely necessary in order to replace the sealed bearings. Even in this case it is often better, because of safety and high-speed accuracy, to purchase a completely new assembly from the manufacturer (Fig. 16-9).

On assemblies with an oil bath lubricating system, bearings may be removed and either cleaned or replaced. Care should be taken that nothing will interfere with oil spray or circulation in this unit.

In many cases the bearing assembly unit is locked in place by tightening a split casting. Care should be taken that this casting is tight enough to avoid any slipping or movement of the sleeve and bearing assembly, yet not so tight as to distort the bearings (Fig. 16-10). Overtightening is one of the most common causes of short bearing life.

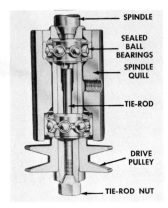

FIG. 16-9

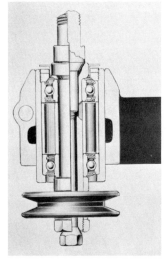

FIG. 16-10

FIG. 16-11

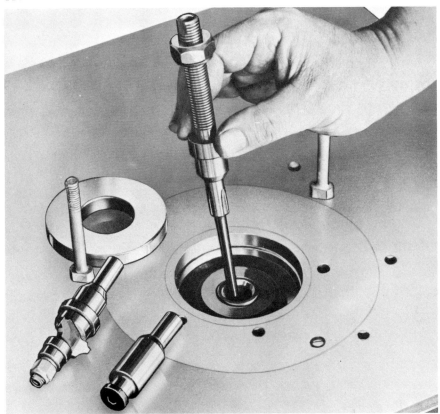

The table should be cleaned with solvent and with steel wool if necessary. The table inserts should also be cleaned and checked for proper fit into the table opening and into each other (Fig. 16-11). All table surfaces and the entire insert nest should be lubricated with hard wax. Starting pin holes and tapered starting pins should be clean and free from gum, pitch, and dirt.

Table extensions should be located and tightened flush with, or in the same plane as, the table itself. If the extension is above or below the table, it should be removed, and the mating edges cleaned before reassembly. All bolts should be drawn up snug, then one end tightened with the surfaces exactly flush. If the extension does not line up automatically, a Jorgenson type of clamp can be used to draw the nonmatching end into line (Fig. 16-12). Tightening should then be done in sequence, loosening or tightening the clamp in order to maintain flush surfaces above each bolt or cap screw.

The movable table on overarm units should be adjusted to move up and down smoothly with no side play. The table or knee usually travels on dovetail ways and should be adjusted accordingly (see Chap. 13, "The Jointer," p. 166), the same as a jointer bed, but with slightly more ease of vertical movement. In some units the foot pedal or table-raising lever is adjustable for operator convenience.

All cast-iron parts of the fence should be cleaned with solvent and the various adjustments lubricated with hard wax. Wood faces should be absolutely straight and square and should also be waxed. If these faces are warped or splintered, they should be replaced, preferably with hardwood rather than softwood (Fig. 16-13).

FIG. 16-12

FIG. 16-13

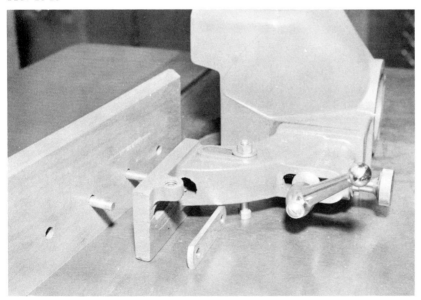

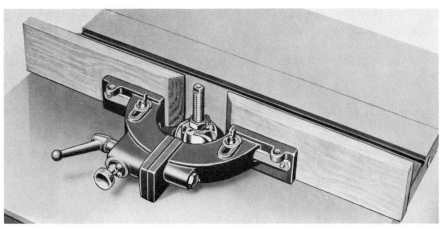

FIG. 16-14

Since most overarm-type shapers have universal motors, the same attention must be paid to brushes, strain relievers, and commutators as in any portable electric tool. (See Chap. 19, "Portable Electric Tools," p. 233.) Chucks and bushings must be clean in order to avoid runout of the bit and excessive bearing wear. The chuck must maintain a firm grip on the shank of the cutter.

All electrical connections should be checked for tightness and the control or switch for fast positive action.

ALIGNMENT

Shaper alignment is basically controlled by manufacturing quality control, adherence to preventive maintenance procedures, and the operator's setup knowledge.

Since the entire drive mechanism is bolted to the underside of the table on a cabinet shaper, vertical alignment is done in the manufacturer's plant. The overarm router/shaper is completely adjustable 360 deg, but at least a scale and often positive stops are provided. A straight rod should be clamped in the chuck and checked with a square in relation to the table. The pointer, scale, and positive stops should then be adjusted for 0 deg.

Although some cabinet shapers are supplied with a height scale, it is not altogether practical because of the great variety of cutters and collars which can be used. It is usually best to make a practice cut in scrap lumber and measure the cut.

There are many styles and types of shaper fences, but basically they fall into two major categories as far as adjustment is concerned: those on which only half of the fence, the front or infeed section, is adjustable, and those on which both sections are adjustable (Fig. 16-14) independently of each other.

The type with only infeed section adjustment or, for that matter, both types are easily adjusted when the edge to be molded or shaped is not completely cut away. When the entire face of the molding is cut away, the following procedure should be followed in adjusting the single-adjustment type:

1. Set the fence faces parallel.

2. Set the entire fence to the desired depth of cut—behind the arc of the knives.

3. Start the cut and move the stock through the cutter until it extends 5 or 6 in. with no support.

4. Stop the machine and move the front fence back and clear of the work.

5. Readjust the complete fence forward until the rear half will pick up or support the work as it leaves the cutter.

6. Readjust the front half to match the original work edge.

7. Check and jog both complete fence and front half adjustments until original depth of cut is matched and cutaway edge is supported.

8. Continue the cut.

For the double-adjustment type the following procedure should be followed:

1. Set the fence faces parallel.

2. Set the entire fence to the desired depth of cut—behind the arc of the knives.

3. Start the cut and move the stock through the cutter until it extends 5 or 6 in. with no support.

4. Stop the machine and move the outfeed or rear fence forward to pick up or support the work as it leaves the cutter.

5. Continue the cut.

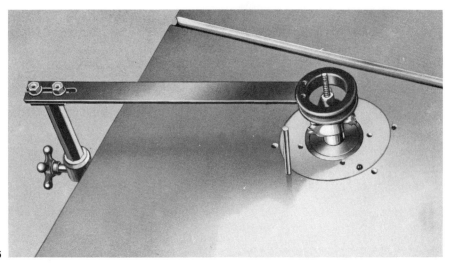

FIG. 16-15

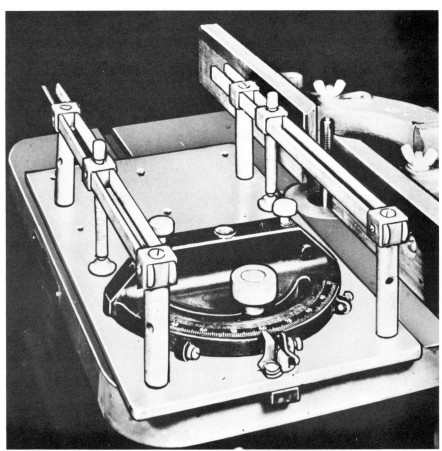

FIG. 16-16

All guards, ring type (Fig. 16-15) or those fastened to the fence, should be clean and adjusted to assure complete safety and yet not interfere with the operation.

Sliding jigs (Fig. 16-16), hold-downs (Fig. 16-17), and similar accessories should be cleaned and dry-lubricated exactly the same as the machine itself. They should all be adjusted so that it is impossible for them to make contact with the cutting tool in spite of their movement or the movement of the workpiece.

The manufacturer's maintenance and adjustment suggestions should be followed for the specific brand and type because of the spindle speeds of over 10,000 rpm.

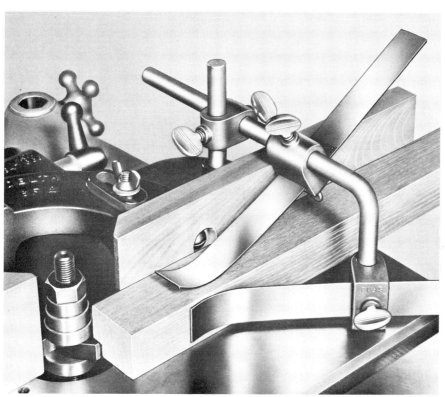

FIG. 16-17

CHAPTER SEVENTEEN
The Wood Lathe

The woodworking lathe (Fig. 17-1) is basically a wood turning machine, although with the proper accessories metal may be turned (Fig. 17-2) or metal spinning operations performed. Sanding, boring, grinding, polishing, and buffing also can be done on the wood lathe. The word "wood" in the accepted name pertains to the material to be turned, not to the basic machine construction, which of course is metal.

The normal pattern shop, home shop, and school shop units are usually 10, 11, or 12 in. in size. The figures indicate the maximum diameter of the work which can be held between centers. Many modern wood lathes have a gap bed (Fig. 17-3) which allows for about four extra inches of potential work diameter close to the spindle nose. Gap bed lathes are often referred to by both size designations—12″/16″. Larger faceplate turning is done "outboard" or at the tail of the headstock spindle.

Most lathes in this general size and price category are under 40 in. between centers, usually 36 or 38 in. Variable-speed models are almost always cabinet or floor units because the drive is mounted in the cabinet. Step pulley models are often available as cabinet or bench lathes.

GENERAL MAINTENANCE

In most school, cabinet, or pattern shop units the head, bed, and tailstock are made of cast iron. These should be checked for cracks and other pos-

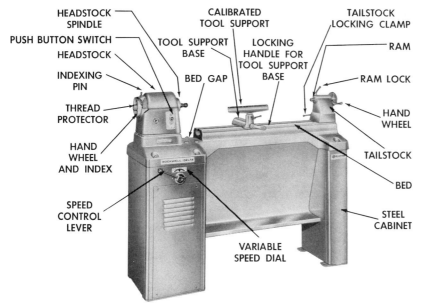

FIG. 17-1

Labels for FIG. 17-1:
- HEADSTOCK SPINDLE
- PUSH BUTTON SWITCH
- HEADSTOCK
- INDEXING PIN
- THREAD PROTECTOR
- HAND WHEEL AND INDEX
- SPEED CONTROL LEVER
- CALIBRATED TOOL SUPPORT
- TOOL SUPPORT BASE
- LOCKING HANDLE FOR TOOL SUPPORT BASE
- BED GAP
- VARIABLE SPEED DIAL
- TAILSTOCK LOCKING CLAMP
- RAM
- RAM LOCK
- HAND WHEEL
- TAILSTOCK
- BED
- STEEL CABINET

FIG. 17-2

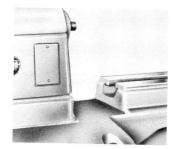

FIG. 17-3

sible problems, primarily nicks and burrs in the bed. The inside edges (Fig. 17-4) of each flat bed section, as well as the top surface, should be smooth. This is because of the mating parts on the tailstock and the underside or flange of the tool support base.

These assemblies should slide smoothly for safe operations. Any burrs should be touched off with a file. Burrs may show up on either the bed or the mating sections.

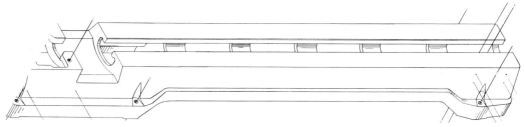

FIG. 17-4

FIG. 17-5

After first sliding the tailstock off the bed, the entire tool support (Fig. 17-5) should be removed by sliding it off the tailstock end of the bed. The tool support assembly can usually be cleaned with a brush and solvent without being completely disassembled. The cam, sliding eyebolt, or other clamp devices should slide free with no interference. All sliding

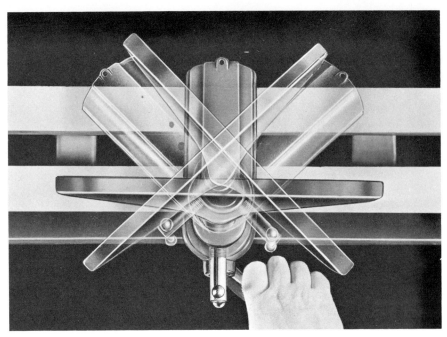

FIG. 17-6

FIG. 17-7

parts, moving parts, the flange, and the base of the casting should be coated with wax. All movement should be smooth and easy when the assembly is not clamped to the bed (Fig. 17-6).

The tailstock should, in most cases, be completely disassembled and all parts cleaned in solvent. Care should be used in removing the ram so that the threads are not damaged, internally in the ram and externally on the quill or ram adjusting screw. Care should be taken also if locking plugs, rather than a split casting (Fig. 17-7), are used to clamp the ram. All washers, plugs, nuts, and other parts should be kept in their correct order. The tapered side of the plug should match the surface of the ram when being reassembled.

If the tailstock is adjustable right and left, the support or base casting and the tailstock casting should be separated. The sliding ways and mating surfaces should be checked, cleaned with solvent, dry-lubricated, and reassembled. The two adjustment screws should hold firm and work properly (Fig. 17-8).

Usually the lead stock can be blown out with air and visually checked for proper functioning. Unless the bearings must be replaced, the spindle should not be removed. Its condition can easily be determined by turning the spindle by hand. Rough bearings can usually be heard as well as felt. Side-play movement also can be checked in this manner. In most cases the pulley is centered inside the casting, but it should always line up for proper belt alignment. The setscrew should be checked for tightness (Fig. 17-9).

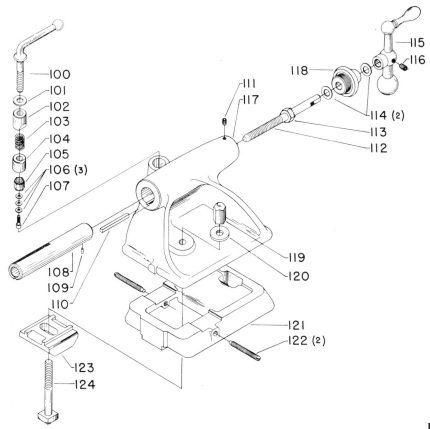

100
101
102
103
104
105
106 (3)
107

108
109
110

111
117

118

115
116

114 (2)
113
112

119
120

121
122 (2)

123
124

FIG. 17-8

FIG. 17-9

FIG. 17-10

In most lathes the headstock bearing is pressed into a seat bored in the casting (Fig. 17-10). The tailstock bearing is often allowed to float (Fig. 17-11). The manufacturer's directions should be checked for shoulders on the spindle or the casting before the spindle is tapped out of the machine; the instructions should indicate which direction to tap. A leather, soft-faced hammer or a wood block should be used to protect the threads at either end of the spindle (Fig. 17-12). Care should be taken that the new bearing or bearings enter the bearing seat straight and even. The pulley and often a key must be repositioned on the spindle after the spindle is half installed.

If the machine is equipped with an indexing mechanism, the positioning holes in the pulley should be cleaned out with solvent (Fig. 17-13). The indexing pin should pull in and out with ease, yet hold in the disengaged position. The movement is often controlled by a spring and steel ball assembly which engages in a recess or shoulder in the pin. These parts must be clean and free to operate by spring load. Care should be taken not to lose the small ball and spring.

Variable-drive systems vary greatly, and the manufacturer's suggestions should be followed. If belt driven, it is important that the drive be in alignment. All mounting brackets should be firmly bolted to the cabinet and the motor to the mounting plate. Lubrication for any particular type of variable-speed pulley assemblies should follow the manufacturer's directions (Fig. 17-14). The only exception might be to use hard wax or a dry lubricant on all adjustments, pivot points, and other similar slow-moving friction areas (Fig. 17-15).

SPINDLE ASSEMBLY

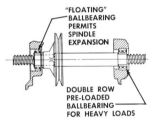

"FLOATING" BALLBEARING PERMITS SPINDLE EXPANSION

DOUBLE ROW PRE-LOADED BALLBEARING FOR HEAVY LOADS

FIG. 17-11

FIG. 17-13

FIG. 17-12

If the variable-speed control is electrical, the manufacturer's directions should be followed exactly in cleaning, adjusting, and lubricating.

On four-speed lathes belt tension and alignment are vital. In most cases adjustment should be made by moving the motor. The spindle pulley is usually centered between the bearings. The motor pulley should be as close to the motor bearing as possible. Sixteen-, twelve-, or other multiple-speed units using jackshafts should be checked for the proper recommended lubrication, belt tension, and belt alignment. The motor-raising mechanism to facilitate belt changing on four-speed lathes should be cleaned and lubricated (Fig. 17-16). This mechanism should not affect either the alignment or tension of the belts. There is usually a positive bottoming stop which can be adjusted for correct belt tension.

The cabinet, usually made of sheet steel (Fig. 17-17), should be checked for open weld joints or any other signs of weakness or buckling. Cabinet doors or panels should fit tightly.

All electrical connections should be checked both at the motor and at the controls. The controls should be checked for proper, safe, and fast action. If safety or slow-start mechanisms are incorporated, they should work as intended and absolutely without fail. It may be necessary to check electrical controls inside the cabinet. Switch or control covers should be dustproof or located in as dust-free a position as possible.

FIG. 17-14

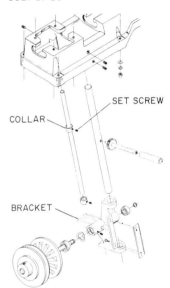

COLLAR

SET SCREW

BRACKET

FIG. 17-15

FIG. 17-17

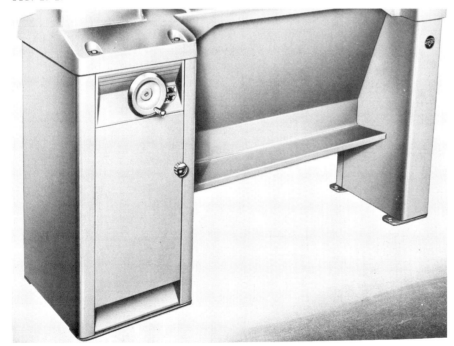

FIG. 17-16

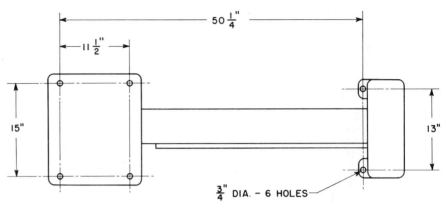

FIG. 17-18

ALIGNMENT

Because a woodworking lathe is by rule of thumb a power tool, in contrast to a machine tool, alignment is not as complicated or critical. Accuracy in wood turning is directly controlled by the skill of the operator, not the machine.

In spite of this fact, certain checks should be made beginning with installation. Although not absolutely necessary, it is certainly good practice to level the unit and bolt or lag it to the floor. Most manufacturers provide at least six points either inside or outside the cabinet on enclosed models (Fig. 17-18). The bed should be checked across the ways at the lead and tailstock end, and lengthwise in the center of the bed (Fig. 17-19). Shims should be used between the cabinet and the floor to bring the bed into proper alignment.

FIG. 17-19

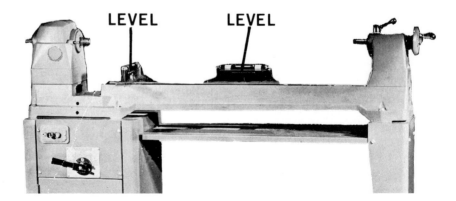

FIG. 17-20

New lathes are sometimes delivered with the belts in a separate package, not installed. This is because belts, either variable-speed or V type, have a tendency to become preshaped if stretched over the pulleys for any length of time. This is not really harmful, but it may take a few days for the slight bumping sound and accompanying vibration to level out and become smooth. Worn V-belts can usually be changed by removing the spindle far enough to allow the belt to slip between the spindle and the casting (Fig. 17-20).

Pulleys should be checked for proper straight alignment of all belts. This is naturally more difficult when a jackshaft or a sixteen-speed unit is involved, but the methods are exactly the same as when checking a single belt on a four-speed pulley lathe. Usually the headstock pulley or sheave should be considered not movable, and all alignment adjustments should be made by moving the jackshaft pulley or pulleys and the motor pulley or the motor itself. The manufacturer's instruction or parts manual can be checked for the correct position of the lead stock pulley, the accuracy of which is extremely important because of the related stress on both inboard and outboard bearings, possible spindle whip, and allowable spindle expansion. Correct positioning is often visually obvious while the spindle and pulley are checked.

Centers should be inserted in the headstock taper and the tailstock ram. The centers should be clean and smooth. The inside of the headstock and ram also should be free from chips, dirt, and burrs. All these surfaces are usually hardened, but they are usually not hard enough to omit using a small file to clean off burrs or excess material around a nick. If the taper is too hard for a file, a small hand grinder can be used carefully to take off only the excess metal. If the taper is well worn and not basically accurate, a new spindle or ram must be installed.

FIG. 17-21

The tailstock should then be moved along the bed until the points of the centers are within 1/64 in. of each other (Fig. 17-21). These points should line up exactly. Most lathe tailstocks are basically two castings,

FIG. 17-22

and shims can be placed between them. This adjustment should be made frequently, especially on older machines, because of wear on the underside of the base casting from continuous sliding on the bed. Usually the bed wear is much less because the wear is spread over a much greater area. If the tailstock center is too low to be corrected by shims, a new tailstock should be purchased. Any difference in the center point alignment from front to rear can usually be corrected by loosening one adjusting screw in the base tailstock casting and tightening the other. Tailstocks without this adjustment depend upon original manufacturing accuracy and bed straightness for perfect alignment. The tailstock clamp, if cam controlled, should be adjusted for positive clamping action (Fig. 17-22).

Although sometimes it is possible to move or change the position of the lead stock on the bed, it is usually not advisable. Mounting bolts should be checked for tightness, and alignment is assumed to be correct. All adjustments are made from this reference point or fixed assembly.

The tool rest should slide level and parallel with the bed. Any inaccuracy is usually caused by burrs in the base casting which supports the tool rest. The burrs should be filed out without distorting any of the bearing or mating surfaces. The underside of the base casting should fit snugly and clamp tightly to the bed. A cam action clamping assembly can usually be adjusted by tightening or loosening a nut on the eyebolt under the flange (Fig. 17-23). Other systems merely require tightening of an acorn nut in the center of the base casting, but no actual adjustment.

Accessories should be checked for proper alignment with the actual lathe on which they are to be used. These might include a metal cutting compound slide rest, a gap filler block, metal spinning tool support, steady rests, floor stand, or wood turning duplicator. These and all similar accessories intended to increase the usefulness of the lathe should be clean and lubricated with wax or other dry lubricant where appropriate.

FIG. 17-23

Faceplates (Fig. 17-24) should be checked visually for obvious runout or wobble. If such a condition is found, the area around the hub should be checked for cracks or defects. Cracked or damaged faceplates should be broken and thrown away. If the plate is slightly bent and the face thick enough, a fine facing cut can be taken (on a metal lathe) in order to true up the surface. This is often not possible or advisable, not only because of insufficient stock thickness, but primarily because the balance of the faceplate is changed and thus can cause lathe vibration, which in turn causes excessive bearing wear, a bent spindle, or danger to the operator by weakening the face and holding areas.

Headstock covers and other guards should be adjusted to fit properly and stay firmly in place during operation. Broken alignment pins should be drilled, removed with a screw extractor, and replaced with a duplicate pin or a roll pin (Fig. 17-25).

FIG. 17-24

FIG. 17-25

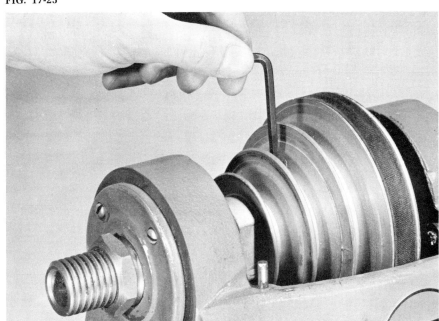

CHAPTER EIGHTEEN
The Grinder

The bench grinder (Fig. 18-1), used primarily to keep cutting tools sharp, is indispensable in a shop. With the proper wire or cloth wheels, buffing and polishing can be done. The two grinding wheels are usually of different grades, classified as to coarseness of abrasive action; they are guarded except for the working face. Basically the bench grinder is a motor with extended threaded shafts (Fig. 18-2). Eye shields are usually provided and are often incorporated in a lighting system (Fig. 18-3). Adjustable tool rests provide a control surface at each wheel face (Fig. 18-4). The name "bench grinder" indicates that this unit is often lagged to a bench top, rather than mounted on a cabinet or pedestal (Fig. 18-5).

The size is usually designated by grinding wheel diameter and horsepower. Common sizes found in the average school, home, or cabinet shop range from 6 to 10 in. and from ¼ to 1 hp. The speed is usually 1725 or 3450 rpm.

The most common accessory for the bench grinder is the edge tool or plane blade grinding attachment (Fig. 18-6). Diamond wheel dressers, drill grinding attachments, buffing wheels, and wire wheels are available.

The buffer is really a grinder with the tool rests, eye shields, and guards removed. Often the shaft is extended even farther than for a grinder to provide greater clearance (Fig. 18-7).

Small bench tool grinders (Fig. 18-8) are often called carbide grinders because they are often used with diamond grit wheels to sharpen carbide cutting tools. Aluminum oxide and silicon carbide wheels are also

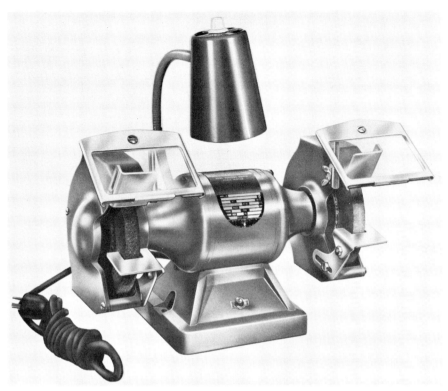

FIG. 18-1
FIG. 18-2

FIG. 18-3

FIG. 18-4

FIG. 18-6

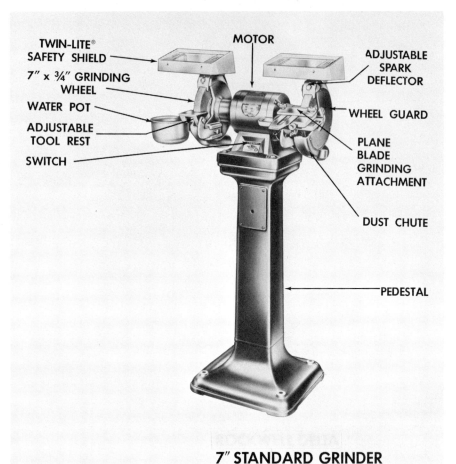

TWIN-LITE® SAFETY SHIELD

MOTOR

ADJUSTABLE SPARK DEFLECTOR

7" x ¾" GRINDING WHEEL

WATER POT

ADJUSTABLE TOOL REST

SWITCH

WHEEL GUARD

PLANE BLADE GRINDING ATTACHMENT

DUST CHUTE

PEDESTAL

7" STANDARD GRINDER

FIG. 18-5

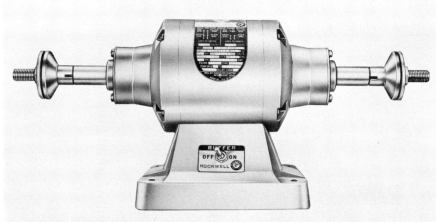

FIG. 18-7

220

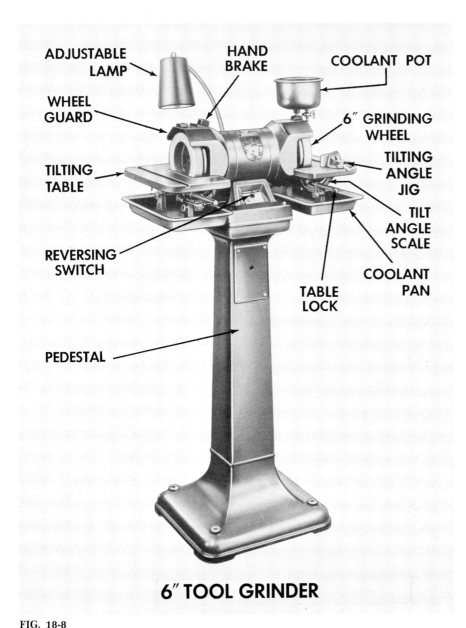

ADJUSTABLE LAMP

HAND BRAKE

COOLANT POT

WHEEL GUARD

6″ GRINDING WHEEL

TILTING TABLE

TILTING ANGLE JIG

REVERSING SWITCH

TILT ANGLE SCALE

COOLANT PAN

TABLE LOCK

PEDESTAL

6″ TOOL GRINDER

FIG. 18-8

All wheels are mounted on a balanced flange assembly with mounting bolts for greater accuracy.

The tool grinder (Fig. 18-9), although often needed for sharpening saw blades (Fig. 18-10), tool bits (Fig. 18-11), shaper cutters, jointer blades, planer blades, and other precision sharpening jobs, is seldom found in a woodshop. By rule of thumb this unit is a machine tool. Sharpening jobs requiring a grinder of this type are usually sent out to a machine shop or to a distributor with tool sharpening service.

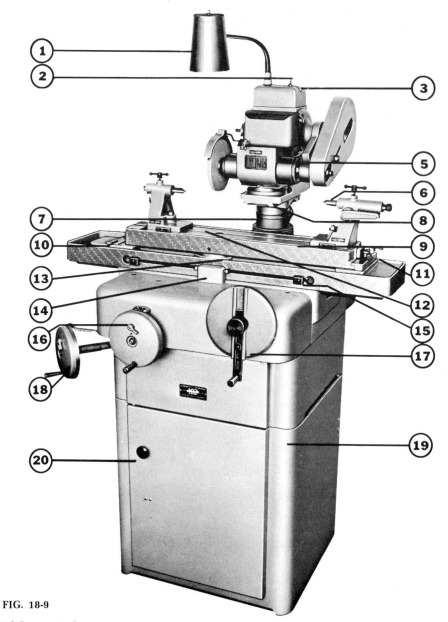

FIG. 18-9

(1) Lamp attachment,
(2) reversing switch,
(3) motor assembly,
(5) quill assembly,
(6) interchangeable centers,
(7) column,
(8) wheel head swivel,
(9) coolant trough,
(10) table calibrations,
(11) table adjustment screw,
(12) T-slot,
(13) table swivel,
(14) table stop,
(15) adjustable stop,
(16) cross feed hand wheel,
(17) traverse hand wheel,
(18) vertical column movement wheel,
(19) cast iron base, and
(20) storage compartment.
(K. O. Lee Company)

FIG. 18-10

FIG. 18-11

GENERAL MAINTENANCE

Since most bench grinders are basically motors, all normal maintenance pertaining to electric motors should be followed. Bearings are usually special and have felt or extra shields in order to keep dirt and grit from the grinding process out of the motor assembly. Any replacement should adhere exactly to the manufacturer's recommendations (Fig. 18-12). These specifications may be provided by the complete tool manufacturer or the actual motor manufacturer.

The cast-iron parts, such as end bells or brackets, bases, guards, and tool rests, should be checked for cracks or defects. Broken parts should be replaced. Unlike the brackets on a normal motor, end bells are often extended, and they may be oval in cross section to provide extra clearance. Because of equal spacing of the tie rods running through the motor and holding the complete unit together, they can be assembled in any one of four possible positions. The correct position can be checked by at-

FIG. 18-12

tempting to mount the guard or by matching the mounting holes in the guard with those in the bracket or end bell.

Threads should be checked in the cast-iron parts of the mounting holes. If guards, tool rests, spark arresters, and lamp attachments are loosely mounted, both accuracy and safety are seriously impaired. Holes can be retapped or redrilled and tapped to a larger size in most cases. Commercial products are available to take up the space between poorly fitting threads.

Both fabricated and cast-iron tool rests should be cleaned and checked for nicks, burrs, and worn edges. The entire surface area should be filed flat and smooth. This can be done easily on a belt finishing machine by holding the face of the tool rest flat against the belt for a few seconds.

All welded areas should be checked for open or broken welds. In some cases guard parts are made of welded sheet steel rather than cast iron. The base and tool support brackets of many small bench grinders also are fabricated instead of cast.

Replacement of light bulbs should be considered a definite part of general maintenance. Whether the eye shield has two bulbs or one bulb, or the lamp attachment is a separate accessory (Fig. 18-13), the exact recommended size and type of bulb must be used. This is necessary primarily because of the amount of heat generated by the lamp within the fixture, and also because of the additional amp draw. Any extra light necessary for a specific grinding job should be supplied by additional fixtures, not brighter bulbs.

FIG. 18-13

Spring clips or other fastening devices holding the glass into the frame of the eye shields should be checked for tightness. Broken glass or defective clips should be replaced. Shatterproof glass is required. Supporting brackets, clips or rods, and the various fasteners should function properly and hold firmly, while being, in many cases, still easily adjustable (Fig. 18-14).

All accessories should be cleaned and checked for obvious defects. Sliding or moving parts should fit snugly and be free from nicks. All adjustment features should move freely and lock tightly.

The cord and plug or other electrical connections, including the ground connection, should be checked. Switches or other controls should operate quickly and with positive action. If the grinder is mounted on a pedestal with controls in the pedestal, all electrical connections between the grinder and the remote control unit should receive

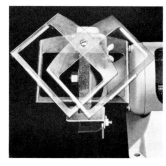

FIG. 18-14

special attention. On 220- or 230-volt single-phase units, light fixtures are often wired in series, each receiving 110 or 115 volts of power, like many Christmas tree light strings. If one bulb burns out, the others will not light, and the defective one must be found by trial and error. A single-phase 110- or 115-volt grinder has the light fixtures wired in parallel, and the two or more bulbs will light independently. The type of wiring can easily be checked visually by unscrewing or unplugging one bulb in the system. Three-phase grinders usually have a separate 115-volt single-phase lighting system independent of the grinder's power source.

ALIGNMENT

The basic alignment in a bench grinder is controlled by the manufacturer of the motor itself. The quality of the bearings and the amount of end play in the armature are probably the two major factors. Unless the unit is defectively manufactured, it should run smoothly at the correct speed and have little or no end play when new.

After extended continuous use, end play or runout may occur. End play can usually be corrected by replacing worn fiber or wave washers in the end bells of the motor unit. Runout is usually due to worn bearings or a bent shaft. Bearings can easily be checked, often by turning the armature by hand or attempting to move it up and down. If roughness is felt when turning, or movement is felt or even heard when checking side play, the bearings should be replaced. In many cases other parts also are worn, and it is usually worthwhile to take the motor unit to an authorized repair station for a complete check. Since a bent shaft is almost impossible to straighten, a new armature, including new bearings, is usually required.

FIG. 18-15

Grinding wheels should be refaced periodically with a diamond dresser (Fig. 18-15) or a star wheel dresser. Refacing is necessary for both accurate tool grinding and proper wheel balance. All broken wheels and extremely worn grinding wheels should be completely broken and thrown away. New wheels should be carefully specified when purchased, according to the rated rpm of the grinder or fpm of the grinding wheel. (See conversion formulas in Chap. 1, "Definition of Terms," p. 13.)

Runout can be checked easily by watching the relationship between the tool rest and the grinding wheel, particularly when the unit is about to coast to a stop. If the wheel moves from side to side, first check the nut and the flanges. The inside flange in particular must be clean, smooth, and exactly perpendicular to the shaft. Any roughness or burrs on the inner flange or shoulder should be carefully touched off with a file. Grinding wheels often have a heavy paper disk on each side extending about one-third of the way from the arbor hole to the face. Usually this disk bears the specifications and is glued to the abrasive wheel. It should be checked to ensure its not being wrinkled, bent, or only half there. If it is not perfectly smooth and intact, it should be completely removed, to avoid wheel runout.

For general or all-purpose grinding, the tool rests should be positioned slightly above the center line of the wheel and at a 15-deg angle to the face, although this is almost a matter of personal opinion (Fig. 18-16). Support assemblies for accessories should be set and adjusted according to the manufacturer's recommendations. The individual and specific directions should be followed also for accessories such as drill grinding, edge tool sharpening, and wheel dressing attachments. These items are usually quite differently manufactured and designed by various companies. They are not supplied by the motor manufacturer, as a rule.

FIG. 18-16

Spark deflectors should be adjusted as close to the grinding wheel as possible (Fig. 18-17). This can be done easily by inserting two or three sheets of paper between the wheel and the deflector. The cap screw or other fastening devices should be loosened to allow the deflector to drop and square itself with the face of the dressed wheel. The cap screw or screws can then be tightened and the paper gage removed by slowly moving the wheel forward and downward. If the deflector has shoulders or surrounds the wheel face, it should be carefully centered (Fig. 18-18).

In order to save costs or to gain extra clearance, grinding heads can be obtained from manufacturers. These units are belt driven from the rear or underneath the head through an opening in the cabinet or bench (Fig. 18-19). Guards, spark deflectors, tool rests, and accessories should receive the same attention as an integral motor-driven grinder. The setscrew in the arbor pulley should be tight and the belt in proper straight alignment. Care should be taken to figure the speed of these units carefully so that the rpm or fpm does not exceed the limits of the grinding wheels.

FIG. 18-17

The small tool grinder, commonly called a carbide grinder, is built to closer tolerances and therefore by rule of thumb is more accurate than the normal bench grinder. The grinding wheels are actually a ring mounted on a precision backing plate. This assembly is fastened to the wheel flange with machine screws or socket head screws. It is automatically centered on a centering ring (Fig. 18-20). Extreme care should be taken not to strip threads, nick the grinding wheel, or damage the wheel flange or centering ring. Balance is critical for accurate work. The arbor nuts usually require a spanner wrench which is supplied by the manufacturer. They should not be tapped on or off with a hammer and punch.

The coolant pans should be unbolted or unclipped and cleaned as often as necessary, possibly once a week. The entire area around the wheel flange should be wiped or brushed clear of all chips, dirt, and coolant. Even though manufacturers go to great lengths to protect the motor and bearings (Fig. 18-21), constant attention to this problem area is recommended.

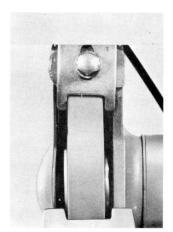

FIG. 18-18

The table grooves must be aligned parallel to the outer surfaces of the grinding wheels. Alignment can be checked by measuring the distance or by holding a block of wood in the sliding jig and using it as a gage at either

FIG. 18-19

FIG. 18-20

end of the tables. The tables can be adjusted or aligned by loosening the cap screws holding them to the trunnion assemblies. A square should then be placed on each table with the blade extending up the wheel surface. The positive stops can then be set at 0 deg and the pointers or the tilt scales moved to match this reading.

To assure initial accuracy or to correct wheel wear, the wheels must be dressed carefully with a diamond dresser controlled by the table slots; very light passes should be taken across the faces of the grinding wheels during this operation. This should be done only on the downside of the moving wheel.

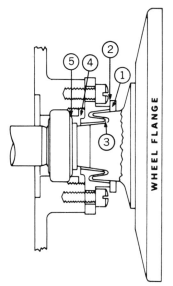

FIG. 18-21
(1) Neoprene slinger washer,
(2) positive contact of washer against seal,
(3) labyrinth type seal interlocks with wheel flange,
(4) space between seal and bearing is packed with grease, and
(5) motor bearing is sealed.

CHAPTER NINETEEN
Portable Electric Tools

Portable electric tools (Fig. 19-1) require less preventive maintenance than stationary machines, and they have fewer alignment problems. With reasonable care there is usually a minimum of trouble. It is recommended that serious or major servicing always be done by an authorized factory branch or franchised service distributor. Such branches or service centers are located in major cities throughout the world.

FIG. 19-1

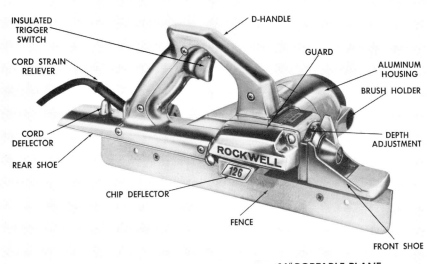

16″ PORTABLE PLANE

There are several reasons for relying on outside service. First, if serious problems arise, the required servicing and primarily the necessary electrical testing equipment are not available in the average cabinet, machine, and school shops or to the average contractor. Second, there are usually several tools of the same type in the shop, e.g., drill, sander, router, grinder, or saw; this is not true, of course, of most stationary equipment. It is therefore not inconvenient if one portable sander, for example, is being fixed while two or three others are still in operation. Third, the small size and weight of portable tools, in comparison with stationary machines, make it easy to take or ship a defective unit to a service outlet.

It is normally recommended that a specific brand of tool be returned to the original manufacturer's service center or branch for major overhaul or repair, for obvious reasons. Nevertheless, most service branches or distributors will repair competitive equipment and stock at least the high-mortality parts needed to service various brands. Some authorized distributors actually have service and parts franchises for more than one major manufacturer of portable electric tools.

There are many technical variables, both mechanical and electrical, that influence the price, the quality, and the operation of portable electric equipment. Aside from these, the overall reputation of the manufacturer and the availability of parts and service are probably the best criterion in choosing a portable tool. In general, tools rated as "domestic" or "utility" are for light duty or home use. Tools rated "industrial" are built for continuous service and are found in the average industrial, commercial, or school shop. Price is also a good guide, for the old adage "You get what you pay for" is quite applicable to equipment.

The following list of details should be considered, even prior to purchasing, in order to eliminate or reduce future service problems:

Reputation of the manufacturer
  What is the guarantee?
  What do present owners and users think?
Reputation of the distributor or dealer
  Does he stand behind the product?
  What do his present customers think?
  Does he repair portable tools?
  Does he stock high-mortality parts?
Location of factory service branch
  Is the authorized center or actual factory branch in the customer's area?
  Is it within easy shipping distance?
  Will a competitive factory branch work on all brands?
  Does it stock high-mortality competitive parts?
Amp rating
  Rule of thumb indicates 7 amp = 1 hp. Will the tool do your job without strain on working parts?

Bearings
   Are ball bearings and roller bearings used, or is the tool equipped
   with sleeve bearings? (Fig. 19-2a)
   Is there a ball thrust bearing?   (Fig. 19-2b)

Construction
   Is the case die-cast aluminum? (Fig. 19-3)
   Is it plastic?
   Is it grounded or insulated? (Fig. 19-4)
   Is it breakproof?
   Is it shockproof?
   Is there a separate motor frame?

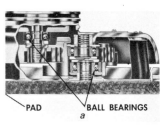

FIG. 19-2a

BALL THRUST BEARING

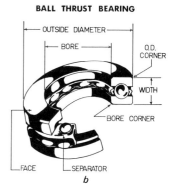

FIG. 19-2b

FIG. 19-3

INSULATED
TRIGGER
SWITCH

FIG. 19-4

Switch
   Is the switch separate and easy to replace in case of failure, or must
   other parts also be replaced?

Brushes
   Are the brushes easy to replace? (Fig. 19-5)
   Is the general area protected from excess dust or dirt?
   Are the brush caps recessed or protected?

Ventilation
   Is the fan adequate to cool the equipment properly? (Fig. 19-6)
   Are blades reasonably protected?

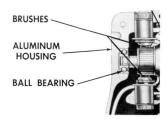

FIG. 19-5

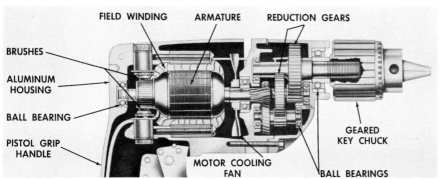

FIG. 19-6

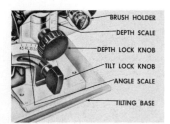

FIG. 19-7

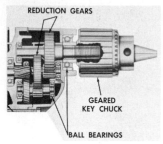

FIG. 19-8

FIG. 19-9

Controls
Are wing nuts, levers, or handles easy to replace? (Fig. 19-7)
Are they protected or out of the way while operating?

Vibration
Is excessive torque or vibration noticeable or objectionable?

Drive
Are reduction or drive gears easy to lubricate and easy to check or replace? (Fig. 19-8)
Are drive belts easy to install? (Fig. 19-9)

Lubrication
Is proper lubrication easy or difficult?
Are gear housings protected from dust and dirt?
Are grease seals adequate?

Motor
Is armature wire resin-coated and bonded? (Fig. 19-10)
Are commutator/coil connections welded?
Is pinion gear separately replaceable?

Cord
Is strain reliever provided? (Fig. 19-11)
Is cord the three-conductor type on all but double insulated tools?
Is the wire size correct for its length?

Rating
Is the tool UL (Underwriters Laboratory) or CSA (Canadian Standards Association) approved?
Is approval not possible because of nonvital reason?
Is the cord approved separately?

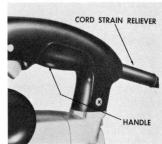

FIG. 19-11

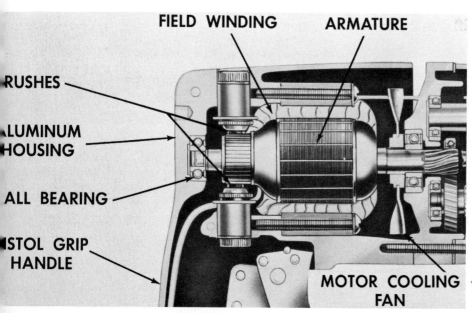

FIG. 19-10

GENERAL MAINTENANCE

One of the major causes of the failure of portable electric tools is the accumulation of dirt both outside and inside the case or housing. The tool should be blown out occasionally with an air hose to prevent the build-up of dust, grease, resin, and dirt. Eventually foreign material can cause serious overheating, lack of electrical contact, or physical and mechanical wear, shortening the life of the equipment considerably. The outside case also should be wiped clean after each use of the tool. This not only prevents dust from entering the case but also allows the operator to keep a firm grip on the tool. Many housings or cases are broken because the tool simply slipped out of the operator's hand.

Proper grounding should be checked periodically. The internal ground connection and the three-conductor plug can be inspected visually. The condition is normally satisfactory, but at least once a year it should be electrically checked for continuity with a meter, either by the operator or at a service branch (Fig. 19-12*a*).

Brushes should be checked or inspected every 50 hours (Fig. 19-12*b*). This might be as often as every two weeks in a cabinet shop or wood production shop, particularly for belt or finishing sanders. In a school shop it is a good policy to check the brushes on all portable electric equipment at least once a month.

After disconnecting the tool from the power supply, remove the brush caps. In some cases the spring and brush will come out with the cap. Since brushes have a tendency to wear in to fit the commutator exactly, care should be taken to remember which spring and brush were removed from each side of the tool. They should be replaced exactly as they came out—not reversed. If a number of tools are being checked by students or inexperienced operators, it is well to remove only one brush at a time. Carbon brushes should have at least 3/16 in. of usable material left; otherwise they should be replaced. Regardless of the exact wear on each brush, if one is replaced, both must be replaced. Never replace just one brush in a portable tool. Make sure the new brushes slide freely in the guides. The spring and the shunt wire should also be inspected and replaced if damaged (Fig. 19-13).

Replacement of these items, if worn or damaged, should be made only with original manufacturer's parts. Spring size, spring tension, actual brush size, hardness, and type are all carefully engineered to work best in each specific tool. It is a good idea for both school and industrial users to purchase and stock replacement brushes and springs. Doing this can help eliminate downtime or tool damage. Using the wrong brushes or springs can cause serious damage to the commutator.

All universal or ac/dc motor brushes will arc or spark when running, but excessive sparking usually indicates a rough or dirty commutator (Fig. 19-14). The commutator should be dressed or cleaned with special abrasive strips or flexible abrasive sticks made specifically for this pur-

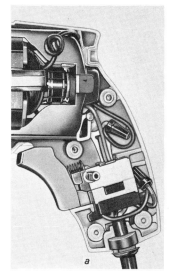

FIG. 19-12*a*

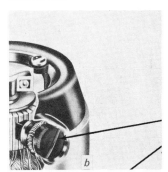

FIG. 19-12*b*

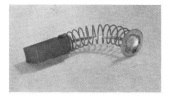

FIG. 19-13

FIG. 19-14

233

pose. Some care should be used in the cleaning operation. No attempt should be made to reshape or literally machine the commutator surface. Emery cloth or aluminum oxide should not be used because the abrasive material may produce electrical shorts in the future.

If replacing brushes and cleaning the commutator do not eliminate excessive sparking, the tool should be checked out at a service branch or authorized repair station. Such a condition indicates the possibility of an open, shorted, or grounded armature or field.

Lubrication should be done in strict accordance with the manufacturer's instructions. Special lubricants, if recommended, should be purchased and used (Fig. 19-15). Specifications for them carefully take temperature rise, type of materials, and other operating factors into consideration. The recommended hours of operation before change and the amount of lubricant to add should be strictly observed. Overfilling of gearboxes can cause a pumping action or increase pressure and break internal grease seals. In removing gear box or gear case covers, care should be taken not to damage the cover seals (Fig. 19-16). If not damaged or torn they can normally be used over and over again. The tool should be thoroughly blown out and wiped off clean before lubricating to prevent dirt, dust, or chips from accidentally entering the gear chambers.

If your portable electric tool fails to operate or will not start, the following checks should be made:

1. Check master electric panel for a blown fuse or tripped circuit breaker.

2. Make sure plug is making proper contact in wall receptacle.

3. Click the switch rapidly on and off as an initial check on a defective switch.

4. Disconnect the power and check for damaged, broken, or worn brushes. Make sure they slide freely in their guides or holders.

5. Check for large chips or other foreign material wedged between working parts.

6. Check for broken or damaged gears or belts in the drive system.

7. Check the power cord for broken internal conductors or wires. If bending the cord will stop and start the tool, replace the cord.

If after these initial checks the tool still fails to start, it should be inspected and repaired by a service branch.

Low speed, lack of power, or erratic operation can often be traced to the use of extension cords. The wrong size of wire or extended distances have a very definite effect on the power available at the tool. This is known as voltage drop. Up to 10 percent less than the rated voltage is usually not damaging to the motor, but it will affect the speed and power.

The sample chart shown in Fig. 19-17 is a good guide for wire sizes and distances recommended to avoid a damaging voltage drop.

FIG. 19-15

FIG. 19-16

RECOMMENDED EXTENSION CORD SIZES FOR USE WITH PORTABLE ELECTRIC TOOLS
(For Rubber Types S, SO, SR, SJ, SJO, SV, SP & Thermoplastic Types ST, SRT, SJT, SVP, SPT)

Nameplate Amperes	25	50	75	100	125	150	175	200	225	250	275	300	325	350	375	400	425	450	475	500
1	16	16	16	16	16	16	16	16	16	16	16	16	16	16	16	16	16	16	16	14
2	16	16	16	16	16	16	16	16	16	16	14	14	14	14	14	12	12	12	12	12
3	16	16	16	16	16	16	14	14	14	14	12	12	12	12	12	12	10	10	10	10
4	16	16	16	16	16	14	14	12	12	12	12	12	12	10	10	10	10	10	10	10
5	16	16	16	16	14	14	12	12	12	12	10	10	10	10	10	8	8	8	8	8
6	16	16	16	14	14	12	12	12	10	10	10	10	10	8	8	8	8	8	8	8
7	16	16	14	14	12	12	12	10	10	10	10	8	8	8	8	8	8	8	8	8
8	14	14	14	14	12	12	10	10	10	10	8	8	8	8	8	8	8	8	8	
9	14	14	14	12	12	10	10	10	8	8	8	8	8	8	8	8				
10	14	14	14	12	12	10	10	10	8	8	8	8	8	8	8					
11	12	12	12	12	10	10	10	8	8	8	8	8	8	8						
12	12	12	12	12	10	10	8	8	8	8	8	8	8							
13	12	12	12	12	10	10	8	8	8	8	8	8								
14	10	10	10	10	10	10	8	8	8	8	8									
15	10	10	10	10	10	8	8	8	8	8										
16	10	10	10	10	10	8	8	8	8											
17	10	10	10	10	10	8	8	8	8											
18	8	8	8	8	8	8	8	8	8											
19	8	8	8	8	8	8	8	8												
20	8	8	8	8	8	8	8	8												

NOTES: Wire sizes are for 3-CDR Cords, one CDR of which is used to provide a continuous grounding circuit from tool housing to receptacle.
Wire sizes shown are A. W. G. (American Wire Gauge).
Based on 115V power supply; Ambient Temp. of 30°C, 86°F.

FIG. 19-17

CHAPTER TWENTY
Portable Air Tools

Portable air tools (Fig. 20-1) are less complicated than most portable electric tools or stationary power tools, and they require less maintenance or preventive maintenance. The normal air motor (Fig. 20-2) is a relatively simple assembly although built to extremely close tolerances. Governors, clutch assemblies (Fig. 20-3), planetary gearing (Fig. 20-4), and torque control systems (Fig. 20-5), which provide the control necessary for specific tool and job applications, are more complicated.

The primary problems with air equipment are often related to the entire system of air supply, the compressor, the air lines, the fittings and couplings, the filters, the lubricator, and the air regulator. Therefore the complete system should be periodically checked as a definite part of the preventive maintenance program. The tool itself is only the final part of this package.

The lubricator (Fig. 20-6) is necessary for proper operation of air tools. This unit, which is placed in the air line, should be checked at least once a day. Any standard nonoxidizing oil, SAE 10 or 20, or an emulsifying oil can be used to fill the bowl. It should be kept full. Oil in the air stream provides many benefits and is essential to the preventive maintenance required.

When oil mixed with the air moves through the tool, a low-friction film is left between moving surfaces, providing lubrication and creating a sealing action between high and low pressure areas in the motor. Rust is retarded, and dirt is pushed out or flushed through the line, the hose, and

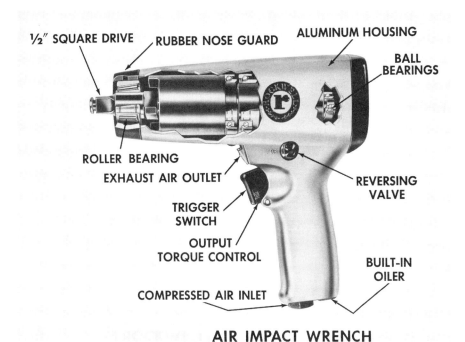

½" SQUARE DRIVE
RUBBER NOSE GUARD
ALUMINUM HOUSING
BALL BEARINGS
ROLLER BEARING
EXHAUST AIR OUTLET
TRIGGER SWITCH
OUTPUT TORQUE CONTROL
COMPRESSED AIR INLET
REVERSING VALVE
BUILT-IN OILER

AIR IMPACT WRENCH

FIG. 20-1

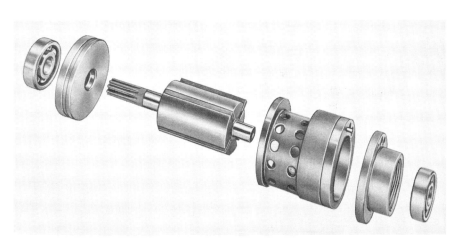

FIG. 20-2

FIG. 20-3

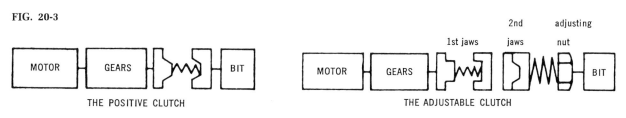

MOTOR | GEARS | BIT

THE POSITIVE CLUTCH

1st jaws | 2nd jaws | adjusting nut

MOTOR | GEARS | BIT

THE ADJUSTABLE CLUTCH

237

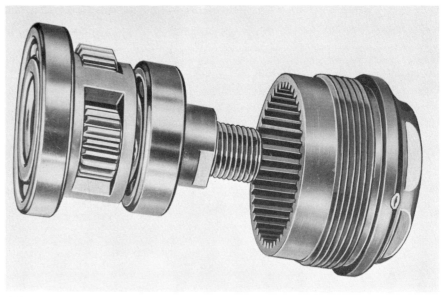

FIG. 20-4

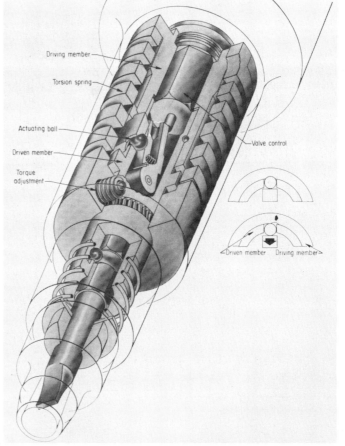

Driving member

Torsion spring

Actuating ball

Driven member

Torque adjustment

Valve control

Driven member   Driving member

FIG. 20-5

KEEP OIL LEVEL
BELOW LINE

Micro-Fog

FIG. 20-6

the motor. Oil acts also as a coolant, dissipating heat from specific areas.

Filters (Fig. 20-7) in the line and screens in hose couplings should be checked and cleaned as often as necessary. If screens are pierced or broken, dirt can enter the tool freely. If the filter or a screen is loaded, the air supply or pressure is reduced and tool speed and efficiency are seriously affected. A filter and oiler installed in an air line, together or as a package, are often called a vitalizer (Fig. 20-8a).

Lines, hoses, and couplings should be checked for correct size. Pressure drops, caused by undersize fittings and couplings in particular, cause many problems. The normal and continuous pressure needed is 90 psig, in addition to a sufficient quantity of air. Correction of a pressure problem may be related to the number and type of tools being operated at any given time. This in turn requires a possible check of the compressor, its capacity, and even storage tanks which may be in the system (Fig. 20-8b).

In most cases the hose connection at the tool indicates the correct size of hose recommended by the manufacturer (Fig. 20-9). Beyond this point

FIG. 20-7

FIG. 20-8a

FIG. 20-8b

FIG. 20-9

it is recommended that the manufacturer or distributor be contacted for an engineering opinion. Most air tool salesmen are well versed in system capacities and proper installation from compressor to tools.

Air tools should be kept clean. Dirt should not be allowed to collect around exhaust parts or fitting connections. The air motor should be taken apart and cleaned with solvent at least once a year when used in a school shop and as often as every three or four months in a cabinet or industrial woodshop (Fig. 20-10). Dirt and gum should be removed from all parts of the motor, governor, clutch, and other operating parts. Blades should be checked for wear. They should be no less than .004 in. shorter than the cylinder, otherwise these blades or vanes should be replaced. Excessive wear on the leading edge is usually an indication of insufficient oil in the air supply.

The bearings used in air tools are usually sealed and cannot be cleaned. They should be checked for roughness and replaced if found to be rough in turning or to have even a slight amount of side play. Because close tolerances are necessary, this is vital. Open bearings should be washed in clean solvent and oiled or lubricated according to the manufacturer's recommendations.

Governors (Fig. 20-11), clutch assemblies, and planetary gear units should be carefully disassembled and cleaned in solvent. Care should be taken to remember or otherwise note how these items came apart in order to reassemble them correctly. They should be lubricated as the manufacturer suggests before reassembly. Bushings in most governors should be inspected for wear and replaced if necessary. The correct speed not only is necessary for efficient operation but can also be a safety factor.

Most schools or small shops rely on the manufacturer for actual service or major maintenance. This saves the expense of stocking parts and the time lost in experimenting to find out what is wrong, what is worn, what is broken, and what must be replaced. Since air tools are expensive to purchase, regardless of the benefits, they are also usually expensive to have repaired. Most manufacturers will submit an estimate covering both parts and labor after checking the tool. The user can then judge for himself whether the tool should be fixed or a new unit should be

FIG. 20-10

FIG. 20-11

purchased. Most air tool users consider replacing the tool when repair costs are in excess of 50 percent of the cost of a new tool. When this point is reached, the equipment is usually outdated after continuous use for a period of many years. Most efficient and better tools have probably been designed meanwhile, making the consideration of a new tool a must.

All guards should be in good condition and properly fastened to the tool (Fig. 20-12). Moving parts and assemblies should be dry-lubricated and operate as the manufacturer intended.

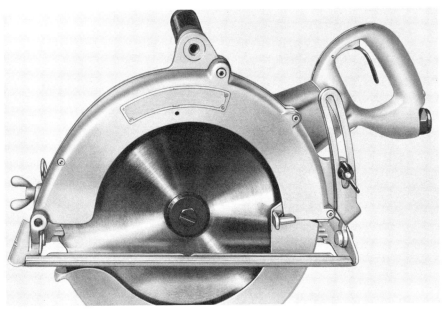

FIG. 20-12

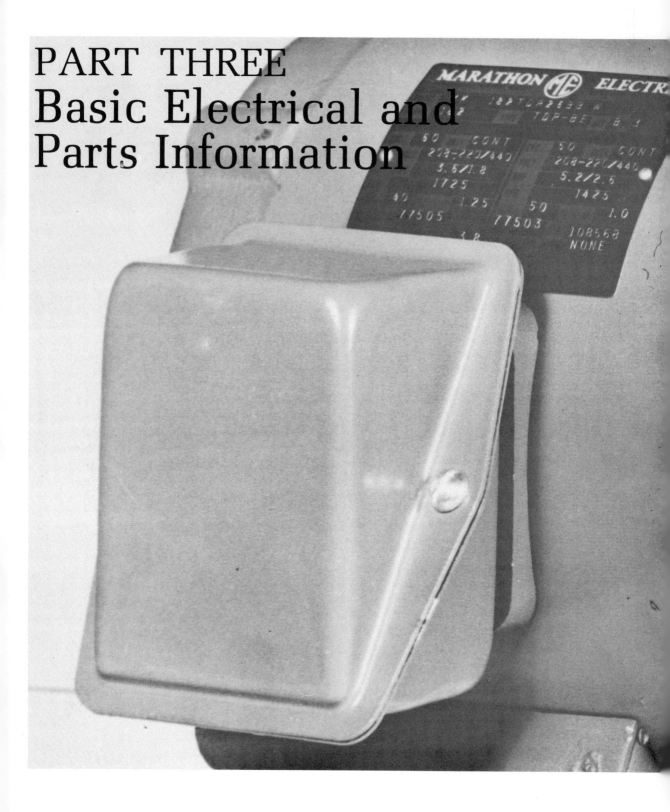

PART THREE
Basic Electrical and
Parts Information

CHAPTER TWENTY-ONE

Motors—Wiring and Controls

In general little actual maintenance is necessary on modern electric motors or controls. Usually the lack of cleanliness, the cause of most problems, should be the major concern.

It is sometimes necessary, however, for the teacher or operator to move stationary machines, rewire or originally connect motors and controls, or purchase new stationary or electrical equipment. A general or layman's understanding of motors, controls, and wiring is therefore almost a necessity. Successful operation, continued operation, safe operation, and even an absence of maintenance or service problems are often the rewards of basic and simple understanding. This knowledge should be applied to purchasing, operating, and maintaining even more than to the equipment itself.

MOTORS

In purchasing it is reasonable to select the lowest-cost motors and motor controls which will give satisfactory service, not only at the start but throughout the anticipated life of the equipment. The lowest-priced motor and control can of course be selected by referring to price lists, but some understanding of the machine and its actual use is needed to choose the motor or controls which will be the lowest in cost over the long run without failure to give the quality of service required.

In motors as in most other things, you get about what you pay for, in quality. Two motors of different makes, both rated ½ hp on the name-plate, may vary a good deal in such important factors as efficiency, starting torque, temperature rise, breakdown torque, rating as to continuous or intermittent service, interference with lighting systems or radios and television sets, freedom from failures and costly repairs, freedom from vibration, speed constancy, type of bearings, and shaft diameter. A "cheap" motor and a "good" motor may both be correctly rated at ½ hp by National Electrical Manufacturers Association (NEMA) standards, and yet the low-priced motor may consume more current and require more repairs, actually costing more to own and operate. The quality motor will run much longer than the cheap one in laboratory tests. It will run much longer also when driving a machine in actual shop use, and besides it will give better performance right from the start. Although these factors are usually considered only when purchasing, they all are directly related to maintenance and service.

There are two basic kinds of electric motors, and many varieties of each type are available. The specific motor to be chosen depends on many details, not only of the motor itself, but of the machine and its use. The following information in layman's language spells out both the differences and the purposes.

UNIVERSAL (AC/DC) MOTORS

These motors are called universal because they will run on either direct or alternating (single-phase) current. The speed, which is not regulated, builds up dangerously high when there is no load and slows down tremendously in proportion to increasing load. This inconsistency in speed could make machines inaccurate, inconvenient, and unsafe, depending, of course, upon the application. Universal motors do have a use, however. They are often used for stationary equipment accessories like a knife grinding attachment or a vacuum cleaner type of dust collector. They are used also by all manufacturers of portable electric tools because they can be plugged in on alternating or direct current and will automatically run slower under a heavier load (Fig. 21-1). They also allow the designer to provide more horsepower in a smaller and more portable package. Through gearing it is now possible to use universal motors in applications formerly considered not advisable if not impossible.

CONSTANT-SPEED MOTORS

Direct-current (DC) Motors

This is the oldest type of motor, but it is used very infrequently today because alternating current is more commonly available. Direct current,

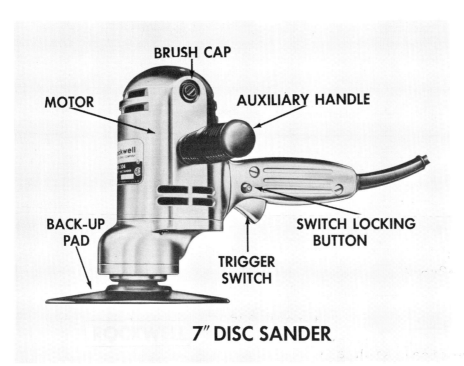

BRUSH CAP

MOTOR

AUXILIARY HANDLE

BACK-UP
PAD

SWITCH LOCKING
BUTTON

TRIGGER
SWITCH

7" DISC SANDER

FIG. 21-1

for one thing, cannot be transmitted over long distances as high-voltage alternating current can be. Generally, the only reason for wanting a dc motor is that only direct current is available; in fact, some plants generate their own dc electricity. Because of the very limited demand, dc motors are expensive and often hard to obtain. They do not hold a constant speed as well as ac motors, they cause radio and TV interference, and they require maintenance of commutator and brushes. They are also larger than the more common ac motors of the same horsepower rating.

Alternating-current (AC) Motors

Alternating current is current that reverses its direction at regular intervals; i.e., the power fluctuates (at a fast rate), causing an instant peak of power followed by an instant of low power. For single-phase current this can be graphically drawn (Fig. 21-2). Three-phase alternating current means that there are three surges or phases of current going through the wire simultaneously and the fluctuations are timed so that one peak occurs when another phase is at a lower power period (Fig. 21-3). Three-phase current, therefore, maintains a much more steady flow of peak power.

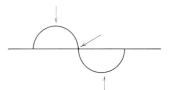

FIG. 21-2

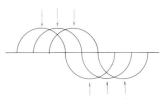

FIG. 21-3

Three-phase Motors

Generally speaking, the three-phase motors (Fig. 21-4) are recommended whenever three-phase current is available. An exceptional case

FIG. 21-4

would be a contractor who has both three- and single-phase current in his shop but might want to take the machine out to a job where only single-phase is available. Most cabinet shops, tool and die shops, and school shops would choose three-phase motors and controls. Not only is the power cost lower, but more usable torque is obtained from a three-phase motor than from a single-phase motor in the same horsepower category. A three-phase motor and starter cost a little more than a single-phase motor and switch, in the fractional horsepower sizes, and a little less in the integral horsepower sizes. It has a medium to high starting torque and a very high breakdown torque.

As for maintenance, the three-phase motor is in a class by itself in respect to freedom from failures and repair costs. This is only natural because it has no brushes, no commutator, and no internal starting switch—in fact no starting mechanism at all. In short, it is the best of the motors under discussion.

Two-phase Motors

Mechanically and electrically the two-phase motor is similar to the three-phase motor, but so few of them are sold that delivery is slow and the price is high. In the average shop they are for all practical purposes nonexistent.

FIG. 21-5

Single-phase Motors

There are three types of single-phase motors. Each one has starting characteristics adapted to a certain kind of load.

Repulsion-start–induction-run motors: This was the first successful type of single-phase induction motor in regular commercial use and was popular from 1896 until 1930 or so. Repulsion-induction (RI) motors are still used on some equipment because by lever they can be reversed quickly without tools or a switch (Fig. 21-5). They are still used on some tilting arbor saws because they have no capacitor to take up needed space on either the inside or the outside of the motor frame. They are also used for hard-to-start equipment because they have a starting torque 3 to 4 times the running torque and the starting current is 2½ to 3 times the running current. The RI motor has a wound rotor with commutator and brushes. When the motor reaches about three-quarters full speed, the commutator bars are short-circuited and the motor runs as an induction motor. All this requires maintenance. The motion must be kept clean and possibly blown out with air periodically. Around 1933, capacitor-start motors began to take the place of the RI motors, especially in fractional horsepower ratings, until now with few exceptions RI motors are not made in fractional sizes. The RI motor is very efficient but also the most expensive single-phase motor.

Split-phase–induction-run motors: The term "split-phase" refers to the method used to get the motor started. There is a starting winding as well as a running winding. When the motor reaches about 80 percent of

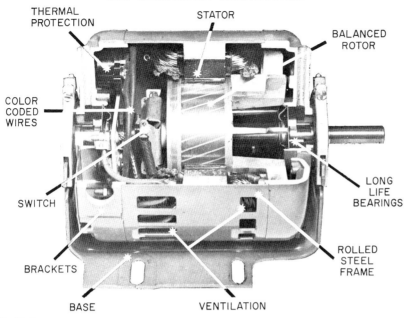

THERMAL PROTECTION

STATOR

BALANCED ROTOR

COLOR CODED WIRES

LONG LIFE BEARINGS

SWITCH

BRACKETS

ROLLED STEEL FRAME

BASE

VENTILATION

FIG. 21-6

its operating speed, the starting winding is disconnected by a centrifugal switch and the motor operates as an induction motor (Fig. 21-6).

Split-phase motors are most often used as small fractional-horse-power motors—from $\frac{1}{20}$ to $\frac{1}{2}$ hp—and are the most widely used kind of single-phase motor, especially the $\frac{1}{4}$-hp rating as used on washing machines.

These are the least expensive of the three kinds of single-phase motors and have been in commercial use very successfully almost as long as the RI motor. They have a low starting torque and a medium break-down torque and are therefore ideally used for machines that start under a light load and run continuously under an even load not heavy enough to cause the motor to fall back on the starting winding. In general they are not recommended for a cabinet or school shop because of the extremely intermittent use there. This slowly but surely wears out the internal centrifugal switch. If on the same circuit, they often cause lights to dim while starting because of the high starting current needed. They require some maintenance cleaning and even replacement of the internal starting switch. If they are repeatedly stalled or started under too heavy a load, a major repair job is usually required.

Capacitor-start–induction-run motors: This motor uses a condenser connected in a series with a starting winding. It starts very well under a load and pulls back up to speed after a brief overload. It is an efficient motor with a high starting torque and a high breakdown torque.

The direction of rotation may be reversed by interchanging the leads to the starting winding. Capacitor-start motors do not use brushes, and they are so designed that they do not cause lights to dim when starting and do not cause radio interference.

Like the split-phase motors, they have an internal starting switch that needs some maintenance or replacement, and a starting winding; but they have also one item the split-phase lacks—the condenser (which rarely needs replacement) (Fig. 21-7). The capacitor-start motor starts much easier than the split-phase under a load, and it pulls back up to speed much faster after a brief overload. There is much less chance of burning out the starting winding than in the split-phase motor.

FIG. 21-7

This motor has been in successful commercial use since the development of inexpensive and reliable electrolytic condensers in about 1930, and its popularity has grown rapidly since about 1933. At first, there were many old-timers who still wanted the RI motor and had sales resistance to the capacitor-start motor. There was some basis for this prejudice because at first the condensers gave some trouble. Now the capacitor-start motors are very popular, and little trouble is given by them. In fact the major motor manufacturers have stopped making RI motors entirely in the general-purpose fractional-horsepower class. Previously the choice among single-phase motors was between the split-phase and the repulsion-induction, but now it is between the split-phase and the capacitor-start when selecting a fractional-horsepower motor. When starting torque is considered and performance in general is compared, the RI and capacitor motors are similar.

The capacitor-start motors cost quite a bit more than the split-phase, but they are not quite as expensive as the repulsion-start motors. A capacitor-start single-phase motor and switch cost less than a three-phase motor and starter in fractional-horsepower ratings.

Very possibly the best rule of thumb is to purchase the specific motor recommended by the machine manufacturer. You can then be certain that all the factors have been checked out by engineers in the relationship of the motor to the machine itself and the job it was designed to do. Short specific rules of thumb are:

1. Check the machine and the horsepower needed for the work to be done.

2. Check the current available.

3. Reach a quality or price level.

4. Choose the type of motor which will satisfy the first three requirements.

The major problems incurred by not using the exact motor specified by the machine manufacturer are related to the actual dimensions of the

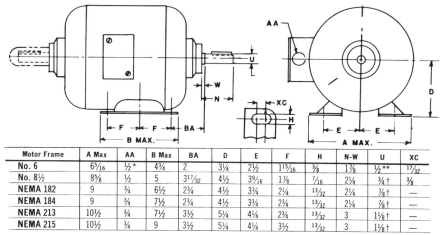

Motor Frame	A Max	AA	B Max	BA	D	E	F	H	N-W	U	XC
No. 6	$6\frac{5}{16}$	$\frac{1}{2}$ *	$4\frac{3}{4}$	2	$3\frac{1}{4}$	$2\frac{1}{2}$	$1\frac{15}{16}$	$\frac{3}{8}$	$1\frac{1}{8}$	$\frac{1}{2}$ **	$\frac{17}{32}$
No. 8½	$8\frac{5}{8}$	$\frac{1}{2}$	5	$3\frac{17}{32}$	$4\frac{1}{2}$	$3\frac{9}{16}$	$1\frac{7}{8}$	$\frac{7}{16}$	$2\frac{1}{4}$	$\frac{3}{4}$ †	$\frac{3}{8}$
NEMA 182	9	$\frac{3}{4}$	$6\frac{1}{2}$	$2\frac{3}{4}$	$4\frac{1}{2}$	$3\frac{3}{4}$	$2\frac{1}{4}$	$\frac{13}{32}$	$2\frac{1}{4}$	$\frac{7}{8}$ †	—
NEMA 184	9	$\frac{3}{4}$	$7\frac{1}{2}$	$2\frac{3}{4}$	$4\frac{1}{2}$	$3\frac{3}{4}$	$2\frac{3}{4}$	$\frac{13}{32}$	$2\frac{1}{4}$	$\frac{7}{8}$ †	—
NEMA 213	$10\frac{1}{2}$	$\frac{3}{4}$	$7\frac{1}{2}$	$3\frac{1}{2}$	$5\frac{1}{4}$	$4\frac{1}{4}$	$2\frac{3}{4}$	$\frac{13}{32}$	3	$1\frac{1}{8}$ †	—
NEMA 215	$10\frac{1}{2}$	$\frac{3}{4}$	9	$3\frac{1}{2}$	$5\frac{1}{4}$	$4\frac{1}{4}$	$3\frac{1}{2}$	$\frac{13}{32}$	3	$1\frac{1}{8}$ †	—

FIG. 21-8

frame or enclosure, the mounting feet or brackets, the total length, and the shaft length (Fig. 21-8). In most cases differences will make it inconvenient, difficult, or actually impossible to mount the motor. Although there are standards, many equipment manufacturers use "custom-made motors" which are similar to the standard but slightly different in one or more dimensions; their object is better conformance to a specific machine design or purpose.

The bearings used in the motors generally supplied with the stationary power tool or machinery are the sealed-for-life ball bearing type, which cause few or no problems. There is really no maintenance involved, only possible replacement after a long period of time. Ball bearing motors can be mounted in any position, vertical or horizontal. Sleeve bearing motors are still used for some light-duty applications. These units require proper lubrication and are supplied with oil cups (Fig. 21-9). A typical application is a fan motor. In most cases, unless specifically designed, the sleeve bearing motor must be used in the horizontal position only.

FIG. 21-9

There are probably as many types of motor enclosures or case configurations as there are motor manufacturers. The two most common types, found in the average school shop, tool and die shop, cabinet shop, or experimental laboratory, are the guarded dripproof (GD) and the totally enclosed–fan-cooled (TEFC). Neither type requires any real maintenance, but the open or GD motor should occasionally be blown out with air to prevent any buildup of dust or dirt. The machine manufacturer will always specify the type of motor enclosure best suited to the dirt, dust, or moisture conditions normally associated with the machine's operation (Fig. 21-10).

If dust and dirt are blown out of open motors, and belts and pulleys are kept in alignment, modern motors should be practically maintenance-

Catalog Number	H.P.	R.P.M.	Volts	Cycles	Shaft	Frame Size	Switch	Cord & Plug	Enclosure	Duty	Wt. Lbs.
96-429	5	3450	230/460	60	1⅛" Single	NEMA 213	—		TEFC	Heavy	133
96-449	7½	3450	230/460	60	1⅛" Single	NEMA 213	—		TEFC	Heavy	150
96-629	3	1725	230/460	60	1⅛" Single	NEMA 213	—		GD	Heavy	74
96-659	3	3450	230/460	60	7/8" Single	NEMA 184	—		GD	Heavy	120
96-679	3	1725	230/460	60	1⅛" Single	NEMA 215	—		TENV	Heavy	125
96-729	5	1725	230/460	60	1⅛" Single	NEMA 215	—		GD	Heavy	110
96-749	5	3450	230/460	60	1⅛" Single	NEMA 213	—		GD	Heavy	106
96-779	5	1725	230/460	60	1⅛" Single	NEMA 215	—		TENV	Heavy	132
96-849	7½	3450	230/460	60	1⅛" Single	NEMA 215	—		GD	Heavy	106

FIG. 21-10

free. If you think a good cleaning is necessary, it is not difficult to carefully remove the end belts or brackets and the rotor from the stator. Care should be taken with internal centrifugal switch parts, brushes, etc., depending on the specific type of motor (Fig. 21-11).

WIRING

Most wiring problems in motors and controls are easily solved by *reading* and *following* the information found on the motor plate (Fig. 21-12) or on the inside of the control box cover (Fig. 21-13). Tool manufacturers include wiring information for the specific motors they sell or recommend in the instruction or parts manuals issued with the machine. They often also publish separate wiring manuals for groups of machines which use the same motor or controls (Fig. 21-14). If a wiring problem is obviously due to a motor, a reversing switch, and a magnetic starter from three different manufacturers, the best solution is to draw your own diagram on paper before attempting any actual work. By reading the nameplate instructions and drawing lines from terminal to terminal on the component parts, you will find the correction solution automatically.

State and local codes regarding electrical work should be checked, particularly in school or public buildings. The following is a suggested checklist:

What size of wire is required for different voltages or amp draw?

Are wire nuts or similar connectors allowable?

Must wires be soldered, and where?

What type of insulation is required for the short connections between motor and starter?

Are extensions allowable?

Are Hubble or Twistlock connections allowable?

Is flexible sheathing or BX required or allowable?

252

STATER

DIE-CAST ROTOR

FIG. 21-12

BRACKETS

BEARINGS

FIG. 21-13

FIG. 21-11

Is thin wall tubing or conduit required?

Can you do your own wiring? If so, must it be inspected?

Must a registered electrician do this work?

Is any special grounding required?

Are double-pole switches required for single phase?

Is there a length limit on single phase extensions?

Will any additional equipment exceed the allowable amp draw at the entrance box?

Is UL (Underwriters Laboratory) or CSA (Canadian Standards Association) or NEMA (National Electrical Manufacturers Association) approval required on the equipment?

Are magnetic starters required for both single- and three-phase, only three-phase, or neither?

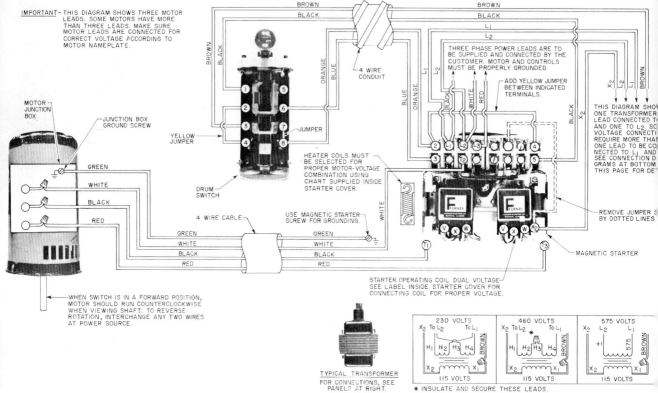

REVERSING DRUM SWITCH AND MAGNETIC STARTER
WITH LOW VOLTAGE CONTROL
FOR THREE PHASE MOTORS

IMPORTANT— THIS DIAGRAM SHOWS THREE MOTOR LEADS. SOME MOTORS HAVE MORE THAN THREE LEADS. MAKE SURE MOTOR LEADS ARE CONNECTED FOR CORRECT VOLTAGE ACCORDING TO MOTOR NAMEPLATE.

THREE PHASE POWER LEADS ARE TO BE SUPPLIED AND CONNECTED BY THE CUSTOMER. MOTOR AND CONTROLS MUST BE PROPERLY GROUNDED

ADD YELLOW JUMPER BETWEEN INDICATED TERMINALS.

MOTOR JUNCTION BOX

JUNCTION BOX GROUND SCREW

YELLOW JUMPER

JUMPER

HEATER COILS MUST BE SELECTED FOR PROPER MOTOR-VOLTAGE COMBINATION USING CHART SUPPLIED INSIDE STARTER COVER.

DRUM SWITCH

4 WIRE CONDUIT

THIS DIAGRAM SHO ONE TRANSFORMER LEAD CONNECTED T AND ONE TO L_2. SO VOLTAGE CONNECTI REQUIRE MORE THA ONE LEAD TO BE CO NECTED TO L_1 ANI SEE CONNECTION D GRAMS AT BOTTOM THIS PAGE FOR DET

GREEN
WHITE
BLACK
RED

4 WIRE CABLE

USE MAGNETIC STARTER SCREW FOR GROUNDING.

REMOVE JUMPER BY DOTTED LINES

MAGNETIC STARTER

GREEN
WHITE
BLACK
RED

GREEN
WHITE
BLACK
RED

STARTER OPERATING COIL DUAL VOLTAGE— SEE LABEL INSIDE STARTER COVER FOR CONNECTING COIL FOR PROPER VOLTAGE.

WHEN SWITCH IS IN A FORWARD POSITION, MOTOR SHOULD RUN COUNTERCLOCKWISE WHEN VIEWING SHAFT. TO REVERSE ROTATION, INTERCHANGE ANY TWO WIRES AT POWER SOURCE.

TYPICAL TRANSFORMER FOR CONNECTIONS, SEE PANELS AT RIGHT.

230 VOLTS	460 VOLTS	575 VOLTS
X_2 To L_2 To L_1	X_2 To L_2 To L_1	X_2 L_2 L_1
H_1 H_2 H_3 H_4	H_1 H_2 H_3 H_4	
X_2 X_1	X_2 X_1	X_2 X_1
115 VOLTS	115 VOLTS	115 VOLTS

* INSULATE AND SECURE THESE LEADS.

FIG. 21-14

FIG. 21-15

CONTROLS

On-and-Off Toggle Switches

As the name implies, these are switches operated by a manually actuated lever or toggle, for the simple purpose of turning a motor on or off. This is the type of motor control regularly used on fractional-horsepower single-phase ac motors (Fig. 21-15). Two kinds are in common use, one-pole switches and two-pole switches, both possibly UL approved, but one better than the other.

Both will turn the motor on and off, and since the one-pole switch is a little cheaper, it is often used. When the one-pole switch is turned off, only one of the two hot wires from the wall receptacle to the motor is broken. The other wire is still connecting the receptacle to the winding of the motor. Because of this, there may or may not be a hot wire into the motor even when the switch is off, depending on which way the plug prongs are inserted into the receptacle. In an attempt to solve this

254

problem, many receptacles and plugs were made with one blade of the plug and one slot in the receptacle wider. This works only if the connections on the switch break the correct line, and so actually the success of this polarized plug depends on who did the wiring.

The modern and accepted three-prong grounding plug and receptacle (Fig. 21-16) are by far the safest method because if properly wired, the machine is definitely grounded at all times. It is well to check the outlet or receptacle to make sure it is definitely grounded inside the box. Needless to say, the grounding plug should never be clipped off to make it fit into an older receptacle. Adapters are available (Fig. 21-17), and the pigtail should be grounded or fastened to the box and checked before using. The best solution, of course, is to replace the old receptacle with the modern three-prong grounded type, being sure to connect the ground to the box. In all cases check or test before using.

There is more chance of a dangerous short with a single-pole switch than with a double-pole switch, which breaks both sides of the line. The manufacturer's catalog should indicate the type of any standard equipment switches supplied with the machine. Many of the small switches are totally enclosed in plastic and require no cleaning or maintenance.

FIG. 21-16

FIG. 21-17

Reversing Switches

Reversing switches are used where it is necessary to change the direction of rotation of a motor frequently, in order to get full use of a machine.

These switches are applicable to dc, three-phase, split-phase, single-phase, and capacitor-start single-phase motors. They cannot be used with repulsion-start single-phase motors. RI motors are reversed by shifting the brush rigging, which usually requires the use of wrenches and takes time. This problem has been solved neatly on some RI motors by fastening a lever on the brush rigging and providing two notches for the lever, one for forward and the other for reverse. This not only makes it possible to reverse the motor in a second or two, but makes it unnecessary to spend the money for a reversing switch when single-phase current is available.

The reversing switches have three positions: forward-off-reverse. The catalog recommendations should be followed as to whether a separate on- and off-control should be used.

Reversing switches may be drum type (Fig. 21-18) or push-button type. Choosing between these is often a matter of personal preference or familiarity with one or the other.

Manual Starters

Like the on-and-off toggle switches, these starters serve to turn on the current to start the motor and turn it off to stop the motor. The contacts are made or broken by the manual or hand action of pressing on push buttons.

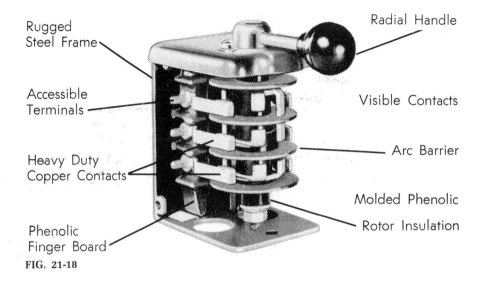

Rugged Steel Frame

Radial Handle

Accessible Terminals

Visible Contacts

Arc Barrier

Heavy Duty Copper Contacts

Molded Phenolic Rotor Insulation

Phenolic Finger Board

FIG. 21-18

Manual starters perform one other important function—giving the motor overload protection (Fig. 21-19).

This means that the motor itself is protected because the power will be shut off automatically before the motor heats up to the point of burning out. Without such protection it is possible for a fire to start in the shop from a badly overheated motor.

These starters have thermal elements consisting of heater coils and a eutectic (low melting point) material so that a *sustained* overload causes the power to be shut off. This occurs when more than the full load current of the motor passes through the heater coil for a long enough period of time to melt the eutectic material. Nothing is destroyed in the starter, and after a waiting period the starter can be reset and used as before. Needless to say, it is recommended to check and remove the cause if automatic shutoff occurs repeatedly.

Heater coils from one brand of starter normally cannot be used in another brand because each electrical manufacturer has a slightly different system.

The overload protection of these starters is far better than fuse protection alone, as explained by the word "sustained." The starter shuts off the power neither while the motor is drawing more than full load current in normal starting nor under a short period overload. A fuse small enough to give the motor full protection would burn out while the motor was starting, and a fuse large enough to allow the motor to start would allow the motor to heat up to the danger point when running. A fuse protects only against a very extreme overload on the line or a dead short.

Any one starter can be supplied with a large selection of thermal elements ranging from small to large current ratings. It is most important that the supplier of the starter know the full nameplate data of the motor for which the starter is to be used. With this information the supplier

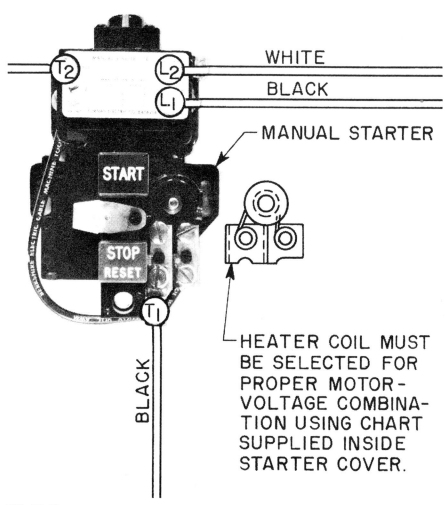

GREEN

WHITE

BLACK

MANUAL STARTER

HEATER COIL MUST
BE SELECTED FOR
PROPER MOTOR-
VOLTAGE COMBINA-
TION USING CHART
SUPPLIED INSIDE
STARTER COVER.

FIG. 21-19

will know the full load amperage rating from which the proper element size is selected. In the case of dual voltage motors, the voltage to be used must be stated, because a motor on 230 volts has about twice the full load amperage rating of the same motor on 460 volts, etc. If the thermal element is too small, the power will be shut off automatically under conditions of normal starting or safe overload currents. If the thermal element is too large, the motor is simply not going to get the protection which is needed, but the operator probably will not complain at all unless the motor burns out.

Manual starters are used with all the kinds of motors—dc, three-phase ac, two-phase ac, and single-phase ac. Most single-phase ac general-purpose motors come with on-and-off toggle switches, and in most cases a manual starter or magnetic starter is not considered necessary. This is a specific option. For instance, some schools require a magnetic starter on all equipment regardless of the size or type of current, strictly for safety. The real problem is that the manual starter, although providing protection for the machine, provides little or none for the operator in no-voltage or low-voltage situation. For instance, if the power were to fail for two minutes and the operator did not physically push the off button or throw the lever to "off," the machine would automatically start when the power came on again. This could create an extremely unsafe situation in a school shop or in any shop with inexperienced operators. This is true regardless of the type of current. Safety regulations everywhere require that a manual starter or magnetic starter be used with three-phase and two-phase motors.

Magnetic Starters

Like the manual starter, the magnetic starter starts and stops a motor by turning the current on and off, and it gives the motor overload protection. It also performs one additional important function, no-voltage and under-voltage protection (Fig. 21-20). If the voltage drops below a certain level even momentarily or if it is entirely interrupted even momentarily, the power is automatically cut off by the magnetic starter and remains off. The motor must be intentionally started again by pressing on the start button, after the trouble has been corrected. The power will not come on automatically. This is a real safety feature for the machine operator.

When you press the start button of a magnetic starter, contacts are made and current flows, both through a magnetic coil in the starter and through the motor. As soon as you remove your finger from the start button, a spring or springs immediately try to break the contacts but are prevented from breaking the contacts and shutting off the motor, only as long as a steady and sufficient current flows through the magnetic coil.

The supplier of a magnetic starter needs to know the complete motor nameplate data and the line voltage in order to provide the proper size of thermal element. This is the same as for the manual starters, with the same bad results if the thermal element is too small or too large. The supplier must know the line voltage in order to supply a magnetic coil of corresponding voltage specifications.

Magnetic starters are used with all the kinds of motors—dc, three-phase ac, two-phase ac, and single-phase ac.

A magnetic starter does everything to control and protect the motor that a manual starter does, but because it also provides the safety of no-voltage and undervoltage protection, it is frequently specified for schools, where there may be a number of inexperienced people in the shop. Magnetic starters are available also with low-voltage control, or 115 volts at the switch (Fig. 21-21).

PUSH BUTTON SWITCH AND MAGNETIC STARTER
FOR SINGLE PHASE MOTORS

IMPORTANT – THIS DIAGRAM SHOWS TWO MOTOR LEADS. SOME MOTORS HAVE MORE THAN TWO LEADS. MAKE SURE MOTOR LEADS ARE CONNECTED FOR CORRECT VOLTAGE ACCORDING TO MOTOR NAMEPLATE.

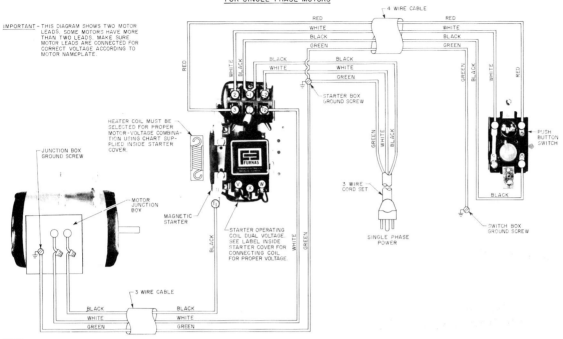

FIG. 21-20

PUSH BUTTON SWITCH AND MAGNETIC STARTER
WITH LOW VOLTAGE CONTROL
FOR THREE PHASE MOTORS

THREE PHASE POWER LEADS ARE TO BE SUPPLIED AND CONNECTED BY THE CUSTOMER. MOTOR AND CONTROLS MUST BE PROPERLY GROUNDED.

IMPORTANT– THIS DIAGRAM SHOWS THREE MOTOR LEADS. SOME MOTORS HAVE MORE THAN THREE LEADS. MAKE SURE MOTOR LEADS ARE CONNECTED FOR CORRECT VOLTAGE ACCORDING TO MOTOR NAMEPLATE.

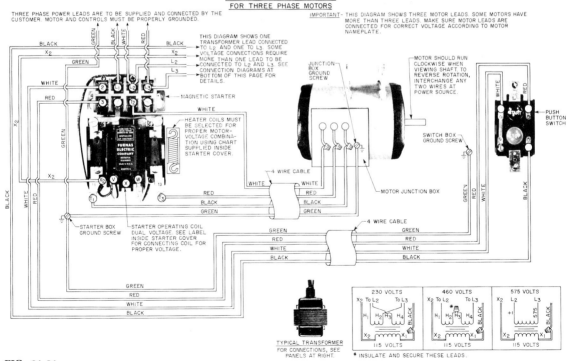

FIG. 21-21

259

Separate control stations, for both manual and magnetic starters, are available with all the elements in one enclosure. Some manual starters have the overload in a separate box or enclosure; this feature may be useful in solving a space or design problem. Because the real work is done electrically, magnetic starters often have the push buttons or control station completely separate from the actual starter. For example, when the control station is separate, it may be a push-button station for on-off control only, as for a drill press (Fig. 21-22), or it may provide on-off reversing for a metal lathe.

The great variety of starters, switches, and control stations meets every conceivable need. They come in a wide electrical range and in all shapes and sizes. They can be specified as oil-tight, dustproof, or explosionproof, for example, and of course the price is commensurate with the purpose and value. The actual control mechanism recommended by the machine manufacturer is probably the best choice because it is engineered to work with the recommended motor on the specified machine.

It is probably a good idea to clean or blow out the dust inside the starter every few weeks. An accumulation of dirt on the electrical contacts can cause burning of the contacts, a voltage drop to the motor, or complete failure of the control.

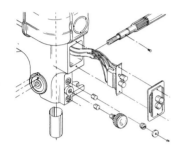

FIG. 21-22

CHAPTER TWENTY-TWO
Parts and Service Information

KEEPING A FILE

In a large industrial shop, a complete file is kept for each piece of equipment. This is often the responsibility of the maintenance department or a maintenance foreman. Even for a tool and die shop, cabinet shop, or school shop or laboratory, which may not be as large or as well departmentalized, making a permanent file is an excellent idea (Fig. 22-1).

A separate file or file folder should be made for each item in the shop which might eventually need service, regardless of size or cost. In addition to data on both stationary and portable tools or equipment, a folder might well be made for all so-called capital equipment, including such items as workbenches, vises, switches, motors, overhead doors, ventilating fans, electric control panels, and similar equipment vital to the functioning of the shop.

The following list indicates some of the information which might be included in the folder:

1. Instruction manual
2. Parts manual
3. Original specifications
4. Folder on accessories available
5. Date of purchase
6. Date of installation

FIG. 22-1

7. Warranty information
8. Catalog page, picture, and listing
9. Manufacturer's address, phone number
10. Manufacturer's representative—name and phone number
11. Factory branch—address and phone number
12. Distributor where purchased—address and phone number
13. Distributor's salesman—address and phone number
14. Original cost of the unit
15. UL-CSA-NEMA information
16. Lubrication information chart
17. Lubrication history—frequency
18. Model number, name, and size
19. Serial number
20. Casting numbers
21. Amp rating—wiring diagram
22. Original color
23. Weight
24. New—used—surplus
25. Service history—parts replaced
26. Motor manufacturer and repair station—address/phone
27. Manufacturer of original belts
28. Manufacturer of original bearings
29. Manufacturer of accessories

If this type of information is filed in the first place and kept up to date, it can be invaluable. This is true not only from an operating and maintenance viewpoint, but also when expecting to trade or sell. Parts can be ordered correctly and quickly. Actual operating or maintenance costs can be figured and analyzed. Future problems can be minimized, anticipated, or budgeted.

In many small shops, particularly school shops, no records are kept or, even worse, the entire file system is taken by the instructor to his next teaching position. Most of the information is actually valueless except when related to the specific equipment to which it applied. Oftentimes, when a file system is started in an older shop after years of operation, much of the history is not available. A reasonable, accurate guess is at least a good start on many points, and these can be revised after specific facts or dates are discovered.

Most equipment manufacturers will mail parts manuals free of charge, and often instruction manuals and other information. It is recommended that the request be written on school or business stationery and indicate in some detail exactly the tool or equipment in question (Fig. 22-2).

McGINNLEY CONSOLIDATED SCHOOL DISTRICT #77
LINDQUIST, FLORIDA 02159

Stryker Tool & Manufacturing Company
824 Harden Drive
North Hills, New York 13542

Gentlemen:

We have the following Stryker tools in our shop. Would you please send
us parts and instruction manuals covering this equipment.

MODEL	DESCRIPTION	SERIAL NUMBER
218	19" Drill Press (Floor Model, Slow Speed)	AM 23386
882	11" Tilting Arbor Saw (About 18 Years Old)	?
?	7" Jointer (No Nameplates--Polaroid Picture Attached)	BX 37119

Thank you for your help.

Sincerely,

B. Harris

B. Harris
Industrial Arts Instructor

FIG. 22-2

Many variations, often in the hundreds, may exist within the same size category of drill press, circular saw, pistol drill, or similar equipment. For this reason, requesting a parts manual for a "15″ drill press" might present real problems to a manufacturer.

Aside from the normal information which might be given, a polaroid picture often helps to identify an older machine. Numbers are usually cast into the unit (Fig. 22-3), and these manufacturer's casting codes pinpoint a specific machine in most cases. These two suggestions are particularly helpful when nameplates are missing, when colors have been changed, and, of course, when no records have ever been kept. In some cases, this information may have to be sent to more than one company before you are successful.

The file belongs to the shop and not to the instructor, operator, or foreman. It is as permanent as the equipment it covers and should leave the shop only when the equipment is sold or traded.

FIG. 22-3

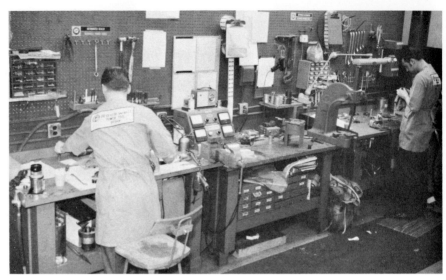

FIG. 22-4

SERVICE PARTS

The quick availability of parts is important to every school and industrial customer. For a cabinet shop, metal fabrication shop, tool room, or contractor, downtime on a machine can quickly be tabulated in dollars. In an industrial education shop, the same downtime is not as easy to cost out, but it is certainly education time which can never be made up. Discipline problems and other factors are also involved. Because of this, it is important to the potential purchaser or present owner to investigate the method of parts distribution utilized by various manufacturers.

There are basically three methods used: factory branches or service stations (Fig. 22-4), authorized parts distributors, and the direct factory handling of all orders.

Most portable tool manufacturers have factory or service branches scattered throughout the country. These branches are not only stocking parts depots; they also repair tools and are often regional sales headquarters. For stationary equipment manufacturers, these branches are normally only local parts distribution centers, because of the size and weight of the tools. When a manufacturer makes both types of equipment, the same branch usually serves both purposes.

Authorized parts distributors for stationary equipment and authorized parts distributors and repair stations for portable tools furnish both parts availability and service at a more local level. A town, population area, or marketing area which could not support a factory branch might well have two or more authorized parts distributors or repair stations. Needless to say, these picked distributors or dealers would also stock and sell the actual equipment.

Some manufacturers prefer to ship all parts directly out of their plant, whether the orders come from distributors or from actual users. Quite possibly, the greatest advantage is the elimination of paper work, but the delay in receiving a needed part is usually extended. Often, the distance between the plant and the customer creates a time problem in mailing or shipping.

Naturally, there are as many variations in these three basic methods as there are manufacturers; some companies use two or even all three of the systems at the same time.

Machine tool and stationary tool manufacturers do not actually produce their own belts, bearings, or motors, just to name three major items. Normally these items are actually guaranteed by the original equipment manufacturer (OEM). In the case of belts and bearings, this responsibility may be accepted by the tool manufacturer or the OEM may receive a back charge for defective items. In either case, the customer or user is not involved, and the item is replaced by the factory branch or authorized parts distributor.

In most cases, the warranty responsibility for constant-speed motors is retained by the actual motor manufacturer. A defective motor or control unit should be returned to the motor manufacturer's repair station, not to the equipment manufacturer's branch or parts distributor. The special nature of the problems, along with the testing and repair equipment needed, requires a separate warranty. Usually, a list of motor repair stations is included with the original equipment. If not, the specific motor manufacturer should be contacted and the closest motor repair station should be noted in the file. The yellow pages in the telephone directory are another good source of reference.

Motor manufacturers often supply special name or instruction plates for OEM use, but in most cases they include also their own name somewhere on the plate (Fig. 22-5).

Many portable electric tool manufacturers make their own motors and therefore assume the warranty responsibility themselves. The factory branch or authorized service station is equipped to handle both the mechanical and the electrical problems which may arise.

FIG. 22-5

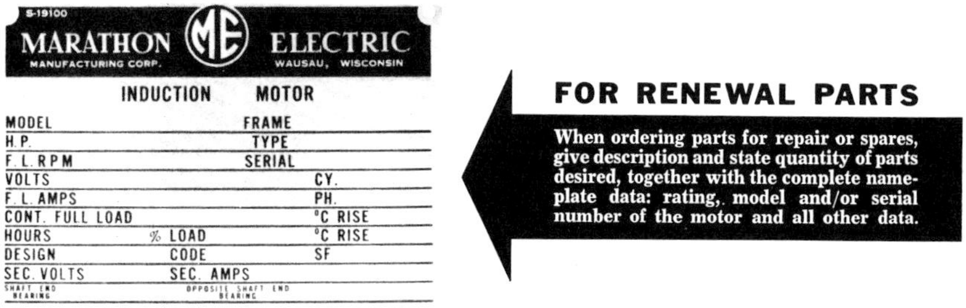

WARRANTY—GUARANTEE

Every reputable manufacturer makes a statement of policy, usually in writing, concerning his product's quality, merchandising, or fitness for a particular purpose. There is often a specific time limit and often a promise concerning repair or replacement. The actual legal difference between the terms used, such as warranty or guarantee, is of no real consequence to the actual user although the term "warranty" is usually preferred in reference to inanimate objects such as machines.

The warranty or guarantee should be read and understood not only when tool failure occurs but when the equipment is purchased. It is often helpful to note in the file on the machine what actual parts or items are covered and also what the time limit is. What is not covered and what action on the user's part will void the warranty should also be noted. In most cases, manufacturers of machine tools and stationary power tools in particular are reasonably lenient in this regard. A serious attempt to repair or replace parts by the user will not usually violate any agreement, even if the effort fails. Overloading, homemade or competitive parts, and flagrant misuse of the equipment could release the original manufacturer from his promise. Since the warranty is a two-way agreement, the user should follow the manufacturer's directions exactly in any warranty claim.

No manufacturer issues a warranty or guarantee which he cannot easily keep. The extent of his obligation might be compared to the weight restrictions on a bridge, which are well under the absolute maximum weight it can bear. In most cases, the replacement promise is restricted to actual defects in either workmanship or materials when the equipment left the manufacturing plant. Since parts, assemblies, and units are normally inspected many times during the manufacturing and assembly process, the user is reasonably protected from the expense of replacing defective merchandise. A typical warranty statement might read as follows:

> The manufacturer warrants its products only against defects in materials or workmanship and makes no implied warranty of any kind with respect to the products except as set forth herein. The manufacturer's liability and dealer's exclusive remedy under this warranty or any warranty extends for a period of one (1) year from the date of the manufacturer's shipment and is expressly limited to repair or replacement or repayment of the purchase price, at manufacturer's option, during said period, upon proof satisfactory to the manufacturer and upon Dealer's returning and prepaying all freight charges on such products to factory, warehouse or service station designated by the manufacturer. Our warranty will not apply on any material that has been altered or changed by outside mechanics.

The time limit on the warranty indicated by most machine tool and power tool manufacturers is one year. This is more or less a standard industry practice. Most defective parts not obviously defective by visual inspection at the time of delivery will fail well within the period of the warranty.

Portable electric tool manufacturers have used the time limit on the guarantee or warranty as a selling feature, in addition to its normal purpose. For this reason, portable electric tools have guarantees that run from one year to "guaranteed for life" and "guaranteed forever." This is possible because in most cases the equipment is less expensive than stationary tools and defective parts, or, for that matter, even the complete tool can be replaced more easily.

In every case, the actual decision concerning a warranty replacement rests with the manufacturer. The user merely presents his case or his problem in accordance with the warranty policy and trusts that an original defect was definitely the cause.

All equipment is subject to eventual failure, but it is more likely in machines with moving parts. The failure can normally be traced to one of these four causes:

1. After a long and useful life, the equipment finally wears out.

2. The equipment is overloaded—forced to do more than its designers and manufacturers ever intended.

3. The equipment is poorly maintained, ending in failure by neglect.

4. The failure is due to some fault in materials or manufacturing procedure.

The responsibility for the first three recognized reasons rests largely with the owner or user of the equipment. The manufacturer is responsible for the last one, but only within the time limit of his written guarantee or warranty. Thus most of the responsibility for the continued and satisfactory operation of the equipment is placed squarely on the shoulders of the cabinetmaker, carpenter, machinist, school shop instructor, or home owner.

FORCE MAJEURE OR EXCUSE OF PERFORMANCE

This part of a manufacturer's policy takes care of the many unforeseen and literally uncontrollable events which affect delivery, not only of machines but also of replacement and repair parts. A typical policy statement might read as follows:

Force Majeure

The consequences, direct or indirect, of labor troubles, fires, accidents, floods, hostilities, shortage of transportation, failure, suspension or curtailment of production due to shortage of supply of raw materials, or other economic factors, government acts or requirements, and any and all like or different causes beyond the control of the parties hereto shall excuse performance by either party to the extent by which performance is prevented thereby.

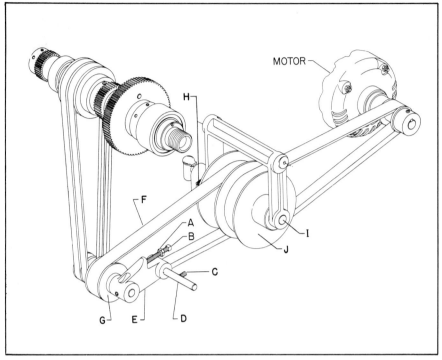

FIG. 22-6

The manufacturer may, during any period of shortage due to any of said causes, prorate its supply of such goods among all its buyers in such manner as may be deemed equitable in the sole judgment of the manufacturer.

PARTS AND INSTRUCTION MANUALS

Every equipment manufacturer issues, with the machine, a parts manual or parts sheet of some type. It is often included in an instruction manual or folder. The instructions usually pertain to properly setting up, adjusting, or repairing the equipment, rather than to operating it. Many companies include line drawings or photographs to illustrate various procedures clearly (Fig. 22-6). The actual parts breakdown is shown in an isometric or pulled-apart style, which is especially helpful during assembly and disassembly (Fig. 22-7).

All such information should definitely be a part of the file on each piece of equipment. In some cases, the parts manual and instruction manual are printed separately, and it is therefore a good policy to request both when writing to a manufacturer. In most cases, manuals are available also from the distributor or a factory branch.

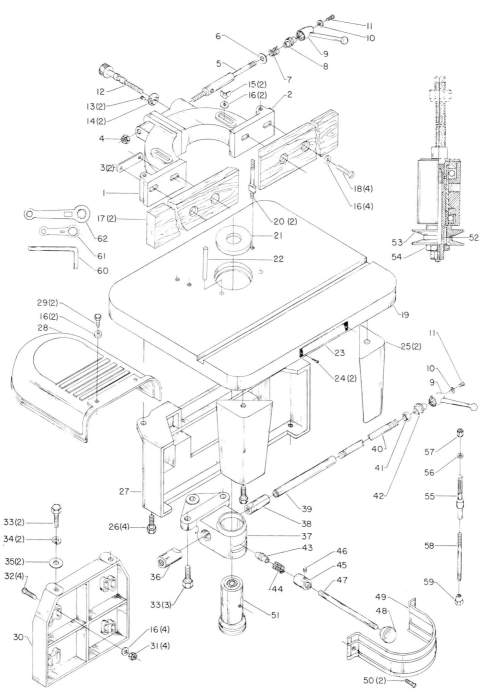

FIG. 22-7

269

PART NUMBERS

Because of modern order entry systems and accounting systems, most manufacturers ship both equipment and parts strictly by catalog or part number. Formerly, descriptions were read by order editors, discrepancies between numbers and descriptions were detected, and all orders and billing papers were typed. This is no longer true in many cases, and therefore the correct number is essential in an order. No descriptions are needed.

The part numbers used by many manufacturers in the past were a combination of letters and numbers. The letters often indicated the machine itself, as D for drill press. The number was taken from a strictly numerical list of available items, usually starting with 100 (236 in our example), and possibly with a letter at the end indicating that this part was actually an assembly (A). If this were a drill assembly, the order would read:

One D-236-A Drill Assembly

Under a computerized system, the same part might well be designated as a seven- or even a twelve-digit number and the order would read only:

One 361-248-972-006

This system is helpful, of course, to the manufacturer in terms of billing, inventory control, cost, and speed. All these factors help to hold down costs and improve service to the customer, but there are serious drawbacks. The major problem is obvious. With shipment and billing based on the number alone, unbelievable errors are possible. If only one digit in the series is wrong, the customer could conceivably receive a 200-lb casting instead of a washer.

There is, of course, some chance of error when a parts numbering system is changed. Usually, for a few years, comparison lists are furnished to both customers and distributors. They should be placed with the original parts manual in the equipment file.

Oftentimes the parts on an isometric drawing are merely numbered in order, e.g., 1-2-3-4. These numbers are used only to clarify the drawing in a minimum amount of space; they cannot be used in ordering parts. The actual part number is always given on an accompanying reference list, usually on the same sheet or in the same manual (Fig. 22-8).

STANDARD PARTS

Every equipment or machine manufacturer uses many items which are considered "standard parts." They are usually purchased by the manu-

Ref. No.	Part No.	Description
86	402-04-057-5009	Head Casting
87	SDP-49	Column Clamp
88	SDP-21	Clamp Sleeve
89	CBL-447	33/64 x 7/8 x 1/16"Washer
90	SP-1282	1/2"-13 Hex. Nut
91	907-01-050-5239	Oiler
92	928-08-011-8868	Pinion Clock Spring
93	DP-528	Clock Spring Housing
94	902-01-281-7295	1/4"-20 Hex. Lock Nut
95	DP-875	Ball Crank
96	DP-527	Adjusting Screw
97	SD-18	1/4"-20 Hex. Nut
98	SDP-22	Clamp Sleeve

FIG. 22-8

Part No.	Description
SP-201	5/16-18 x 5/16 Hex. Soc. Set Scr.
SP-1300	5/16-18 Hex. Nut
SP-1620	11/32 x 11/16 x 1/16 Washer
SP-2951	Tinnerman Nut
SP-834	5/16-18 x 3/4 Carriage Bolt
SP-609	5/16-18 x 1 1/2 Hex. Hd. Cap Scr.
DP-515	Motor Plate
SP-1620	11/32 x 11/16 x 1/16 Washer
400-00-057-5001	Head Casting
SP-2851	Rubber Bumper

FIG. 22-9

facturer and are not unique or specifically made for one kind or brand of machine. They include a great variety of nuts, bolts, cap screws, washers, keys, wing nuts, thumbscrews, pins, snap rings, and other similar items. Because of stocking or warehousing costs and shipping costs, it is usually much faster and less expensive to purchase such items locally. It is slightly ridiculous to order "two 1/4-20 × 1/2" Hex Hd. Screws" from a factory hundreds of miles away or even a branch 30 miles away, wait days for delivery, and be charged 20 cents each. The same screws are most probably available from a small hardware store or local mill supply house, instantly, and for a few cents each. If standard parts (SP) are not specifically indicated as such by the manufacturers, it is quite easy to judge for yourself by the catalog description (Fig. 22-9).

OBSOLETE PARTS

Any reputable manufacturer realizes that future business depends upon service and the availability of service parts. Therefore most equipment manufacturers make every attempt to have available service parts, as long as a reasonable demand exists. Most service parts are normally produced at the same time as the production run of the machine or accessory for which they will be required. After a specific tool or piece of equipment is discontinued, it is naturally more expensive to produce replacement parts. The production run is then only large enough to meet the service requirements.

Machine tools, power tools, and other equipment used commercially, industrially, or in industrial education are not subject to the same continuous pressure for change as home tools. This heavier and, of course, more expensive equipment is built to perform a specific job over a longer period of time. Unless the job specifications change or there is a radical development in method, this equipment is not forced into obsolescence by frequent or unnecessary model changes.

After a specific model of machine has not been manufactured for some time, the situation is carefully analyzed before a decision is made to obsolete or not produce replacement parts. At least the following three factors would be considered:

1. What is the total number of original machines produced? It would stand to reason that the more machines or units produced, the longer the demand for parts.

2. Can the part be replaced by a different or redesigned part (not actually interchangeable) with a minimum of cost to the user for additional parts needed to make the substitution? It is often advantageous to install the redesigned part as well as the additional parts necessary, because availability of the new parts will be assured for a longer period of time.

3. Can the user fabricate or have fabricated locally a replacement part? Many items or parts can be made in the user's own shop at a fraction of the cost of the manufacturer's producing, stocking, cataloging, and shipping them.

In most cases, there is no legal termination of a manufacturer's obligation, although for some unknown reason there is a very popular misconception that seven years is the limit.

STOCKING PARTS

Besides the factory, factory or service branches, and authorized parts distributors, many local dealers stock parts. In most cases, they are restricted by both space and cost, but high-mortality items are often stocked in some quantity. This is a real service to the customer, primarily saving him time, but also building a good service reputation and good customer relationships.

It is quite easy, through your own or others' past experience, to ascertain the mortality of specific parts needed to keep the equipment operating. These items should be purchased by the user, industrial, commercial, or school, in the anticipated quantity, not one at a time. For instance, if the V-belt in a specific application is replaced twice a year, then it is logical to purchase three at a time and keep the extras in stock, right in the shop. This can mean more economical purchasing, depending on the item, and certainly it can solve the downtime problem instantly. There are probably no more than ten high-mortality parts in the complete shop. The convenience and time saving more than compensate for the small investment in such vital parts. In order to build a stock of these parts gradually, a good rule of thumb might be "when you need one, buy two."

It should be understood that a so-called high-mortality part may be specifically engineered and manufactured to be exactly that. It may wear at a fast rate intentionally to save wear on an expensive assembly; or it may be designed to break under undue strain for a similar reason or even as a safety factor in regard to the machine or the operator (Fig. 22-10).

Because of acquisitions, mergers, and address changes, it is difficult to keep a completely accurate list of sources of supply and service. Current information on the names of manufacturers and tools is given in Appendix A, and a list of supplementary printed material in Appendix B, in the hope that they may provide some guidance in locating parts, manuals, and other items that are not readily available. Some of the brands listed are no longer on the market, and others that are still being built are now sold under different trade or brand names.

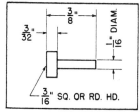

NOTE: You can make a new shear pin out of low carbon screw stock by following the above illustration.

FIG. 22-10

APPENDIX A
Tool Sources

BRAND NAME	TYPE OF TOOL	CONTACT
Acme	Stationary belt sanders	R. A. Ness & Company 5083 N. Elston Avenue Chicago, Ill. 60630
Aget	Dust collectors	Aget Manufacturing Company 3346 Church Street Adrian, Mich. 49221
Airetool	Portable air	Air Tool Corporation of America 2209 South Berry Avenue Los Angeles, Calif. 90064
Amco	Stationary wood	American Machine & Tool Company Royersford, Pa. 19468
American	Stationary wood	American Woodworking Machinery Company 100 Liberty Street Hackettstown, N. J. 10019
Apex	Disk sanders	Apex Specialties Company 1117 Douglas Avenue Providence, R. I. 20904
Arco	Hacksaws Sanders	Arco Manufacturing Company Box 817 Grand Forks, N. D. 58201

Aro	Portable air	The Aro Corporation 400 Enterprise Street Bryan, Ohio 43506
Baldor	Grinders Motors	Baldor Electric Company 4353 Duncan Avenue St. Louis, Mo. 63110
Belsaw	Grinders Planer molders	Belsaw Power Tools Field Building Kansas City, Mo. 64111
Berkroy	Sheet metal	Berkroy 1177 East 32nd Street Los Angeles, Calif. 90031
Black & Decker Atlas DeWalt Master	Portable electric Stationary wood Radial saws Portable air	Black & Decker Manufacturing Company Towson, Maryland 21204
Blount	Wood lathes Stationary wood	Bowl-More Company J. G. Blount Division Everett, Mass. 02149
Boice Crane	Stationary wood (except drill presses, band saw)	Boice Crane Industries, Inc. P.O. Box 283 Gothenburg, Nebraska 69138
Boyar-Schultz	Grinders	Esterline Corporation Boyar-Schultz Division 2003 South 25th Avenue Broadview, Ill. 50153
Bridgeport	Milling machines	Bridgeport Machines 500 Lindley Street Bridgeport, Conn. 06606
Buffalo	Drill presses	Buffalo Forge Company Machine Tool Division 465 Broadway Buffalo, N.Y. 14204
Burlington	Stationary sanders Buffers	Will Krumbach Corporation Burlington, Wis. 53105
Caldwell	Milling machines	Caldwell Industries P.O. Box 170 Luling, Tex. 78648
Chicago Pneumatic	Portable air	Chicago Pneumatic Tool Company 6 East 44th Street New York, N.Y. 10017

BRAND NAME	TYPE OF TOOL	CONTACT
Cincinnati	Machine tools Milling machines Metal lathes Grinders	Cincinnati Milling Maching Company Cincinnati, Ohio 45209
Clausing Colchester	Metal lathes Milling machines Drill presses Metal lathes	Atlas Press Company 2019 N. Pitcher Street Kalamazoo, Mich. 49001
Cleco	Portable air	Reed International, Inc. P.O. Box 40430 Houston, Tex. 77040
Comet	Radial saws	Comet Industries Corporation 2000 Imperial Street Los Angeles, Calif. 90021
Covel	Grinders	Covel Manufacturing Company Graham Avenue & Shore Drive Benton Harbor, Mich. 49122
Craftool	Dust collectors Buffers Lapidary equipment	Craftools, Inc. 1 Industrial Road Wood-Ridge, N.J. 07075
Craftsman Dunlap	Stationary wood Portable electric Stationary wood	Sears, Roebuck and Company 925 South Homan Avenue Chicago, Ill. 60607
Dara James	Stationary wood	Toolcraft Corporation P.O. Box 157 Brightwood Station Springfield, Mass. 01107
Diston	Portable electric	H. K. Porter Company Diston Division Porter Building 601 Grant Street Pittsburgh, Pa. 15219
DoAll	Band saws	DoAll Company 254 North Laurel Avenue Des Plaines, Ill. 60016
Duro	Stationary wood (except routers)	Duro Metal Products Company 2651 North Kildare Chicago, Ill. 60639
Engelburg Huller	Stationary belt sanders	The Engelberg Huller Company, Inc. 831 West Fayette Street Syracuse, N.Y. 13204
Enterprise	Machine tools Metal lathes Shapers	Enterprise Machine Tools 1309 South Clover Drive Minneapolis, Minn. 55420

BRAND NAME	TYPE OF TOOL	CONTACT
Foley	Grinders Sharpening equipment	Foley Saw & Tool 3300 N.E. 5th Street Minneapolis, Minn. 55418
Gardner/Denver	Portable air	Gardner/Denver Gardner Expressway Quincy, Ill. 62301
General Electric	Portable electric	General Electric Company 1285 Boston Avenue Bridgeport, Conn. 06610
Gilliom	Stationary wood	Gilliom Manufacturing Company St. Charles, Mo. 63301
Gorton	Milling machines	George Gorton Machine Company 2810 Racine Street Racine, Wis. 53403
Greaves	Milling machines	Greaves 2300 Eastern Avenue Cincinnati, Ohio 45202
Grobe	Band saws	Grobe, Inc. 10th Avenue Grafton, Wis. 53024
Hamilton	Metal lathe-mill	Hamilton Associates, Inc. 1716 Whitehead Road Medows Industrial Park Baltimore, Md. 21207
Hardinge	Metal lathes	Hardinge Brothers, Inc. 1934 Anderson Street Elmira, N.Y. 14902
Harrison	Metal lathes	REM Sales, Inc. West Hartford, Conn. 06107
Heston & Anderson	Swing saws	Fairfield Engineering and Manufacturing Company Heston & Anderson Division Fairfield, Iowa 52556
Houdaille		Houdaille Industries, Inc. One M & T Plaza Buffalo, N.Y. 14203
Burgmaster	Drilling machines	Burgmaster 15003 South Figueroa Street Gardena, Calif. 90247
Di-Acro	Sheet metal	Di-Acro 928 Eighth Avenue Lake City, Minn. 55041

BRAND NAME	TYPE OF TOOL	CONTACT
Logan	Machine tools Metal lathes	Logan Engineering Company 4901 West Lawrence Avenue Chicago, Ill. 60630
Powermatic	Stationary wood Stationary metal	Powermatic Highway 55 McMinnville, Tenn. 37110
U.S. Burk	Milling machines	U.S. Burk Machine Tool 5055 Brotherton Road Cincinnati, Ohio 45227
Index	Milling machines	Index Machine & Tool Company 559 Mechanics Street Jackson, Mich. 49204
Ingersoll-Rand Miller Falls	Portable air Portable electric	Ingersoll-Rand 11 Broadway New York, N.Y. 10004
Jiffey	Portable air	Jiffey Manufacturing Company 360 Florence Avenue Hillside, N.J. 07205
J-Line	Stationary wood	Brodhead Garrett Company 4560 East 71st Street Cleveland, Ohio 44106
Johnson	Band saws	Kysor Johnson Manufacturing Kysor Industrial Corp. 1013 Barnes Street Albion, Michigan 49224
Kalamazoo	Horizontal band saws	K T S Industries, Inc. Machine Tool Division 2062 Harrison Street Kalamazoo, Mich. 49001
Karle	Wood and spinning lathes	Karle Spin-Shop Company 105 South State Street North Warren, Pa. 16365
Keller	Power hack saws	Sales & Service Manufacturing Co. Keller Division 2365 University Avenue St. Paul, Minn. 55114
Kerney & Trecker	Machine tools Milling machines	Kerney & Trecker Corporation 11000 Theodore Trecker Way Milwaukee, Wis. 53214
K. O. Lee	Grinders	K. O. Lee Company Aberdeen, S.D. 57401

BRAND NAME	TYPE OF TOOL	CONTACT
LeBlond Fosdick Regal	Metal lathes	The R. K. LeBlond Machine Tool Company 1947 Edwards Road Cincinnati, Ohio 45208
Lynn	Band saws	Lynn Engineering, Inc. Albion, Ind. 46701
Master Craft	Portable electric	Master Craft Benson, Minn. 56215
Micor	Table saw	The Micor Corporation 230 South Evergreen Street Bensenville, Ill. 60106
Milwaukee	Portable electric	Milwaukee Electric Tool Corp. 13135 West Lisbon Road Brookfield, Wis. 53005
Mumert-Dixon	Grinders	Cam Industries, Inc. Hanover, Pa. 17331
Newman Whitney	Wood planers Wood planers	Newman Machine Company, Inc. P.O. Box 3428 Greensboro, N.C. 27402
Niagara	Sheet metal	Niagara 1000 Erie Avenue North Tonawanda, N.Y. 14120
Northfield	Stationary wood	Northfield Foundry and Machine Co. Lock Box 140 Northfield, Minn. 55057
Oliver	Stationary wood	Oliver Machinery Company 445 Sixth Street, N.W. Grand Rapids, Mich. 49504
Onsrud	Routers	Danly Machine Corporation Onsrud Machine Works, Inc. 7720 North Lehigh Avenue Niles, Ill. 60648
Parker-Majestic	Grinders	Parker-Majestic, Inc. 147 Jos. Campau Avenue Detroit, Mich. 48207
Parks	Wood planers	Parks Woodworking Machinery 1501 Knowlton Street Cincinnati, Ohio 45223
Penncraft	Stationary wood Portable electric	J. C. Penney 1301 Avenue of the Americas New York, N.Y. 10019

BRAND NAME	TYPE OF TOOL	CONTACT
Pet	Portable electric	G. W. Murphy Industries, Inc.
Shopmate	Radial saws	Portable Electric Tools
		1200 E. State Street
		Geneva, Ill. 60134
Pexto	Sheet metal	The Peck, Stow & Wilcox Company
		Southington, Conn. 06489
Powrkraft	Stationary wood	Montgomery Ward
		619 West Chicago Avenue
		Chicago, Ill. 60607
Pryor	Jointers	Pryor Special Machine
		La Habra, Calif. 90631
Ram	Portable electric	Ram Tool Corporation
		2110 West Walnut Avenue
		Chicago, Ill. 60612
Rockwell	Metal lathes	Rockwell Manufacturing Company
	Milling machines	Power Tool Division
Buckeye	Portable air	Rockwell Building
Crescent	Stationary wood	Pittsburgh, Pa. 15208
Delta	Stationary wood/metal	
Driver	Stationary wood	
Duro	Stationary routers	
Homecraft	Stationary wood	
Multiplex	Radial saws	
Porter-Cable	Portable electric	
Red Star	Radial saws	
Sterling	Sanders	
Walker-Turner	Stationary wood/metal	
Rodgers	Stationary belt, sanders, shapers, swing saws, routers	Rodgers Machinery Mfg. Company, Inc. 2600 South Santa Fe Avenue Los Angeles, Calif. 90058
Rotor	Portable air	Copper Industries, Inc.
		Cleveland, Ohio 44132
Sheldon	Metal lathes	Sheldon Machine Company
	Shapers	4200 North Knox Avenue
		Chicago, Ill. 60641
Shopmaster	Stationary wood	Shopco, Inc.
		6600 South Country Road
		18 Eden Prairie, Minn. 55434
Shopsmith	Stationary wood	Magna Engineering Corporation
		Menlo Park, Calif. 94025
Sioux	Portable electric	Sioux Tools, Inc.
		2801 Floyd Boulevard
		Sioux City, Iowa 51105

BRAND NAME	TYPE OF TOOL	CONTACT
Skill	Portable electric and air	Skill Corporation 5033 N. Elston Avenue Chicago, Ill. 60630
South Bend	Metal lathes Milling machines Drill presses	Amsted Industries South Bend Lathes South Bend, Ind. 46623
Sprunger	Stationary wood	Sprunger Brothers, Inc. Ligonier, Ind. 46767
Standard modern	Metal lathes	Standard Modern Tool Company, Ltd. 69 Montcalm Avenue Toronto 10, Ontario, Canada
Stanley Carter	Portable electric and air Routers	Stanley Tools 111 Elm Street New Britain, Conn. 06051
Sunbeam	Portable electric Dust collectors	Sunbeam Corporation 5400 Roosevelt Road Chicago, Ill. 60650
Tanawitz	Stationary wood	Tanawitz, Inc. 315 Front Avenue, N.W. Grand Rapids, Mich. 49502
Thor Speedway	Portable electric and air	Thor Power Tool Company 175 State Street Aurora, Ill. 60507
Toolcraft	Stationary wood	Toolcraft Corporation 700 Plainfield Street Chicopee, Mass. 01013
Tops	Radial saws	Power Tools Inc. King Division 500 South Hicks Road Palatine, Ill. 60067
Torit	Dust collectors	The Torit Corporation 1133 Rankin Street St. Paul, Minn. 55116
Tornado	Dust collectors	Breuer Electric Manufacturing Co. 5100 N. Ravenswood Avenue Chicago, Ill. 60640
Toro	Stationary wood	Toro 8111 Lyndale Avenue South Minneapolis, Minn. 55420
Tree	Milling machines	Tree Tool & Die Works 1601 Junction Avenue Racine, Wisconsin 53403

BRAND NAME	TYPE OF TOOL	CONTACT
U.S. Electric	Grinders	U.S. Electric Motor Company North & Buffalo Street Cadiz, Ohio 43807
Wallace Routeser	Stationary wood Stationary router	J. D. Wallace & Company 800 North Detroit Street Warsaw, Ind. 46580
Wells	Horizontal band saws	Wells Manufacturing Corp. 320 Service Road Three Rivers, Mich. 49093
Wen	Portable electric	Wen Products, Inc. 5810 Northwest Highway Chicago, Ill. 60631
Wilton	Drill press Stationary wood	Wilton Tool Manufacturing Company 9525 Irving Park Road Schiller Park, Ill. 60176
Wizard	Stationary wood Portable electric	Western Auto Supply Company 2107 Grand Avenue Kansas City, Mo. 64108
Yates American	Stationary wood (except J-Line)	Yates American Machinery Company Beloit, Wis. 53511

Supplementary Sources

BOOKS

Compressed Air and Gas Handbook, Compressed Air and Gas Institute, New York, 1961.

Cunningham, Beryl M., and William F. Holtrop: *Woodshop Tool Maintenance*, Chas. A. Bennett Co., Inc., Peoria, Ill., 1956.

Groneman, Chris H., and Everett R. Glazener: *Technical Woodworking*, McGraw-Hill Book Company, New York, 1966.

How to Get the Most out of Your . . . Lathe, Shaper, Abrasive Tools, Radial Saw, Drill Press, Band Saw & Scroll Saw, Circular Saw & Jointer, Rockwell Manufacturing Company, Pittsburgh, 1969.

Le Grand, Rupert (ed.): *The New American Machinists' Handbook*, McGraw-Hill Book Company, New York, 1955. (Based on earlier editions of *American Machinists' Handbook*, eds. Fred H. Calvin and Frank A. Stanley.)

Oberg, Erik, and F. D. Jones: *Machinery's Handbook* (18th ed.), The Industrial Press, New York, 1968.

PAMPHLETS

Anti-Friction Bearings and Their Lubrication, GS109, New Departure Ball Bearings, Division of General Motors Corporation, Bristol, Conn., 1960.

Anti-Friction Bearing Maintenance, AFBMA-100, Anti-Friction Bearing Manufacturers Association, Inc., New York.

Practical Maintenance and Safety Tips for V-Belt Drives, No. 14995, Gates Rubber Company, Denver, 1965.

A Reference Manual for the Repair and Overhaul of Precision Equipment, M2-225, New Departure Ball Bearings, Division of General Motors Corporation, Sandusky, Ohio, 1964.

Timken Engineering Journal, Machine Tool Section, Timken Roller Bearing Company, Canton, Ohio. 1960.

ARTICLES

"Electric Motors," *Industrial Distributor News*, October 1965.

Feiper, John L.: "Equipment: Maintenance, Care and Repair" (editorial), *I.A.V.E. Magazine*, March 1964. (CCM Professional Magazines, Inc., Greenwich, Conn.)

Griffin, Denham R.: "Equipment and Lubrication Records," *I.A.V.E. Magazine*, March 1964. (CCM Professional Magazines, Inc., Greenwich, Conn.)

Hutchings, Gilbert R.: "Units of Study for Woodworking Machinery Maintenance," *I.A.V.E. Magazine*, May 1968. (CCM Professional Magazines, Inc., Greenwich, Conn.)

Kassay, John A.: "Maintenance Checklist for the Wood Laboratory," *I.A.V.E. Magazine*, March 1965. (CCM Professional Magazines, Inc., Greenwich, Conn.)

Krubek, Floyd: "Selection and Maintenance of Power Tools," *Power Tool Instructor*, vol. 13, no. 3, 1964. (Rockwell Manufacturing Company, Pittsburgh)

MANUALS/SHEETS

Specific parts manuals and instruction manuals are available from all manufacturers of power tools, accessories, and working components.

Instructions/Installation, Operation, Maintenance—Standard Induction Motors, Marathon Electric Manufacturing Corporation, Wausau, Wisc.

Selection and Operation of Motors, PM-1554, Rockwell Manufacturing Company, Pittsburgh, 1943.

Index